BETTER
FEEDBACK FOR
BETTER
TEACHING

BETTER
FEEDBACK FOR
BETTER
TEACHING

A Practical Guide to Improving Classroom Observations

Jeff Archer | Steve Cantrell | Steven L. Holtzman

Jilliam N. Joe | Cynthia M. Tocci | Jess Wood

JB JOSSEY-BASS™
A Wiley Brand

BILL & MELINDA
GATES *foundation*

Published by Jossey-Bass
A Wiley Brand
One Montgomery Street, Suite 1200, San Francisco, CA 94104-4594—www.josseybass.com

Jossey-Bass books and products are available through most bookstores. To contact Jossey-Bass directly call our Customer Care Department within the U.S. at 800-956-7739, outside the U.S. at 317-572-3986, or fax 317-572-4002.

Wiley publishes in a variety of print and electronic formats and by print-on-demand. Some material included with standard print versions of this book may not be included in e-books or in print-on-demand. If this book refers to media such as a CD or DVD that is not included in the version you purchased, you may download this material at http://booksupport.wiley.com. For more information about Wiley products, visit www.wiley.com.

Library of Congress Cataloging-in-Publication Data available at:

978-1-118-70198-0 (Paperback)
978-1-118-70196-6 (ePub)
978-1-118-70200-0 (ePDF)

Cover image: © ayzek/iStockphoto
Cover design: Wiley

Printed in the United States of America

FIRST EDITION
PB Printing 10 9 8 7 6 5 4 3 2 1

Contents

Acknowledgments

Numerous experts on classroom observations provided invaluable insights for this book. We greatly appreciate the contributions of: Colleen Callahan (Rhode Island Federation of Teachers); Sheila Cashman (Chicago Public Schools); Melissa Denton, Sandra Forand, and Lauren Matlach (Rhode Island Department of Education); Dennis Dotterer (South Carolina Teacher Advancement Program); Paul Hegre (Minneapolis Public Schools); Sara Heyburn (Tennessee State Board of Education); Dawn Krusemark (American Federation of Teachers); Tyler Livingston and Renee Ringold (Minnesota Department of Education); Catherine McClellan (Clowder Consulting LLC); Stephanie Aberger Shultz (District of Columbia Public Schools); David Steele (retired from Hillsborough County Public Schools, Florida); and Jonathan Stewart (Partnerships to Uplift Communities [PUC] Schools). Consultant Mark Toner provided significant editorial support. Additional design and editorial guidance came from KSA-Plus Communications. Many thanks also to Pamela Oakes (Bill & Melinda Gates Foundation) for her highly valued coordination and project management assistance. Finally, we are grateful to the staff at the New York office of the Brunswick Group for so graciously hosting our many work sessions as we wrestled this book's content into shape.

Left to Right: Steven L. Holtzman, Steve Cantrell, Cynthia M. Tocci, Jess Wood, Jilliam N. Joe, and Jeff Archer

About the Authors

Jeff Archer is president of Knowledge Design Partners, a communications and knowledge management consulting business with a focus on school change issues. A former writer and editor at *Education Week*, he has worked extensively with the MET project to translate the implications of its research for practitioners.

Steve Cantrell, a former middle school teacher, is a senior program officer in the K-12 Education division at the Bill & Melinda Gates Foundation. He has played a leading role in guiding the foundation's investments in innovative research and development focused on improving teaching and learning. He codirected the MET project's groundbreaking study of teacher evaluation methods.

Steven L. Holtzman is a senior research data analyst in the Data Analysis and Research Technologies group at ETS. He served as research lead on the MET project's video-scoring project and several other MET studies.

Jilliam N. Joe runs a research and assessment consulting business, Measure by Design. She is a former research scientist in the Teaching, Learning, and Cognitive Sciences group at ETS. At ETS, she provided psychometric and design support for the MET video-scoring project, and research and implementation direction for the Teachscape Focus observer training and certification system.

Cynthia M. Tocci, a former middle school teacher, spent more than 20 years at ETS, where she worked as an executive director in research. She was the senior content lead for Danielson's Framework for Teaching during the MET video-scoring project, and for the Teachscape Focus observer training and certification system. Now retired from ETS, she runs a consulting business, Educational Observations.

Jess Wood, a former middle school teacher and instructional coach, led development of an observer training system while at the District of Columbia Public Schools. Now a senior policy advisor at EducationCounsel, a mission-driven policy and strategy organization, she works with states and districts to improve the way we attract, prepare, support, and evaluate educators.

Guided by the belief that every life has equal value, the Bill & Melinda Gates Foundation works to help all people lead healthy, productive lives. In developing countries, it focuses on improving people's health and giving them the chance to lift themselves out of hunger and extreme poverty. In the United States, it seeks to ensure that all people—especially those with the fewest resources—have access to the opportunities they need to succeed in school and life. Based in Seattle, Washington, the foundation is led by CEO Susan Desmond-Hellmann and Cochair William H. Gates Sr., under the direction of Bill and Melinda Gates and Warren Buffett.

About the MET Project

The MET project was launched in 2009 as a research partnership of academics, teachers, and education organizations committed to investigating better ways to identify and develop effective teaching. Culminating findings from the project's three-year study were released in 2012. Funding came from the Bill & Melinda Gates Foundation. For more, see www.metproject.org.

BETTER FEEDBACK FOR
BETTER TEACHING

Introduction
Getting from Here to There

Imagine two teachers—Mr. Smith and Ms. Lopez—who work in different districts, and who have very different views on classroom observation. Mr. Smith is skeptical of observations, and for good reason. From his conversations with colleagues about being observed by different evaluators, he suspects the ratings they get have more to do with who does the observing than with the quality of the teaching. Moreover, Mr. Smith has never left a post-observation conference with a clear understanding of the reasons for the ratings that he received. Nor does he have any clear ideas of how to improve his ratings. Not surprisingly, he sees little value in observations and has little faith in evaluation.

Ms. Lopez's experience is different. At first, she too was skeptical of classroom observations. She thought they were primarily a mechanism for accountability and was unsure of the criteria. After experiencing several observations by different evaluators, however, her views have changed. The feedback she received clearly explains how what happened in the lesson aligns with the performance levels that are spelled out in the district's observation instrument, which embodies the district's expectations for teaching. Most important, when she sits down for a post-observation conference, she now expects to leave with a concrete plan for improving her teaching practice.

> *Ensuring that observers can provide accurate and meaningful feedback, in rich conversations with teachers, is essential for improving teaching and learning.*

Both scenarios are playing out across the country. In some schools and districts, teachers report getting meaningful feedback from observations. But not in others. Across some districts, observation results appear to be consistent and accurate. But across other districts, the results suggest that teaching is being judged based on different standards, or that evaluation remains a perfunctory exercise in which virtually all teaching is deemed proficient. On the whole, classroom observation today may be better than in the past, when it was based on simple checklists (e.g., "was the lesson objective posted?"), but the quality of implementation clearly remains uneven.

What will it take for all the Mr. Smiths to have the same experience as Ms. Lopez? A big part of the answer is ensuring that observers have the full set of knowledge and skills that quality observation requires. Observation is a highly challenging task. Observers must filter a dynamic and unpredictable scene in the classroom to find the most important indicators of performance, make an accurate record of them, and then apply a set of criteria as intended. Observation is complicated by the fact that, as educators, we've all formulated our own views of what effective teaching looks like, which can lead us to interpret and apply the same criteria differently. We're not used to seeing things through a common lens. Providing observers with instruments and procedures is not enough; they need the opportunity to learn how to use them effectively.

Ensuring that observers can provide accurate and meaningful feedback, in rich conversations with teachers, is essential for improving teaching and learning. Research indicates there aren't enough clearly low-performing teachers to think that focusing on them alone will result in meaningful gains in student achievement. The overall quality of teaching in the vast majority of classrooms—perhaps 90 percent—is near the middle in terms of performance

FIGURE I.1   To Improve Teaching and Learning, Professional Growth Matters Most

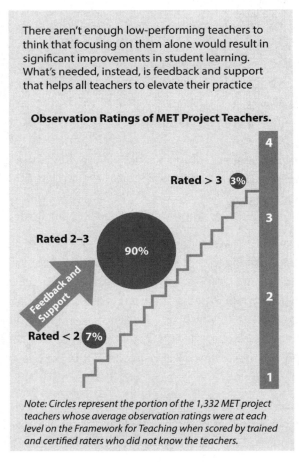

There aren't enough low-performing teachers to think that focusing on them alone would result in significant improvements in student learning. What's needed, instead, is feedback and support that helps all teachers to elevate their practice

Observation Ratings of MET Project Teachers.

Rated > 3 3%

Rated 2–3 90%

Feedback and Support

Rated < 2 7%

Note: Circles represent the portion of the 1,332 MET project teachers whose average observation ratings were at each level on the Framework for Teaching when scored by trained and certified raters who did not know the teachers.

FIGURE I.2 The Observation Process

Collect	**Sort**	**Interpret**	**Provide Feedback**
An observer looks for and records relevant evidence from a lesson.	The observer organizes the evidence by rubric components.	The observer determines ratings by comparing the evidence to the rubric's language.	The observer uses evidence in discussion with the teacher on how to improve.

Sequence adapted from Rhode Island Department of Education training materials.

(see Figure I.1). Significant progress in achievement will require that every teacher gets the individualized feedback and support he or she needs to change practice in ways that better promote student learning. Quality observation provides not only that, but also the data that state and district leaders need to evaluate and improve their systemwide supports for better teaching.

In our field, we've learned a great deal in recent years about what happens in quality observation. Researchers and innovative practitioners have broken down this challenging task into discrete steps, which generally follow the process in Figure I.2. The key ingredient is evidence. Observers collect evidence in the classroom, then use it to rate teaching performance, and refer to it when giving the teacher feedback. The key tool is the observation rubric. How an instrument defines each aspect of teaching and each performance level tells an observer what to look for and how to judge it. By applying clear criteria to objective evidence, different observers can reach the same conclusions about the same lessons.

But quality observation takes a special set of knowledge and skills (see Figure I.3). To collect evidence, you need to know what evidence is, and what kinds of evidence are relevant. To rate performance, you need to understand the conditions under which each rating is merited. To provide feedback effectively, you need to know how to coach. These competencies build on each other. If you fail to ensure that observers have each of these competencies, or if you try to develop a core skill before developing a prerequisite, you'll frustrate not only your observers but also your overall attempts to provide teachers with accurate and meaningful feedback.

You develop these competencies through repeated modeling and practice. To master a skill, you need to see how it's done effectively, then you need to try it yourself, and then you need feedback that tells you how you did. Much of this modeling and practice will include pre-scored video: videos of teaching that have been reviewed and rated by experts before the examples are used in observer training. Pre-scored video makes visible the thinking behind quality observation and lets trainees compare their own work to examples of good

FIGURE I.3 Observation Knowledge and Skills

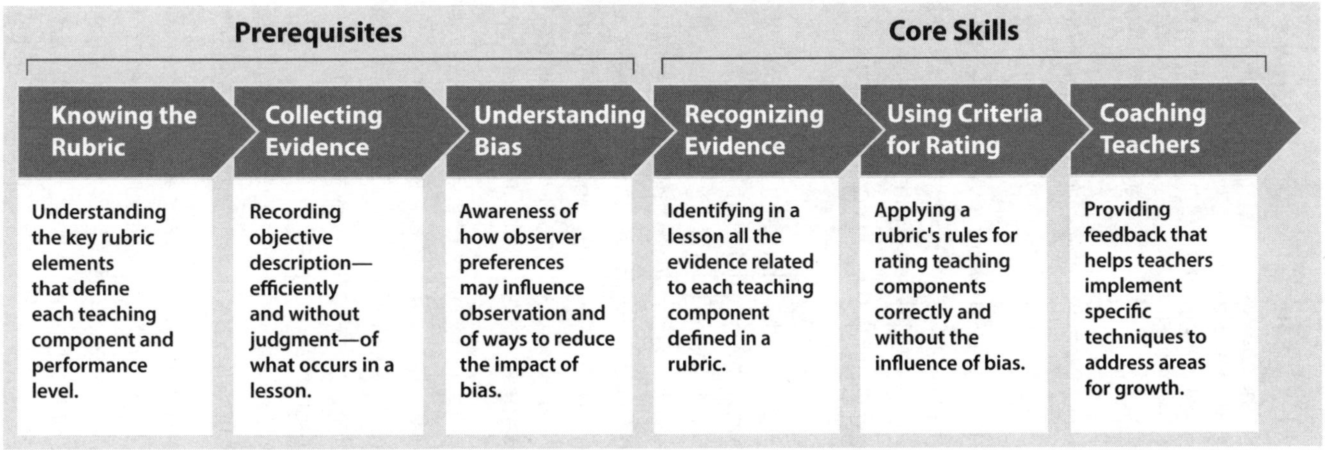

Prerequisites			Core Skills		
Knowing the Rubric	**Collecting Evidence**	**Understanding Bias**	**Recognizing Evidence**	**Using Criteria for Rating**	**Coaching Teachers**
Understanding the key rubric elements that define each teaching component and performance level.	Recording objective description—efficiently and without judgment—of what occurs in a lesson.	Awareness of how observer preferences may influence observation and of ways to reduce the impact of bias.	Identifying in a lesson all the evidence related to each teaching component defined in a rubric.	Applying a rubric's rules for rating teaching components correctly and without the influence of bias.	Providing feedback that helps teachers implement specific techniques to address areas for growth.

practice in using the observation process. But while pre-scored video is indispensable, an observer-in-training needs a certain amount of foundational knowledge before attempting what experts can do.

Using This Book

In this book we explain how to build, and over time improve, the elements of an observation system that equips all observers to identify and develop effective teaching. It's based on the collective knowledge of key partners in the Measures of Effective Teaching (MET) project—which carried out one of the largest-ever studies of classroom observations—and of a community of practitioners at the leading edge of implementing high-quality observations in the field. From this experience, we've unpacked how to build the necessary skills, how to build the capacity to provide quality training, and how to collect and use data to ensure that observations are trustworthy.

This book is for anyone whose work affects the quality of observation and feedback, including:

- State and local managers of teacher effectiveness programs

- Human capital and professional development directors

- Teacher unions and professional groups

- Technical assistance providers

- Principal managers and instructional support leaders

- Administrator preparation and training programs

- Teacher preparation and professional development programs

- School administrators and teacher leaders

The pages that follow speak most directly to those who develop, implement, and improve observation systems, as well as those who prepare, manage, and support individuals who observe and provide feedback to teachers. But observers themselves can deepen their understanding of quality observation and feedback by reviewing the sections in Part III, "Building the Knowledge and Skills for Observation."

> *The knowledge and skills we explain are too important to be limited to administrators and others involved in formal evaluation; peer observers, instructional coaches, and classroom teachers need to know and be able to do what quality observation requires.*

Although we sometimes refer to "evaluators" as the objects of the practices we describe, we use the term broadly to mean anyone whose work entails analyzing and evaluating classroom practice. The knowledge and skills we explain are too important to be limited to administrators and others involved in formal evaluation; peer observers, instructional coaches, and classroom teachers need to know and be able to do what quality observation requires. In addition, while we refer to "states and districts" when describing what to do, and what to avoid, many other actors play a role in developing, managing, and improving an observation system. Our guidance is for anyone whose work affects the quality of observation and feedback.

This book is not meant to be used only once or in only one way. Nor must it be read in its entirety. We recognize that observation systems are in different stages of development and exist in widely different contexts. Hence we've organized the content into 19 stand-alone chapters that each address one issue. These may be reviewed in the order that best serves readers' current needs. Figure I.4 presents approaches tailored to different readers and objectives. Each of the 19 chapters includes ideas for getting started, and for improving on existing work. As needs change over time, readers can look back at the material for ways to strengthen what they've put in place, and for ways to address new priorities.

Each chapter includes several features to support readers in turning ideas into action (see Figure I.5). These are to help practitioners answer for themselves how they can build and improve the elements of a quality observation system, by considering what such a system needs to accomplish and how others have developed a set of practices that does so. There's no one right way to do this work in every situation. But there is a body of knowledge that includes proven strategies, tools, and techniques to borrow and adapt for different contexts. Informed by best practice, and their own data, school systems will find their own path to continuous improvement.

Although the material in this book will be of benefit to individuals, observation and feedback are, by their nature, collaborative endeavors. Essentially, they're about people working together to forge a common understanding of goals and how to meet them. In the same spirit, this guide will best support improvement when it grounds discussion, planning, and implementation among colleagues, diverse stakeholders, and critical friends who are willing to share expertise and resources while learning together. Professional learning is most powerful when it happens in a focused professional community.

FIGURE I.4   Ways to Individualize Your Use of This Book

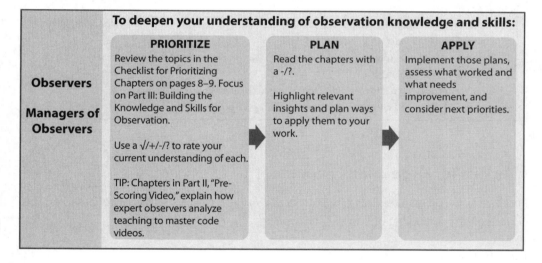

	To improve your observation system to ensure better feedback:		
State/ District Teaching Effectiveness Managers **Observer Trainers**	**PRIORITIZE** Review the topics in the Checklist for Prioritizing Chapters on pages 8–9 Use a √/+/-/? to rate your current efforts/understanding of each. TIP: First use the Observer Training Checklist on pages 287–290 to assess your training.	**PLAN** Read the chapters with a -/?. Respond to the idea-generating prompts at the end of each. Summarize plans across those chapters using the relevant parts of the Planning Worksheet on pages 291–303.	**APPLY** Implement those plans, assess what worked and what needs improvement, and consider next priorities.

	To deepen your understanding of observation knowledge and skills:		
Observers **Managers of Observers**	**PRIORITIZE** Review the topics in the Checklist for Prioritizing Chapters on pages 8–9. Focus on Part III: Building the Knowledge and Skills for Observation. Use a √/+/-/? to rate your current understanding of each. TIP: Chapters in Part II, "Pre-Scoring Video," explain how expert observers analyze teaching to master code videos.	**PLAN** Read the chapters with a -/?. Highlight relevant insights and plan ways to apply them to your work.	**APPLY** Implement those plans, assess what worked and what needs improvement, and consider next priorities.

Ensuring that observers have the necessary knowledge and skills cannot, by itself, guarantee that observations produce better teaching. The practice of observation changes the very notion of what it means to work in the service of student learning. It opens classrooms to peers and instructional leaders, aligns the purpose of evaluation and professional development, and acknowledges that different educators have different strengths and needs. This challenges deep-seated beliefs, mindsets, and cultural norms. Other efforts will be needed to change those beliefs, mindsets, and cultural norms. But working to make sure teachers and observers experience observation as something positive can go a long way toward moving them in the right direction.

FIGURE I.5   Guide Features for Turning Ideas into Action

In Each Chapter:
- **Essential Questions** Key questions at the start of chapters and sections that the material will help readers answer (e.g., How will you teach evidence collection?).
- **Tips** Lessons learned from leaders in implementing quality observation and feedback systems.
- **Snapshots** Concrete examples of how real states and districts are tackling specific issues.
- **Tools** Resources from leading states and districts across the United States that can be adapted for use in different contexts.
- **Techniques** Summaries of key points from each chapter, including ways to begin to address the essential question, and ways to improve on existing work.
- **Putting It into Practice Questions** Prompts to generate immediate ideas for applying the techniques in a particular context.

In the Appendix:
- **Observer Training Checklist (pp. 287–290)** A tool to identify gaps in observer training to prioritize next steps to improve it.
- **Planning Worksheet (pp. 291–303)** A template for summarizing plans for addressing all essential questions in the book.
- **Complete Tools** The full versions of all tools described in each chapter.

* You can download items with from www.wiley.com/go/betterfeedback.

Checklist for Prioritizing Chapters

Prioritize how you read this book by putting a "✓/+/−/?" next to each chapter based on your current efforts or understanding of each topic.

Part I: Making the Big Decisions

☐ **1:** **Building Support for Better Observer Training**
Creating awareness among stakeholders of how robust training supports accurate and meaningful feedback.

☐ **2:** **Finding Enough Observers**
Determining how many observers you need, and expanding the pool as needed.

☐ **3:** **Deciding on Training Delivery Methods**
Determining who should develop and deliver training, and the best modes (online or in person) for your context.

☐ **4:** **Setting Priorities for Observer Training**
Determining a focus for improving your training in the coming year.

Part II: Pre-Scoring Video

❑ **5:** **Understanding Pre-Scoring Video**

Understanding the process, products, and value of pre-scoring video.

❑ **6:** **Planning a Pre-Scoring Process**

Determining a focus for pre-scoring for the coming year.

❑ **7:** **Getting the Right Video to Pre-Score**

Finding videos of teaching with sufficient quality and content to pre-score.

❑ **8:** **Recruiting and Training Master Coders**

Identifying expert observers, and preparing them to pre-score video.

❑ **9:** **Ensuring Quality of Pre-Scoring**

Using quality control checks and data for continual improvement of your pre-scoring process.

Part III: Building the Knowledge and Skills for Observation

❑ **10:** **Knowing the Rubric**

Understanding the key rubric elements that define each teaching component and performance level.

❑ **11:** **Collecting Evidence**

Recording objective description—efficiently and without judgment—of what occurs in a lesson.

❑ **12:** **Understanding Bias**

Understanding how observer preferences may influence observation, and of ways to reduce their impact.

❑ **13:** **Recognizing Evidence**

Identifying in a lesson all the evidence related to each teaching component defined in a rubric.

❑ **14:** **Using Criteria for Rating**

Applying a rubric's rules for rating teaching components correctly and without the influence of bias.

❑ **15:** **Coaching Teachers**

Providing feedback that helps teachers implement specific techniques to address areas for growth.

❑ **16:** **Organizing a Training Program**

Scheduling and sequencing training into a series of manageable chunks that supports observer success.

Part IV: Using Data to Improve Training and Support of Observers

❑ **17:** **Collecting and Using Data from Training**

Analyzing information from training to identify areas for improvement.

❑ **18:** **Assessing Observers to Ensure and Improve Quality**

Determining if observers have sufficient proficiency, and providing additional supports for those who don't.

❑ **19:** **Monitoring Your Observation System**

Checking if procedures are followed, if observers maintain proficiency, and if teachers get useful feedback.

⬇ This item can be downloaded from www.wiley.com/go/betterfeedback

The Components of a Trustworthy Observation System

While most of this guide deals with observer training, it's important to understand how all the components of an observation system work together. Often when people talk about observations they refer only to the tools and procedures used in the classroom. But what makes observations trustworthy and effective are a set of components that support and reinforce each other, detailed as follows:

An Observation Rubric A rubric represents what makes teaching effective. It does so by describing the different levels of performance for important aspects of teaching. It says, "this is what we mean by 'use of questioning,'" and this is how 'effective' questioning differs from 'minimally effective' questioning." A rubric outlines a common language for instructional practice that gets teachers, instructional coaches, and others on the same page about the elements of effective teaching. It defines and guides what observers look for in the classroom. This has a profound effect on teachers' practice. What's in a rubric will shape what teachers do in the classroom.

Observer Training You can't just hand a rubric to people and say "go observe." If you do, you'll get as many interpretations of how to apply it as you have observers. Why? Because without anything else to go on, each person connects the words in the rubric to his or her own ideas and images of effective teaching. Learning to see teaching through the common lens of a rubric takes close study of its structure and language, examples of correct interpretation, and repeated practice. The same goes for feedback. The quality of feedback will be uneven if the elements of effective feedback aren't explicitly taught.

Observer Assessment Just because you taught something doesn't mean it was learned. Assessment is the only way to know if those you've trained have developed the right knowledge and skills. It's also the only way to know who's not yet ready and needs additional support to get there, and where your training program needs to do a better job. Without assessment, an observation system lacks a critical quality control. Without assessment, you have no idea to what extent you can trust the information observers produce.

Monitoring of Observations This is the other essential quality control. You need to know what's actually happening in the field. Are observers following procedures, or are they rushing through them and cutting corners? Knowing problems exist means that you can do something about them (like helping principals with scheduling and time management). The other reason to monitor is that skills naturally rust, unless periodically polished. The point at which observers complete their initial training shouldn't be the only time in their careers where their skills are tested and honed.

These components reinforce each other and allow for continual improvement. A rubric is the basis for training, but while training observers you may discover parts of the tool that need clarification. Observer assessment builds confidence that observers have mastered the requisite skills, but it also exposes the need for enhancements in training. Monitoring what observers do and produce over time helps in maintaining and improving the quality of all parts of the system.

A set of key activities drives each of the four components. For example, a rubric won't work as intended without efforts to ensure that it's clear and manageable for observers. Training won't be successful without pre-scoring video for use in modeling and practicing observation. These activities are shown in Figure I.6.[1] Review them and ask yourself to what extent your observation system currently addresses each (for a more detailed assessment of your system's observer training, see the Observer Training Checklist in this book's appendix). This may lead you to zero in on some chapters in this guide before others. Chances are most states and districts are doing some, but not all of these activities.

Looking at this book's contents, you'll see we devote a lot more ink to some components than others. Training—including pre-scoring video—accounts for about 70 percent of this book. Training requires the most resources and the most know-how. It's what equips observers to do what they need to do to provide accurate and meaningful feedback. The other components are essential in large measure because they support the quality of training. Assessment and monitoring provide credible evidence that training is successful—and that the whole system works—as well as the data to continually improve it.

So where are the chapters on rubrics? There aren't any. Because a research-based rubric is the cornerstone of an observation system, most states and districts have already adopted one. The more pressing need is to support observers in using them well. Moreover, rubrics will, and should, evolve as more is known about the best ways to identify and develop effective teaching, and as the expectations for student learning continue to evolve. What isn't going to change is the need to forge a shared understanding of current best practice.

About the Rubrics in This Guide

While there are no chapters on rubrics in this guide, you'll see excerpts of rubrics throughout. These come from states, districts, and organizations we know well. These include the Teaching and Learning Framework of the District of Columbia Public Schools; the Framework for Teaching, developed by Charlotte Danielson; and the Standards of Effective Instruction

FIGURE I.6 Components and Activities in a Trustworthy Observation System (with relevant chapters)

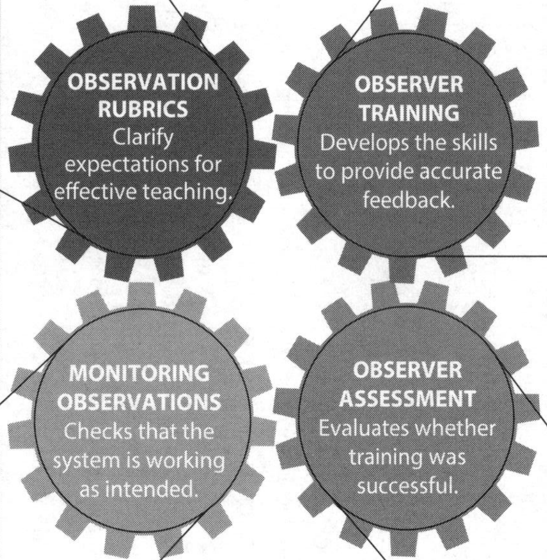

OBSERVER TRAINING
Develops the skills to provide accurate feedback.

- **Pre-scoring video (Chapters 5–9).** Use the rubric to determine benchmark ratings and rating rationales for videos of teaching.
- **Explaining the rubric (Chapter 10).** Provide observers an overview of the rubric's basis, structure, key features, and terms.
- **Minimizing bias (Chapter 12).** Make observers aware of their biases and of ways to counter the possible effects of those biases on rating.
- **Supporting practice (Chapters 11, 13–14).** Develop observer proficiency through explicit instruction, modeling, and practice.
- **Modeling feedback (Chapter 15).** Illustrate how to give teachers productive feedback based on observations.

OBSERVER ASSESSMENT
Evaluates whether training was successful.

- **Determining tasks (Chapter 18).** Create a set of performance activities that measure the requisite knowledge and skills.
- **Defining proficiency (Chapter 18).** Set a minimum standard of performance.
- **Establishing consequences (Chapter 18).** Clarify what happens when observers don't demonstrate proficiency, including what additional supports they'll receive.

OBSERVATION RUBRICS
Clarify expectations for effective teaching.

- **Aligning expectations.** Build buy-in for a set of commonly understood indicators of effective teaching.
- **Ensuring applicability.** Limit indicators to behaviors that can be expected in all lessons and that observers can reasonably track.
- **Ensuring clarity.** Leverage language and structure to support easy comprehension of each indicator.
- **Soliciting feedback.** Ask teachers and observers how well the rubric supports consistency and instructional improvement.
- **Evaluating validity.** Check for evidence that results discern among teachers based on how well they promote student learning.

MONITORING OBSERVATIONS
Checks that the system is working as intended.

- **Verifying process (Chapter 19).** Inspect to see if observation policies and procedures are being followed.
- **Checking agreement (Chapter 19).** Make sure observers maintain their accuracy.
- **Monitoring Feedback (Chapter 19).** Make sure teachers are getting clear, specific, and actionable feedback.

(SOEI), used by Minneapolis Public Schools. Another more recent rubric, developed with a streamlined design, is TNTP Core, created by The New Teacher Project.[2]

You can find complete versions of these rubrics with a quick web search.

We don't advocate these instruments over others. Indeed, many of the rubrics in use are quite similar, since they're based on similar findings about evaluating effective teaching. At the same time, some of the rubrics we refer to are in the process of being updated based on new research and new student learning objectives. Our goal in referring to specific rubrics is to illustrate the techniques that support a shared understanding of how to use such a tool. Those techniques apply no matter what tool is used.

We need feedback, too. *If you've got tools, techniques, or insights for quality observations to share—or comments on the ones in this book—email them to: info@betterfeedback.net.*

PART I

MAKING THE BIG DECISIONS

CHAPTER 1

Building Support for Better Observer Training

ESSENTIAL QUESTION

How Will You Make the Case for Robust Training?

You might wonder why observers need any significant training to provide teachers with accurate and meaningful feedback. After all, most principals and instructional leaders have extensive experience in education. They have long used classroom visits as part of their process for conducting teacher performance reviews. They believe they know good teaching when they see it. Why would they need anything more than their best judgment to accurately evaluate classroom practice? For that matter, why wouldn't some feel their expertise is being questioned by the suggestion that it's not enough?

But longstanding traditions in our profession have masked the extent to which we lack a shared vision of effective teaching and effective feedback. Instructional leaders often think they agree on what good teaching looks like, but that perceived agreement hasn't been tested, nor has it mattered if it didn't exist. Until recently, classroom visits by evaluators were infrequent and of little consequence. They were rarely based on clear or research-based criteria, and the results were almost never analyzed to see if they indicated what they were supposed to. There was little expectation that observations be followed by coaching that changes teacher practice. Now all that's changing. Today, we recognize that teaching drives student learning more than any other factor that schools control. Thus the premium on identifying and developing effective teaching has greatly increased.

When principals and other observers recognize the relevant indicators of a lesson's quality, they are better able to explain a teacher's ratings and how to improve them.

Think about what happens when observations fail to produce credible results and meaningful feedback. In most states, observations now count for half or more of a teacher's overall evaluation, and those evaluations increasingly factor into personnel decisions. Teachers are rightfully concerned when their job performance is determined using different standards, both across schools and within them. Moreover, students pay a price. Teachers cannot improve their practice when they receive inaccurate or confusing feedback. The lack of effective feedback creates an environment that discourages top-performing teachers from wanting to stay. In a study of highly effective teachers, The New Teacher Project (TNTP) found that regular, quality feedback was among the factors that determine how long such teachers plan to stay at their schools.[3]

Finally, observation results often are the only window a school system has into the state of teaching in its classrooms. Without accuracy, it's impossible to know what supports teachers need, or if those supports are working.

There's no magic number for how many hours of training are needed to ensure accuracy and meaningful feedback. But it's safe to say observer training will take school leaders away from their myriad other duties for dozens of hours over the course of a year (at least when they're first trained), and that some observers will take more time, and more reteaching, to get through it. In addition, trainers must be paid. If you use an online off-the-shelf program, you'll pay user fees. And if you build your own training from scratch, there's the significant cost of development: engaging a team to plan and pilot, acquiring video and pre-scoring it, and creating new materials. You need to make a clear case to stakeholders for making such a big investment.

You make the case for training with evidence. Revealing differences in interpretation builds an appreciation of the challenge that training helps address. Ask groups of instructional leaders to rate a video of teaching using your instrument's rubric, and then have them compare the ratings they gave for each teaching component and the evidence they used to determine the rating. The result may be disagreements, or even debates, between the raters. The point is not to question anyone's expertise, but to surface potential inconsistencies that might cause teachers to lose confidence in the observation process and the feedback they receive. Another way to make the case that different standards are being applied is to compare rating distributions across schools and districts. This may show that in some places large numbers of teachers are rated highly effective, while in others almost none are.

But consistency alone is not a strong sell. It is hard to justify the time and resources needed to implement quality observations if the only results are more accurate ratings of teachers' practice. Stakeholders need to see how training benefits their work. When principals and other observers recognize the relevant indicators of a lesson's quality, they are better able to explain a teacher's ratings and how to improve them. School leaders are eager for training that's focused on instruction and that helps them give meaningful feedback. When this effective feedback results in improvement, teachers place a higher value on the source of that feedback, and school leaders are more motivated to provide quality feedback going forward. The message that training makes evaluators better coaches will increase their investments.

Stakeholder groups and school system leaders also need to see observation as professional learning. Although the cost of robust observer training may be higher than what school systems spent in the past on evaluation, it's miniscule when compared with the dollars spent on professional development. By some measures, the overall expense of evaluation in districts with robust observer training is equal to about 1 percent of the total cost of teacher compensation (that includes the expense of other evaluation components, like student surveys, though observations cost more due to the training and time involved).[4] As professional development, observations are a modest investment, with great potential for return.

IN FOCUS:
EMPIRICAL EVIDENCE FOR MAKING THE CASE

The case for observer training isn't just rhetorical. It's empirical. Recent studies have shown students have greater gains in learning when their teachers receive effective observations and effective feedback. The following are two studies worth noting:

Chicago Public Schools Excellence in Teaching Project. When funding issues led Chicago Public Schools to reduce the amount of observer training provided to a group of principals, researchers asked what the impact might have been on student learning. Under the Excellence in Teaching Project (EITP), principals received training on how to rate lessons using a version of Charlotte Danielson's Framework for Teaching. With the assistance of the Danielson Group in the project's first year, that training included:

■ Three days of initial training over the summer on the instrument, evidence collection, and coaching

■ Monthly professional learning community meetings and quarterly half-day professional development sessions to address specific observation skills and challenges

■ The opportunity for principals to compare the ratings they gave with those given by independent expert observers who observed the same teachers at the same time

Participating principals had to provide project leaders with the same feedback they gave teachers. District leaders also personally messaged the importance of the project to improving teaching and learning.

The following year, however, training for the EITP's second cohort of principals was reduced significantly as funding failed to keep pace with growth in participation. This led researchers at the University of Pennsylvania and the University of Chicago Consortium for Chicago School Research to compare differences in student achievement gains among schools in the two principal cohorts. Researchers found that after one year the first group, whose principals received robust observer training, made greater gains than the second group, which at that point hadn't received any training. After two years, the first group made even greater gains than the second, which by then had received the less robust version of training (Figure 1.1). The study is notable because schools were randomly assigned into each cohort, allowing for better comparison.

FIGURE 1.1   In Chicago: Robust Observer Training Translates into Greater Student Learning

Difference between student achievement gains in schools led by administrators who received robust training and student achievement gains in comparison schools

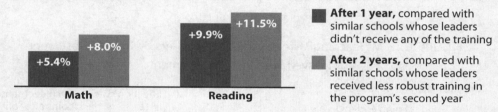

After 1 year, compared with similar schools whose leaders didn't receive any of the training

After 2 years, compared with similar schools whose leaders received less robust training in the program's second year

Note: Student achievement gains are compared in terms of standard deviations.

An article in *Education Next* put the size of the student learning gains into perspective. According to the article, if Chicago's weakest-performing schools made the same learning gains as the schools led by principals who received the most robust training, the lower-performing schools could narrow the gap between their performance and the district's average performance by 25 to 50 percent.[5] To be sure, robust observer training might not, by itself, produce such gains in those schools. (In fact, the researchers found that the schools most likely to improve were also the ones with the least poverty.) But the results suggest that when conditions are right, observer training can have a significant impact.

Video-Based Coaching via MyTeachingPartner. Another study that involved a random design experiment of observation-based feedback also showed that student learning improved in the classrooms of those teachers who received effective coaching. A research team from the University of Virginia and elsewhere randomly assigned teachers from a study group to receive a year of coaching via MyTeachingPartner (MTP), a video-based professional development program built around the Classroom Assessment Scoring System (CLASS) observation instrument.

Teachers received coaching that consisted of eight to eleven highly structured cycles in which teachers submitted videos of their teaching. The teachers then engaged in focused reflection and planning with a coach, and tried new techniques in the class-room. Coaches received extensive initial training and ongoing support that helped them identify relevant evidence of effective performance, prepare for discussions with teachers, and engage in collaborative action planning. Investigators later analyzed student achievement gains in the classrooms of teachers who participated and in the classrooms of a control group of teachers who did not receive coaching.[6] The gains they attributed to the observation-based coaching were equivalent to moving students' assessment results from the 50th percentile to the 59th (see Figure 1.2).

FIGURE 1.2   MyTeachingPartner: Coaching Teachers by Trained Observers Improved Students' Achievement

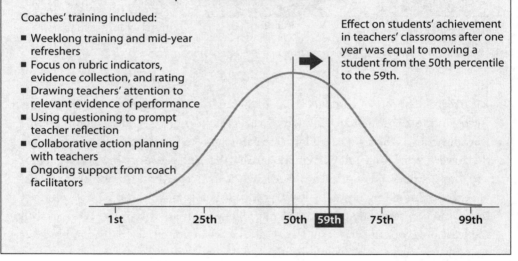

Coaches' training included:

- Weeklong training and mid-year refreshers
- Focus on rubric indicators, evidence collection, and rating
- Drawing teachers' attention to relevant evidence of performance
- Using questioning to prompt teacher reflection
- Collaborative action planning with teachers
- Ongoing support from coach facilitators

Effect on students' achievement in teachers' classrooms after one year was equal to moving a student from the 50th percentile to the 59th.

1st   25th   50th 59th   75th   99th

  TIP

One way to message that observer training is professional development—and not just about evaluation—is to allow participation in the training to count toward required professional development hours for principals and others who take part in observation.

☑ TECHNIQUES:
MAKING THE CASE FOR OBSERVER TRAINING

To Lay the Foundation:

- To make the case with evaluators, prior to training ask small groups to rate the same lesson video using the rubric. Highlight resulting inconsistencies and ask participants what impact those inconsistencies could have on teachers, students, and the school system.

- Collect survey data from teachers on their perception of the feedback they receive and their level of trust in the evaluation system.

- Explain to evaluators and teachers how observer training supports actionable, specific feedback to improve teaching practice.

- With system leaders, stress the importance of accurate information about the quality of teaching to assess the need for and effectiveness of professional development investments. Also clarify that observer training itself represents an investment in teacher professional development, not just in evaluation.

- Point to research, including the studies cited in this chapter, showing that robust observer training improves teaching and learning.

To Build and Improve:

- Share success stories with stakeholder groups on the benefits of your observer training. Collect testimonials from training participants able to articulate how training improved their feedback and made them more effective instructional leaders.

- Look for data to share with stakeholders to suggest the need for and benefits of robust observer training (e.g., if surveys show your system's teachers getting more useful feedback, or observer assessment results show greater consistency).

- Over time, look for and share data showing that teaching practice has improved when evaluators received high-quality training on observation and feedback (e.g., ratings on "use of questioning" gradually increased).

- Share with school system leaders examples of how observation data have helped to better target professional development investments.

Putting It into Practice

To Lay the Foundation:

What do stakeholders in your school system need to understand most so they can appreciate the importance of robust observer training, and what messages would most resonate with them?

To Build and Improve:

Based on the successes and challenges you've experienced with your training, what messages and strategies could you use to build greater support?

This item can be downloaded from www.wiley.com/go/betterfeedback

CHAPTER 2

Finding Enough Observers

ESSENTIAL QUESTION

Who Will You Train to Ensure Sufficient Feedback?

You earn credibility by doing what you say you'll do. When applied to a teacher observation system, that means ensuring that every teacher receives a sufficient number of observations by a trained and trustworthy observer. If your school system promises that each teacher will receive quality feedback from three cycles of 30-minute observations—including written reports and post-observation conferences—then your school system better deliver on that promise. Not only will you earn credibility, but you will reduce teachers' anxiety about the process, avoid lawsuits stemming from not following procedures, and receive more reliable data.

> *Systems must consider a variety of factors that may limit the potential of observers to conduct the required number of observations and proactively plan around them.*

But while the mantra of "do what you say you'll do" is simple, living up to it is not. Having enough evaluators who can perform quality observations is no easy feat. School systems must consider a variety of factors that may prevent observers from conducting the specified number of observations and must proactively plan around these limitations. Smart planning will often require that you train many more observers than you may actually need. More than likely, this will require thinking outside the box about who can observe teachers in the classroom and what these observations might entail, without sacrificing quality.

Quality Is a Heavy Lift

Some potential observers may not be ready to perform quality observations after their initial training. This can be for many reasons, ranging from the quality of their administrator preparation programs to the effectiveness of past professional experiences and training. Observing requires significant instructional expertise and the ability to put aside long-held pedagogical preferences in favor of a shared vision of instructional quality. At the same time, the first few iterations of observer training may not be wholly successful. Even after high-quality initial training is in place, a school system may find that as many as 40 percent of trainees still need additional support.

Carrying out a quality observation also takes time, even for the most highly skilled evaluators. An observer must collect and organize an accurate record of relevant evidence, interpret and judge that evidence using a rubric, and then prepare and deliver meaningful feedback that improves teacher practice. If observers must complete more teacher observations than they think their busy schedules allow, they may cut corners. In some school systems, the result has been observers trying to complete an almost impossible number of teacher observations right before a deadline—not a prescription for positive change.

Facing Up to Supply and Demand

To tackle the twin challenges of skill and time, you need to make sure you have enough observers who can perform enough quality observations within the available time. In the following table are the key variables, the exact values of which will vary from place to place.

Demand Variables	Supply Variables
■ **Time needed to complete a quality observation:** In your system, do observers complete written feedback? Must they complete a pre-observation conference? These steps will take additional time.	■ **The percentage of time observers can dedicate to observation:** Many observers have myriad other responsibilities: engaging parents, leading professional learning, and managing school operations. School systems need to consider how much time is left for observers to spend on observation and feedback and think creatively about ways to increase it.
■ **The number of educators who need to be observed:** Do teachers receive different numbers or types of observations based on past performance or tenure? Are out-of-classroom staff also observed?	■ **The number of individuals who can observe:** States and districts may have rules about who can observe. Is it only school leaders? Instructional leadership teams? Can trained colleagues, central office staff, or retired administrators be leveraged?

First, you should determine how much time is required to complete all observations. Figure 2.1 shows how to calculate the total time required. Include time for each task an observer needs to do: from preparing for an observation through discussing the results with the teacher to writing the necessary documentation. For a full observation, all those steps may take up to four hours. If you don't know how long it takes, ask a group of evaluators to time themselves going through the process. Resist the temptation to think it shouldn't take so long. You'll wind up with a lot of frustrated observers and teachers if you plan based on unrealistic numbers.

FIGURE 2.1   Determining Overall Demand for Observation Time

Time to complete a full observation		Number of teachers required to receive full observations		Number of times each teacher gets a full observation each year		Total hours required for full observations annually
▪ pre-conference ▪ observation ▪ written feedback ▪ post-conference	✖		✖		=	
4 hours		**450**		**3**		**5,400**

➕

Time to complete an abbreviated observation (if permitted)		Number of teachers to receive abbreviated observations		Number of times those teachers are to get abbreviated observations each year		Total hours required for abbreviated observations annually
May be shorter, more focused, require less documentation	✖		✖		=	
1 hour		**150**		**3**		**450**

	Total hours required for all observations	**5,850**

Remember to factor in time for any abbreviated observations that your system permits or requires. A study by the MET project found that combining multiple short observations with one full observation could be as reliable as combining two full observations.[7] Shorter observations may involve less time in the classroom and require less documentation. Using both short and long observations for some or all teachers may help with scheduling. But remember that if you use both short and long observations, you need to train observers how to do each reliably.

Things rarely go completely as intended, so do contingency planning. Some observers will need additional training before they're proficient enough to rate teaching as part of formal evaluation. Some may not get there even after receiving additional training that's generally proven effective with most observers. To avoid falling short, plan to train more observers than you need. To do that, multiply your system's total number of observation hours by some factor based on your expected success rate in getting observers to proficiency after initial training. When training is new, that multiplier may be as high as 1.5.

FIGURE 2.2   Determining the Overall Supply of Observation Time

Number of SCHOOL LEADERS in positions that can observe		Percentage of time these school leaders can observe		Hours in the workday for these school leaders		Total days in the year when observations can take place*		Total supply of hours available for observation
22	✖	10%	✖	8	✖	140	=	2,464

➕

Number of PEER OBSERVERS who can observe		Percentage of time peer observers can observe		Hours in the workday for these observers		Total days in the year when observations can take place*		Total supply of hours available for observation
10	✖	15%	✖	8	✖	140	=	1,680

Typically observations take place within certain windows of time during the school year; remember to subtract from those times testing days, holidays, and professional days when observations are not possible.

= Total hours available for observation   **4,144**

Next, figure out how much time you currently have to work with. Figure 2.2 gives an example of this. The key is knowing what portion of each observer's time is available for observation. To determine how much time each observer has available, you may need to review written job expectations, conduct a survey, or discuss with some of those to be trained how much time they have available. The percent of time that may be allocated for observation will vary by position; the example in Figure 2.2 shows how to figure out the observation time available for two positions, that of school leader and peer observer, but you may have more positions for which you need to determine the time available for observation. Don't forget also that there are many days during the school year that aren't appropriate for observing: on testing days, at the beginning of the school year and at the end, and so on.

What if your hours available for observation are less than the hours you need? First, know you're in good company. Ensuring quality observations for all teachers is a significant undertaking. It's an ongoing and core aspect of people's jobs—one that changes the very nature of leadership and professionalism in schools. Virtually all school systems that implement quality observations find they need to reallocate time and resources to make sure those observations happen for every teacher.

Second, don't sacrifice quality. Faced with a gap in resources, it may be tempting to reduce expectations for preparing for observations and conferences—or to reduce the number of observations a teacher gets. But this reduces the amount of meaningful feedback in a system and can erode the reliability of evaluation. Consistent quality feedback is needed to support all teachers—those who struggle, those who excel, and the vast majority in the middle who represent the greatest potential to shift practice at scale.

Nonetheless, you can change the variables in the formulas in the figures we've shown and still maintain quality. Here are four strategies:

Differentiate observations for different teachers. If your system is providing the same number of observations to all teachers, consider whether differentiating by past performance is feasible. Providing fewer or shorter observations to higher-performing teachers can reduce the anxiety of top performers, while still providing those teachers with feedback and focusing your efforts on those who need more intensive support.

Rethink the requirements. Consider what's required for each observation. Many systems require a pre-observation, a full lesson observation, written feedback, and a post-conference. Is there a way to reduce the burden but keep the parts that ensure quality data and feedback? Each system will need to answer this question on its own, but systems might consider shorter observations, making pre-conferences optional, or reducing the amount that's required in a written evaluation. Some systems require written evaluations only for "full" observations, for example.

Rethink who can observe. Many systems rely exclusively on school leaders to complete observations. But other individuals can be trained to reduce the burden on administrators. Examine your collective bargaining agreements and state legislation to determine if there are restrictions on who may observe. If there are, consider if there are things that might be exchanged—such as fewer or shorter observations for top performers—to provide more flexibility in who can observe. Recent retirees may be another source of potential observers. Providing teacher leaders the opportunity to observe may be a means of providing additional professional development and grooming future leaders.

Leverage video. Filming and uploading lessons to a secure website may be one way to increase the number of people who can observe. Some systems use trained external observers to evaluate lessons, while others are able to use video to evaluate educators in rural settings or in school buildings with a high staff-to-observer ratio. Video may also be helpful in observing specialty content areas, such as some world languages, for which only a small number of observers may have expertise.

Solving the time/human resource puzzle takes collaboration. Convene school leaders—including principals, department heads, union representatives, and other teacher leaders—to consider what's possible given current constraints, and which constraints might be changed. Communicate to such groups that the goal isn't to increase the number of observations; it's to provide sufficient feedback so all teachers can be successful. Having more individuals observe shouldn't be seen as a challenge to the authority of current school administrators; rather, it gives them a manageable load, while increasing the amount of instructional expertise in their buildings.

> *Communicate to stakeholders that the goal isn't to increase the number of observations; it's to provide sufficient feedback so all teachers can be successful.*

As with most aspects of planning for quality observations, determining how many observers you need to train involves a good deal of guesswork at first. To plan better going forward, you need to collect data: How many of the observers that you trained were in fact ready to observe after initial training? How long did it really take observers to work through the observation process? Where in the process does unnecessary friction remain? Could certain administrative tasks involved be automated? The good news is that observations will take less time as evaluators gain experience with the process.

 ## SNAPSHOT:
EXTRA EYES IN MINNESOTA

Minneapolis Public Schools has trained hundreds of "secondary observers" to provide observations. The secondary observers are current teachers and instructional coaches based in school buildings. They provide observations to colleagues and participate in regular training to ensure they are calibrated. The district has been able to repurpose unused coverage funds—designed to compensate schools for substitutes when teachers are out of the classroom—to pay for secondary observers' time.

☑ TECHNIQUES: FINDING ENOUGH OBSERVERS

To Lay the Foundation:

■ Use the example formulas in this chapter to determine if your system has a gap between the total amount of time needed to provide observations and the amount of time your observers can currently cover. Remember to factor in the need to train more observers than required to account for the fact that some will not be ready after their initial training.

■ Put in place a plan to provide additional support and reteaching so that observers who aren't ready after their initial training still have a chance to develop the necessary skills.

■ Review contract language and other policies regarding who can observe to see if they'd allow others to do so.

■ Convene principals, teacher leaders, and other instructional leaders to discuss ways to expand the number of observers, and the amount of time they can spend on observation.

■ If possible, stagger the rollout of observations over two to three years. This will allow more opportunity to build capacity and make refinements before going to scale.

To Build and Improve:

■ Identify and expand the use of training and reteaching strategies that are successful in getting new observers ready to provide accurate and meaningful feedback.

■ Survey and talk to observers about how long the observation process is taking them and where in the process they see opportunities to increase efficiency, including the use of technology to automate some tasks.

■ Capture the value of observer training to those who receive it. Their stories can make for effective recruitment tools.

- Consider if there are additional ways to involve others in observing. For example, could expert teachers volunteer to become trained and provide feedback to colleagues who request it?

- Consider additional ways to "share" observers across schools (e.g., a school's department head might observe in multiple schools as well as her own).

- Look for ways to leverage video to mitigate the challenge of scheduling and geography. This might begin with a small group of teachers who volunteer to be observed based on recordings of their lessons.

🔅 Putting It into Practice

To Lay the Foundation:

What steps can you take to determine the gap between the supply of and demand for observation time in your system, and how can you find ways to fill it?

To Build and Improve:

From your experience, what are some promising strategies your system might use to better ensure a sufficient number of quality observations for all teachers?

⬇ This item can be downloaded from www.wiley.com/go/betterfeedback

CHAPTER 3

Deciding on Training Delivery Methods

ESSENTIAL QUESTION
How Will You Deliver Training?

Before you decide on the content, structure, and design of your observer training, consider how you might deliver your training. The kind of work involved in ensuring sufficient quality will vary greatly depending on who does the training and what methods they use. Developing training requires a different approach from outsourcing it. Creating an online training program involves different tools from developing live training. Your options depend upon the resources, expertise, and policy contexts that are available in your school system. Be sure you understand the implications of each before choosing among them or choosing to combine different options.

One of the biggest decisions related to delivery is whether to build or buy observer training. Ideally, whether or not resources exist to build new training should factor into deciding what instrument to use. When a state or district chooses to create its own observation instrument, the only option is to develop its own training. Off-the-shelf programs will support consistency only when they are used with the instruments they were built to support. When you make even modest changes to an instrument, it may render existing training obsolete because the training is aligned to the original instrument, not to your adaptation of it.

Absent a highly compelling reason, there's too much other work involved in implementing observations to commit staff time and funds to creating a new instrument and training if proven ones can do the job.

While we don't recommend it for most school systems, there can be some benefits when a district or state develops a new instrument and training. It can build ownership when your own instructional experts define expectations. Those who participate in development gain deep insights about the instrument that make them even more valuable instructional leaders.

In addition, districts and states can choose from many new tools that can help them create training for new instruments. Free online services, like Vimeo and Google Drive, allow for password-protected video sharing. The American Federation of Teachers and MyLearningPlan have created a free online tool, EvidencePro, that lets observers enter evidence from an observation and then easily sort it according to a rubric's teaching components. You can purchase access to videos of teaching from, among others, the ETS Classroom Video Library, and the SOE Teaching and Learning Exploratory, run by the

University of Michigan School of Education. Services by companies such as RANDA Solutions, Empirical Education, and Frontline Technologies (which acquired MyLearningPlan) let you organize content in a single platform for viewing video, rating lessons, and comparing evidence and results. Insight Education Group sells similar products. Many of these systems can produce reports showing trends in observer proficiency.

Building from scratch does have its drawbacks, chief among them the resources required to create a quality instrument and training. It takes significant expertise in teaching and assessment to create an instrument whose rubric is clear, manageable, and has data to support its use in evaluating the quality of teaching. It also takes years of testing and tweaking. Then even more time and resources are needed to pilot and build out training to help evaluators learn how to apply it correctly. New platforms can help, but you still need to create all the content. This includes a library of carefully pre-scored video that is extensive enough to help observers become accurate in rating all parts of a rubric. You also need to plan all the learning activities that use those videos.

A school system should build from scratch only after considering alternatives, if any exist, and only if enough time and resources are available. Absent a highly compelling reason, there's too much other work involved in implementing observations to commit staff time and funds to creating a new instrument and training if proven ones can do the job. No matter how training is delivered, a school system must ensure that its evaluators complete it, and that those who do are applying the rubric correctly. You will need to supplement even off-the-shelf training with guidance on local procedures and additional supports that address the specific needs you've identified for your system. Figure 3.1 presents all these considerations in the form of a decision tree.

Considering Different Training Modes

Along with "who will provide the training?" another major question is "how will the training be presented?" Changes in technology have created significantly more options for how observers are trained. Trainees can review video almost anywhere and at any time. They can join live presentations remotely. They can submit their work and quickly get feedback on it without a meeting or phone call. This flexibility in scheduling and location is a boon for already busy principals and for efforts to foster a shared understanding of effective teaching across all schools in a system. It means that more evaluators are able to engage with the same training content, which supports consistency in practice.

But face-to-face training still has its place. In facilitated group sessions, trainers can probe the source of evaluators' misunderstandings. Persistent confusion over how to rate a component

FIGURE 3.1   Considerations in Who Develops Training

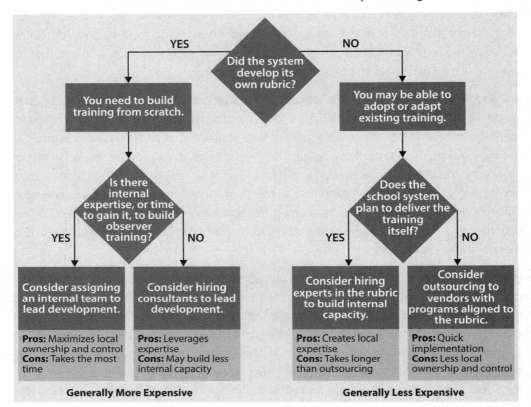

of teaching may relate to particular terms in the rubric, the content of video used to illustrate it, or some other factor. A skilled trainer can determine the cause, clarify, and make adjustments. Group sessions also allow trainees to hear each other's questions, and the answers, and to practice justifying their ratings to others who reviewed the same lesson. Some individuals also simply prefer face-to-face training over independent and online work (though you should weigh the potential for variability in trainer quality when considering face-to-face).

To decide how much use to make of different modes, consider your school system's capacities. To what extent are your evaluators comfortable with online training? Can they stream video on their computers without running into problems with bandwidth or the blocking software that the school has installed? If not, online might not be advisable. But before committing to live training, consider if your school system has access to a sufficient number of experts in instruction, evaluation, and adult learning who can lead high-quality training. To what extent will schedules and geography let you bring evaluators together for extended sessions? The following table outlines the considerations for choosing one mode over another.

Comparing Modes of Training

Mode	Key Strengths	Uses That Leverage Strengths	Considerations
Face-to-face	■ In group settings, allows observers to learn from each other ■ Trainers can make quick adjustments to address specific needs	■ At the start of training, address observers' early questions and allow them to experience some training as a group ■ At a midpoint, get together to gauge trainees' growing understanding and clear up any confusion ■ Review trainees' understanding at the end of training and address remaining issues prior to assessment	■ Can you provide a sufficient number of trainers/training times to keep groups to a manageable size? ■ Can you ensure that all your trainers are able to provide consistent quality of training?
Independent/online work	■ Standardizes the training content for trainees ■ Accommodates different trainee schedules and locations ■ May be less threatening because of anonymity ■ Enables checking of individual understanding throughout, and repeating portions as needed	■ Review videos of teaching to practice the skills of evidence collection, alignment of evidence to the correct teaching component, and scoring ■ Compare trainees' attempts to evaluate teaching with the work of expert observers for the same videos ■ Offer reflective activities to help observers identify personal biases that could affect their scoring ■ Support trainees with different learning needs (e.g., those who need more wait time or reflection time)	■ Can you ensure that trainees are able to use any needed technology? ■ How will you provide feedback to trainees on their independent work? ■ Can you monitor whether or not trainees are devoting sufficient time to independent work?

None of these decisions are either/or. There are many possibilities between outsourcing and doing it yourself. A school system with a new instrument may assign primary responsibility for training development to members of its own staff or to consultants.

None of these decisions are either/or. There are many possibilities between outsourcing and doing it yourself. A school system with a new instrument may assign primary responsibility for training development to members of its own staff or to consultants. Consultants may actually deliver training to evaluators for a period of time while building internal capacity to take over the role. No evaluator training is ever wholly online; some live activities are essential for learning a skill that's ultimately applied in the context of live instruction. But the mix of face-to-face versus independent work can vary, and it may change over time as more is learned about the success of each.

 SNAPSHOTS:
DIFFERENT DELIVERY METHODS

Building Online Training in DCPS: Having developed its own observation instrument—the Teaching and Learning Framework—District of Columbia Public Schools (DCPS) opted to build a training program from the ground up. Doing so would allow the district to make adjustments in training as it refined the observation system it had begun to roll out. With a $2.5 million grant from the Bill & Melinda Gates Foundation, DCPS created eight full-time positions, the "Align TLF Training Team," which spent two years developing a primarily online system, working with RANDA Solutions. After first developing a series of live sessions, the Align Team designed and packaged them into a set of modules using RANDA's web-based platform, Edvisor. Evaluators now work independently through the online modules to learn the rubric's structure and how to identify evidence for each teaching component, and to practice rating pre-scored videos of teaching; they also still come together periodically for in-person sessions to practice and address specific challenges.

Going Live in Minneapolis: Over several years, Minneapolis Public Schools has developed (and continues to refine) an observer training program using only face-to-face sessions. Developed with Teaching Learning Solutions, and delivered by a four-person team of central office staff, the training includes:

■   A four-day workshop for new evaluators, offered eight times a year

- Monthly three-hour sessions that employ pre-scored video to practice evidence collection and alignment and post-observation conference planning

- Annual follow-up support targeted to evaluators' needs, based on assessment of their skills

The district uses a rubric similar to Danielson's Framework for Teaching.

Blending Methods in Rhode Island: The Rhode Island Department of Education (RIDE) has used a combination of commercially developed and homegrown training to support evaluators throughout the state in learning to use Danielson's Framework for Teaching (See Figure 3.2). For the first few years of implementation, RIDE staff led in-person summer academies in which new evaluators were introduced to Teachscape Focus, the online training program built around the Danielson framework. Participants then worked through the Focus modules on their own over several weeks. In the winter and spring, observers from the same district took part in "calibration sessions" led by RIDE staff, in which they reviewed pre-scored videos of teaching and reached consensus on relevant evidence and ratings. Those who completed initial training then took part in annual follow-up training, also led by RIDE staff. Recently RIDE has completed development of a fully homegrown training program.

FIGURE 3.2   Combining Face-to-Face and Online Training in Rhode Island

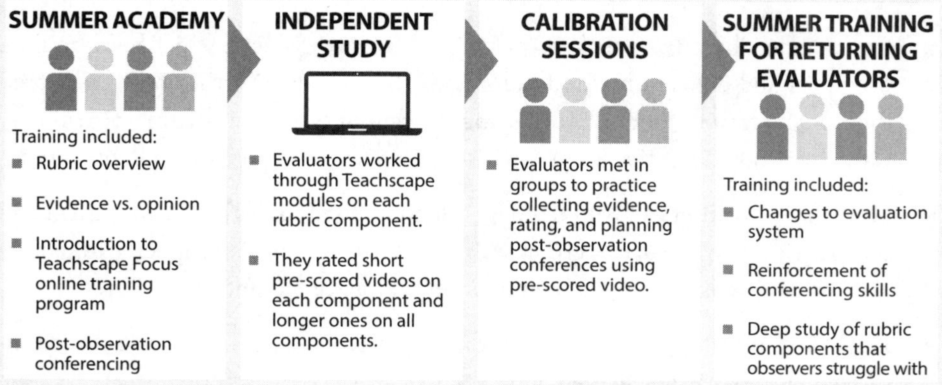

SUMMER ACADEMY

Training included:
- Rubric overview
- Evidence vs. opinion
- Introduction to Teachscape Focus online training program
- Post-observation conferencing

INDEPENDENT STUDY

- Evaluators worked through Teachscape modules on each rubric component.
- They rated short pre-scored videos on each component and longer ones on all components.

CALIBRATION SESSIONS

- Evaluators met in groups to practice collecting evidence, rating, and planning post-observation conferences using pre-scored video.

SUMMER TRAINING FOR RETURNING EVALUATORS

Training included:
- Changes to evaluation system
- Reinforcement of conferencing skills
- Deep study of rubric components that observers struggle with

✓ TECHNIQUES: DECIDING ON DELIVERY METHODS

To Lay the Foundation:

- Use the decision tree in "Considerations in Who Develops Training" on page 38 to weigh your system's objectives, capacities, and time constraints.

- If a provider already offers training aligned to your rubric, determine which of the items in the Observer Training Checklist in this guide's appendix (pages 287–290) are addressed by that training, and which your school system would need to add itself.

- Rely primarily on face-to-face training when first developing it yourself. This allows for learning what works, and what doesn't, in real time and with a minimal investment. Once a set of content and activities is proven, it may be codified in an online platform.

- Assess stakeholders' views on online versus in-person training, and on relying primarily on commercial training versus a homegrown program.

- Talk to system leaders in similar contexts (e.g., geographically spread out, limited internal expertise, etc.) about lessons learned.

To Build and Improve:

- Consider feedback from training participants on the extent to which your training providers and delivery methods addressed their needs. Did they feel it prepared them to observe in their schools, using the school system's instrument? Did they want more opportunities for group discussion, or for more independent study?

- Look for opportunities to build independent-study modules based on content and materials proven to work in group sessions. What parts of training seem to require little or no discussion for trainees to develop the needed understanding?

- Look for ways to shift some group work to pre-work, by creating clear directions for what to do before a live session.

- Continue to rely primarily on face-to-face training for any new parts of a program (e.g., when adding follow-up training for the first time for experienced evaluators). Consider independent study when you've worked out the kinks.

💡 Putting It into Practice

To Lay the Foundation:

What constraints and criteria (expertise, cost, geography, who developed the rubric, etc.) are most important in deciding how training will be delivered in your system?

To Build and Improve:

What's working well in how training is delivered in your system, and how might different approaches address areas for improvement?

CHAPTER 4

Setting Priorities for Observer Training

ESSENTIAL QUESTION

What Will Be Your Goal for Training This Year?

High-quality training doesn't come overnight. It's the result of multiple iterations and capacity building. Your first attempts at observation training probably won't produce the accurate and meaningful feedback that you can expect from later attempts. Observation is too challenging to expect the first attempt to be fully successful. The results may be more trustworthy than when you had no training or research-based criteria for observation. But you should expect version 2.0 to work better than version 1.0, and expect a third version to work better than the second. What matters is that you build on a solid foundation and learn as you go.

From the very beginning of development, training needs to include certain essential activities that help evaluators gain the knowledge and skills they need to observe. These are:

Explaining the rubric, by providing an overview of the observation instrument's criteria, structure, and key features;

Minimizing bias, by making observers aware of their personal preferences and how to mitigate their impact on observation;

Supporting practice, through explicit instruction, modeling, and guided practice reviewing and rating pre-scored videos of teaching; and

Modeling feedback, by illustrating how to give teachers productive feedback based on their observations.

> *Observation that produces accurate and meaningful feedback is too challenging to expect a first attempt at training to be fully successful.*

None of these activities are optional. Leave any one out, and there's a good chance training will fail. Observers who don't understand a rubric's structure or how to keep their biases in check won't produce accurate ratings in guided practice. An observer who hasn't learned to produce accurate ratings cannot provide accurate and meaningful feedback. Without explicit training on how to provide feedback, teachers will receive feedback of uneven quality. Each activity supports and reinforces the effectiveness of the others.

These activities needn't be fully developed for training to have value, but they all must be addressed. Think of it as building a new airplane. To get off the ground, you need wings, an engine, and a rudder. But to get as far as you want to go, you'll need to improve those parts. Hence the first consideration in planning near-term goals for your training is whether you're addressing all four of the essential activities. If not, your first priority should be whatever foundational steps you need to take to make sure you're engaged in all the activities required for a training program to be considered complete.

But by itself a solid foundation won't get you to the point where all teachers are consistently experiencing accurate and meaningful feedback. To build on that foundation, you need to examine what's working with your training, and where you need to try something different. You also need to add to your training to make sure it develops all the knowledge and skills required to observe in whatever situation your observers may find themselves. Once all the pieces are in place, maintaining and improving quality is a matter of ongoing processes for considering changes based on collected data. The overall sequence of steps is outlined in Figure 4.1.[8]

A school system's focus for training in any year will depend on what's already been accomplished. If you're just starting to implement quality observations, you'll want to take the foundational steps across all the essential activities. If possible, stagger the rollout of a new training program to reduce the amount of rebuilding you need to do; you can learn a lot about what works, and what doesn't, by training a small subset of observers. School systems with elements of training already in place will likely focus on foundational steps for some activities, while building and improving for others.

Keep in mind that even after training is well developed, it takes time for those trained to fully master the art and science of observation. Much of what quality observation entails is new to educators: the use of descriptive evidence, interpretation based on common criteria, and the expectation that feedback is meaningful and actionable for teachers. It takes a big mind shift to go from relying on one's best judgment to the idea that any observer should make the same judgment as would anyone else who's rating correctly. Set goals and manage expectations accordingly—and call out progress along the way.

FIGURE 4.1   Key Steps to Address Essential Activities in Training

	Explaining the Rubric	Minimizing Bias	Supporting Practice	Modeling Feedback
Continual Improvement Steps	Establish a yearly process to consider changes to the rubric overview based on participant and teacher input.	Establish a yearly process to consider changes to bias awareness training based on input from participants.	Begin annual follow-up training to keep observers sharp and to develop more sophisticated skills.	Begin annual follow-up training on feedback that focuses on how to handle different situations.
Building Steps	Improve how you introduce the instrument based on participant feedback and any changes to the rubric.	Train observers to identify and counter their own biases.	Codify, enhance, and build out effective activities for modeling and practicing observation.	Require observers to practice giving feedback, and give them feedback on their feedback.
Foundational Steps	Explain the instrument's basis, structure, and the importance of using it correctly to rate practice.	Explain what bias is in the context of observation and why it's important to address.	Review types of evidence relevant to each teaching component, and let trainees practice observation with pre-scored video.	Show how use of a rubric to collect and rate evidence from the classroom supports quality feedback.

⌖ Putting It into Practice

To Lay the Foundation:

How would you restate the foundational steps in Figure 4.1 as a set of overarching first-year goals that you could communicate to others in your system?

To Build and Improve:

Which steps in Figure 4.1—foundational, building, and continual improvement—has your system accomplished for each of the essential activities? What does this suggest as a focus for the coming year?

This item can be downloaded from www.wiley.com/go/betterfeedback

PART II

PRE-SCORING VIDEO

CHAPTER 5

Understanding Pre-Scoring Video

ESSENTIAL QUESTION

What Is "Pre-Scored Video"?

Picture this scene: As part of their training, a group of observers are asked to rate a video of instruction using their district's observation rubric. They each review the clip, take detailed notes, and seek to align what they saw and heard with the right level of performance. But the discussion quickly turns into debate over how to rate the teaching on a key component in the rubric.*

One camp says the video showed *proficient* performance for "use of questioning." Another says *needs improvement*. Drawing on years of experience that have shaped their visions of effective instruction, both camps cite evidence they feel is most relevant to their interpretation of the teacher's practice. Despite extended conversation, no clear consensus is reached when the session ends.

This scenario, which likely echoes similar ones in many school systems, poses some major problems. The observers leave with significantly different interpretations of the same practice, undermining the fairness of observations and the quality of the data they produce. The resulting inconsistencies will soon be apparent to teachers. The observers themselves may be frustrated by not having had the opportunity to learn how to accurately rate the video. They haven't been set up to provide consistent and specific feedback.

Fortunately, there's a way to avoid these outcomes. To build a common understanding of what it looks like when teaching is demonstrated at particular levels takes practice with examples of teaching for which accurate ratings have been determined. This is why pre-scored video is foundational to observer training. Pre-scored video is used to clarify parts of a rubric, to practice evidence collection and scoring, and to assess observer proficiency. Learning to assign the right score for the right reasons isn't just about accuracy. It allows observers to clearly explain *this is your score, this is why, and this is how to improve it*. Giving teachers access to pre-scored video also helps them better understand a school system's expectations and demystifies the observation process.

States or districts that adopt an existing rubric may use training that includes already pre-scored video, but an understanding of pre-scoring is important in any trustworthy

---

* Some material in Chapters 5–9 is borrowed from the MET project brief, "What It Looks Like: Master Coding Video for Observer Training and Assessment," by Catherine McClellan of Clowder Consulting, LLC. In her former role at ETS, McClellan led the team that designed the online observer training, assessment, and scoring system used by ETS for the MET project's classroom observation research.

observation system. Where a rubric is new or modified (e.g., to align with new college- and career-ready standards), pre-scoring should be part of the instrument's development; attempting to score actual lessons consistently is an important test of applicability. Commercially available observer training also may need augmenting with video examples from the local context. Moreover, the pre-scoring process—in which individuals reach agreement on how to accurately rate videos—can be a powerful professional learning opportunity for teachers and instructional leaders, sharpening a shared vision of effective teaching.

A FOUNDATIONAL PROCESS

Pre-scoring video serves multiple purposes in an observation system:

- To inform development of a new rubric, or revisions to an existing one

- To identify challenges to target in observer training

- To give concrete examples of a rubric's components, performance levels, and terms

- To let observers compare their own attempts to rate with accurate ratings

- To assess observer accuracy at the end of training and on a periodic basis

- To build a cadre of experts in a rubric who can play leadership roles in a system

---

So what is pre-scored video? Pre-scored video anchors an observation rubric to actual examples of teaching. Expert reviewers do much the same when they score and annotate examples of students' written responses to anchor a common understanding of how to evaluate answers to open-ended questions on a standardized test. With pre-scored video, segments of recorded lessons are anchored to the correct performance rating for each teaching component the video segment illustrates. (Other terms for pre-scoring include "anchor rating," "master coding," and "master scoring.") Pre-scored video makes concrete the written definitions in a rubric. The video makes the written descriptions of practice and different levels of performance come alive for observers.

But you need more than just the correct rating for pre-scored video to serve its purpose. Observers must also understand the justification for each rating. When observers watch a recorded lesson, they can see what classroom behaviors align with a particular rating. Thus they are better able to rate other lessons accurately and in a variety of contexts. In addition, when observers understand why a different performance rating would not be correct for a given set of observed behaviors, then they can more clearly communicate to teachers what would result in a higher performance rating. Pre-scored video supports both accuracy in

FIGURE 5.1   Well-Supported Ratings for a Pre-Scored Video Segment

USE OF QUESTIONING: **Effective**	
Evidence	**Score Rationale**
Teacher questions: 14:02 "What tools would a scientist use?"	**Why the rating is *effective.*** Most of the questions the teacher asks are open in nature and engage students in deeper thinking and further discussion.
16:58 "What would a butterfly do?"	**Why a lower score is wrong.** The teacher does not use a combination of open and closed questions, with only some questions inviting thoughtful response.
17:59 "How is the pollen going to come off the flower and go to another?"	**Why a higher score is wrong.** The teacher's questions do not provide students an opportunity to demonstrate reasoning for formulating their own questions.

ratings and actionable feedback. For this reason, a quality pre-scoring process produces clear justifications not just for why a rating is correct, but also for why other ratings would not be correct.

The example in Figure 5.1 shows the key elements of well-supported ratings for a pre-scored video. This example looks at the teaching component "use of questioning" in a four-minute segment, or excerpt, from a lesson video. The score rationale in this example justifies a rating of *effective* based on the observation rubric. It uses the language of the rubric and specific evidence from the lesson to explain why observed behaviors were rated *effective*, and why other ratings would be incorrect. Observers learn that the key indicator for a performance rating is the extent to which the teacher's questions invite student thinking and ask students to explain their reasoning. Exact quotes of the teachers' questions, with time stamps for when they were asked in the video, show that although the questions invited student thinking and discussion, none of the questions encouraged students to demonstrate their reasoning.

Pre-scored video sets the gold standard for accurate performance rating with a rubric. Given that, you need to make every effort in your pre-scoring process to ensure that the ratings and justifications produced are both clear and correct, based on the rubric. If they are not, then observers will not receive the support they need to provide accurate ratings and effective feedback. For this reason, the pre-scoring process involves multiple expert observers, or coders, who score the same video segments individually, and then compare notes to reach an agreement on an appropriate score and rationale for the teaching demonstrated in the segment—a process called reconciliation. (See Figure 5.2.) Without this process, a single master coder may overlook relevant evidence or fail to notice a key difference in how a rubric distinguishes between two performance levels.

FIGURE 5.2   Steps in Pre-Scoring Video

1. **Expert observers independently review video segments and submit score rationales based on the rubric.**

2. **Submissions are compared and differences reconciled to produce a single set of scores and rationales.**

3. **Video segments are used in training with reconciled scores and rationales to align trainees' understanding of the rubric.**

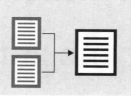
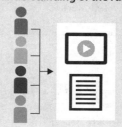

But your success in producing useful pre-scored video also depends on many other factors, such as the expertise of your master coders and their understanding of the pre-scoring process, the audio and video quality of the recording to be scored, the specificity and language of written score justifications, and the use of data for continual improvement of the process. You also need strategic planning that builds support for the process, identifies the required resources, and builds your capacities in a way that best meets your school system's ongoing needs. Each of these issues is addressed in the chapters that follow, with advice on how to start a pre-scoring process and how to strengthen it over time.

SNAPSHOT: PRE-SCORING VIDEO AND THE AMERICAN FEDERATION OF TEACHERS

The American Federation of Teachers (AFT) has included pre-scoring video as part of its teacher evaluation work, funded by a U.S. Department of Education Investing in Innovation (i3) grant. AFT state affiliates in New York and Rhode Island have worked with a dozen districts to pre-score video to support teacher and evaluator training aligned to rubrics shared across the participating school systems within each state. Taking part in the pre-scoring process have been teacher leaders, peer evaluators, principals, and central office administrators.

> *"It makes you think about the rubric so much more deeply—which makes you think about practice so much more deeply. It allows you to verbalize expectations and make it real for folks."* —Katrina Pillay, a participant from Cranston Public Schools in a pre-scoring process organized by the Rhode Island Federation of Teachers and Health Professionals

"It improved our rubric. There were pieces where we felt the language needed to be fine-tuned. When you actually start using the rubric is when you say, 'I really don't know how to find this.'" —Robin Hecht, a participant from the Marlboro Central School District in a pre-scoring process organized by the New York State United Teachers

Putting It into Practice

To Lay the Foundation:

Which parts of the pre-scoring process do you have the most questions about?

To Build and Improve:

In which parts of your pre-scoring process do you see the greatest need for improvement or refinement?

See page 108–111 for guidance on using data to answer this question.

This item can be downloaded from www.wiley.com/go/betterfeedback

CHAPTER 6

Planning a Pre-Scoring Process

ESSENTIAL QUESTION

How Will You Create Support for Pre-Scoring Video?

The investment required to pre-score video is significant. You will need time to prepare videos of teaching for scoring, to train master coders, and to let them review video segments repeatedly to record relevant evidence, align this evidence to the correct indicators of a rubric, and then come to an agreement on performance ratings. This time commitment is ongoing. Typically, master coders are teachers, principals, and other instructional leaders who may devote several hours a month to pre-scoring video throughout the year. Moreover, you may find that it takes up to two years before the process runs smoothly and consistently yields high-quality examples of well-justified ratings. Such an effort will succeed only if your stakeholders appreciate its value.

> *Teachers' trust in the whole evaluation system suffers when different observers apply the same rubric differently. Without clear, evidence-based explanations, even accurate performance ratings are little help to teachers who want to improve their practice.*

In many states and districts, classroom observations count for half or more of a teacher's overall evaluation. Teachers' trust in the whole evaluation system suffers when different observers apply the same rubric differently; teachers are left knowing that their ratings depend more on who does the observing than on how their teaching compares with a set of common expectations. Teachers' trust also falters if these observations fail to produce actionable feedback. Without clear, evidence-based explanations, even accurate performance ratings are little help to teachers who want to improve their practice. For observation to improve teaching and learning, observers must be skilled at providing teachers with well-supported performance ratings.

To develop this skill, pre-scored video is almost essential. Your observers are able to accurately rate teacher performance when they understand why a particular instance of teaching merits a specific rating and how their own attempts to rate performance compare with the ratings that experts gave the same instruction. You would find this very hard to accomplish with live observations of teachers in the classroom. In a live teaching observation with one or more observers, a trainer must determine the correct rating on the fly. Classroom space also severely limits the number of evaluators who can observe the same live lesson. In contrast, video examples allow for:

- Pre-scoring by multiple expert observers to confirm the correct rating and rationale;

- Unpacking all the relevant evidence in a few minutes of teaching;

- Rewinding and reviewing an instance of teaching multiple times; and

- Exposing all observers to the same examples, regardless of where and when training takes place.

How you build support for pre-scoring video will evolve over time. When you're starting out, your state or district will have few results to point to in making the case for this investment. To lay a strong foundation of support, you need to educate your stakeholders about the importance of consistent evaluations and actionable feedback and about how both are advanced by examples of well-supported performance ratings. Later, your state or district can point to the benefits it experienced to build on that foundation. Participants in the pre-scoring process can be especially effective in communicating its value. Creating support means building trust among stakeholders in the pre-scoring process, in the master coders, and in what they produce.

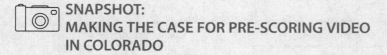

SNAPSHOT:
MAKING THE CASE FOR PRE-SCORING VIDEO
IN COLORADO

The Colorado Department of Education (CDE) created a set of summary documents to explain how and why it manages a master-scoring process. A short fact sheet explains who serves as "master scorers," why consistency in evaluation is important, and how the state is making pre-scored video available to teachers and school leaders through an online platform called Elevate Colorado. The two-page document states: "This process builds clarity in understanding and identifying high-quality teaching and thus consistency in evaluation."

No one formula can determine the cost of pre-scoring video in every context. The biggest factors are the time for people to manage the process and the time of master coders, who are typically paid a stipend. Figure 6.1, with 2015 figures from the CDE, shows the cost in dollars and time for each of the state's master scorers. In its first year of pre-scoring, Colorado trained and worked with six master scorers. Now with 11 master scorers, the state reviews and pre-scores about 12 videos a year. The time required for review and reconciliation may vary significantly among states and districts, depending on the complexity and specificity of the rubrics.

Additional expenses include the time of department personnel who recruit and train master scorers, plus training-related travel expenses. Colorado also pays three experts in the state's rubric to review the work of master scorers as a form of quality control. The cost of getting video of teaching to pre-score depends on the source. Colorado has both purchased access to lesson videos from commercial vendors and contracted with a videographer to record new lessons.

FIGURE 6.1   Costs per Master Scorer in Colorado

Stipends	Time Commitments	
$2,250	Spring and summer training to learn process and begin pre-scoring	Eight work sessions during year to compare and reconcile ratings
	■ 3.5 days for initial training, plus a one-day refresher midyear	■ Up to 3 hours for each session
	■ Plus pre-work (includes reviewing video)	■ Plus pre-work (1.5–3 hours to review video)

☑ TECHNIQUES: BUILDING SUPPORT FOR PRE-SCORING VIDEO

To Lay the Foundation:

■ Craft a concise message for funding proposals, information sheets, and recruit-ment efforts about how pre-scoring video supports consistent evaluation and actionable feedback.

■ Build credibility for pre-scoring video among teacher and administration groups by explaining how multiple instructional experts work together in a structured process to pre-score each video. Share how important this work is to building a consistent vision for effective instruction across the system.

■ Ask groups of educators not trained with pre-scored video to score part of a video and compare the ratings. Use examples of inconsistency to make the case to the group for pre-scoring.

■ Cite research, including studies by MET project partners, showing that observers trained and assessed with pre-scored video can produce consistent performance ratings. (See the MET project research paper "Gathering Feedback for Teaching: Combining High-Quality Observations with Student Surveys and Achievement Gains" [2012] Seattle, WA: Bill & Melinda Gates Foundation.)

To Build and Improve:

■ Share testimonials from teachers and administrators about how working as master coders has improved their own teaching and instructional leadership. Have them talk about the rigor of the pre-scoring process.

■ When using pre-scored video in training with observers new to the process, briefly explain how the correct ratings were determined by multiple instructional experts.

■ Communicate the professional backgrounds of master coders and how represen-tative they are (from different grade levels, regions of the state or district, etc.).

■ Communicate examples of how the pre-scoring of video has improved parts of the observation system (e.g., identifying rubric components to clarify).

■ Share observer assessment data from your own state or district on the amount of consistency among observers trained with pre-scored video.

💡 Putting It into Practice

To Lay the Foundation:

What case for pre-scoring would be most compelling to multiple perspectives (teachers, school leaders, administrators) in your school system?

To Build and Improve:

How can you more effectively communicate the benefits of pre-scoring video to educators across your system?

⬇ This item can be downloaded from www.wiley.com/go/betterfeedback

ESSENTIAL QUESTION

What Is Your Goal for Pre-Scoring Video This Year?

Pre-scoring video is not a one-time activity. It's an ongoing process in your state or district's efforts to foster a shared understanding of effective teaching. It's also a capacity that can be developed only through practice. With each round of pre-scoring video, your participants will get better at producing examples of well-supported performance ratings that can help evaluators do the same. Understanding this evolution helps with your near-term planning. You should determine your goals for pre-scoring video in any given year by basing them on how the process can best add value to your current efforts to improve teaching practice and student learning. That planning changes as you increase the capacity to pre-score video and as your observation system continually improves.

Ideally, the pre-scoring video process should be a part of your rubric's development. When you have observers try to score videos with a new rubric, it "pressure tests" the way the rubric distinguishes among different teaching components and performance levels. Indeed, if you try to get a rubric exactly right before you attempt to score lessons with it, you may find that you've wasted your time. Only when evaluators try to apply a draft instrument to actual teaching will it become apparent where wordsmithing—or more substantive changes—may be needed. Using video makes it easier for developers to understand why different observers might struggle to apply the instrument. If pre-scoring video was not part of your rubric's development, then you should test the rubric with some video scoring before proceeding.

If you have evidence that your evaluators can apply a rubric, then you can train a group of master coders to produce pre-scored videos for observer training. The training of master coders is discussed in Chapter 8, "Recruiting and Training Master Coders," but a key feature of this training is the use of existing pre-scored video to help master coders understand the process. If you do not yet have any trained master coders who are able to produce these videos, then the task must fall to those who have the best understanding of the rubric. This also pressure tests a pre-scoring process before teaching it to others. (At least one of the rubric experts who pre-scores video to train master coders should also lead the master coder training.)

It's unrealistic to expect to pre-score quality examples for most of a rubric in a matter of months. It's also not advisable. A school system's second attempt at pre-scoring is more likely

FIGURE 6.2   Building Capacity to Pre-Score Video

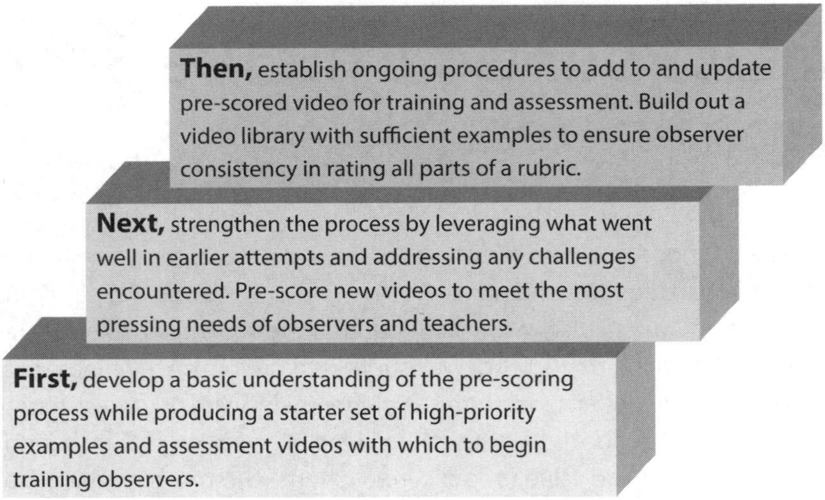

Then, establish ongoing procedures to add to and update pre-scored video for training and assessment. Build out a video library with sufficient examples to ensure observer consistency in rating all parts of a rubric.

Next, strengthen the process by leveraging what went well in earlier attempts and addressing any challenges encountered. Pre-score new videos to meet the most pressing needs of observers and teachers.

First, develop a basic understanding of the pre-scoring process while producing a starter set of high-priority examples and assessment videos with which to begin training observers.

than its first to produce accurate and well-supported ratings—and its third is more likely than its second. Moreover, if a rubric is likely to change (e.g., to better align with new student learning standards), then different video examples of teaching practice will be needed. Be careful when revising your rubrics, as even small changes in wording can alter interpretation. If your rubric changes, then your previously pre-scored video may need to be rescored. Better to learn the process while pre-scoring a limited number of videos than to do extensive rebuilding later.

> *With each round of pre-scoring video, your participants will get better at producing examples of well-supported performance ratings that can help evaluators do the same.*

When a solid understanding of the process is in place, the focus can shift to continually improving your pre-scoring process while building out a video library (see Figure 6.2).[9] At this point, you need to establish ongoing procedures to replace outdated or problematic videos, to refresh the supply of assessment videos, and to prioritize additional parts of a rubric to illustrate with new examples. The pre-scoring process itself should continue to improve as you learn more about the quality of the examples being produced and how effective they are in observer training. Pre-scoring video never ends in a trustworthy system of classroom observations. You will always need additional and updated examples to use in training. The need for any community of educators to better understand what effective teaching looks like is perennial.

☑ TECHNIQUES:
SETTING NEAR-TERM GOALS FOR PRE-SCORING VIDEO

To Lay the Foundation:

- To support a rubric's initial development, ask evaluators to try using the instrument to rate lesson videos. This may suggest where the rubric needs clarifying (e.g., if the rubric doesn't sufficiently define the teaching component "students are generally engaged").

- After a rubric is developed, have a small group of experts who know the instrument best pre-score three to four lesson videos to use in training a first cohort of master coders.

- Train a first cohort of master coders to pre-score a small number of videos that can be used in the first iteration of observer training.

To Build and Improve:

- Establish an ongoing process for pre-scoring new video. Additional examples are always needed to build out and update a video library that supports observer training.

- Replace pre-scored videos that proved to be problematic in training (e.g., if something in them distracted evaluators or they could not see or hear sufficient evidence to rate).

- Replace videos used for assessment so that evaluators do not see the same one multiple times.

- When parts of a rubric change, ask evaluators to score lesson videos to make sure the new language is interpreted as intended. Rubric revisions may require new examples of well-supported ratings.

🔅 Putting It into Practice

To Lay the Foundation:

What do you think are realistic goals for your first year of pre-scoring video?

To Build and Improve:

Which of the techniques for building and improving in the preceding list most resonate as goals for your system?

⬇ This item can be downloaded from www.wiley.com/go/betterfeedback

ESSENTIAL QUESTION

What Pre-Scored Video Do You Need?

Different parts of a job call for different tools. A video segment for illustrating part of a rubric requires different content than does a segment for practicing to rate entire lessons. When you understand which pre-scored videos can best add value to your observation system at a particular stage of implementation, you increase the chance of producing the videos that you need. Granted, pre-scoring video is a lot like mining: You can't know what you'll find before you start digging. You can't tell if a video shows what you need until you review it. But knowing what you need comes first. How to pre-screen video and identify segments for different uses is discussed in Chapter 7, "Getting the Right Video to Pre-Score." In the next few pages, we explain how to set your goals for what to produce.

At any stage of implementation, two categories of pre-scored video are needed: short training videos that show what parts of a rubric look like in practice, and longer assessment videos that allow observers to rate a lesson on multiple rubric components. This range of video supports observer training that builds from scoring parts of a lesson on individual teaching components to scoring entire lessons, as observers do in the classroom. After training, you will need at least two assessment videos to meaningfully measure an observer's accuracy (additional videos may be required when the results from rating two videos appear to conflict).

In the previous pages, we made the case for starting small. When pre-scoring video for the first time, you should focus on building a basic understanding of the process while producing a limited starter set of pre-scored videos with which to begin training observers. The most useful training videos at this point will be short segments that each feature a clear-cut example—called a benchmark—of one teaching component demonstrated at one specific performance level. A benchmark might be a four-minute segment that shows the teaching component "use of questioning" at a "highly effective" level, or it might be a seven-minute clip showing "basic management of classroom procedures" at the "basic" level. Each would be annotated with a rationale calling out clear evidence to support the rating. You should produce your first set of assessment videos in time to gauge your observers' accuracy when they complete the new training; this will provide you with valuable data that will help you improve the training's next iteration.

⌕ IN FOCUS:
RULES OF THUMB FOR PRIORITIZING

Only so many videos can be pre-scored in any period of time. To prioritize goals for the near term, ask: "Where is the greatest need for consistency in ratings?" and "Where is the greatest opportunity to improve teaching and learning across the school system?"

Consider how most teachers currently perform and where observers need the most help to better rate performance. For example, most teachers typically perform in the middle performance categories, yet those are often the hardest to distinguish with consistency. If this is the case in your system, then helping observers to better discern among 2s and 3s on a four-point rubric may result in more accurate and specific feedback for the most teachers.

Use data to identify where greater consistency or clarity on practice will be most beneficial. Before a pre-scoring process begins, ask a group of evaluators to rate a set of unscored lesson videos to see which parts of a rubric produce the most inconsistency. After a pre-scoring process is established, look at observer assessment results and teacher observation scores to determine new priorities.

Over time, you should build out a video library with enough examples to allow for sufficient observer agreement on all parts of a rubric.

After your state or district has used an initial set of videos in training—and has established a basic understanding of the pre-scoring process—then the focus can turn to building out its set of examples, producing more videos to use in practice rating, and replenishing its supply of assessment videos. Most of the training videos that are produced will likely continue to be benchmark examples. These videos may be of additional parts of a rubric, multiple examples of the same parts of a rubric, or replacements of previously pre-scored videos that proved to be problematic when used in training. Variations can address more specific needs, such as clarifying the meaning of a single term in a rubric (e.g., what is meant by "scaffolding"). Borderline examples—called rangefinders instead of benchmarks—can help clarify when teaching is at the low or high end of a rating (e.g., when the evidence of "student engagement" minimally qualifies for an effective rating and not the next lowest rating).

From the outset, it's important to keep in mind that teaching looks different in different places. Evaluators who are going to observe high school teachers should be trained and assessed with videos from high school classrooms. If observers will be rating math instruction, their preparation should include video of math lessons. Moreover, classrooms from the same grade and subject look different in different parts of a school system. The backgrounds of students and teachers differ, facilities differ, and teachers' personalities differ. Any set of videos used for observer training should reflect these differences. Evaluators must be able to recognize a rubric's indicators in any context in which they find themselves.

TECHNIQUES:
PRIORITIZING PRE-SCORED VIDEO TO PRODUCE

To Lay the Foundation:

Training Videos

■ Pre-score a small number of clear-cut examples (benchmarks) that each illustrate one teaching component at one specific performance level (e.g., a level 3 for "maximizing use of instructional time")—often 2 to 12 minutes long.

■ Consider prioritizing what examples to look for first, based on how most teachers in the school system perform and what parts of the rubric are hardest for evaluators to rate. To determine the latter, ask evaluators to rate unscored videos and look for parts of the rubric that produced the greatest inconsistency. (Keep in mind that locating examples of teaching components that show up less often will require reviewing more lessons to find them. See the section "How Much Raw Video Is Needed?" on page 77 in Chapter 7.)

■ From the beginning, make sure any set of videos used for observer training covers a range of grades, subjects, classroom compositions, and teacher backgrounds.

Assessment Videos

■ Pre-score segments that show clear examples of multiple teaching components in a rubric—or all the components—and that are similar in length to the observations to be carried out in the classroom—often approximately 20 minutes.

■ Pre-score at least two such assessment videos for each grade band in which observers will be evaluating. So if observers will be rating performance in two grade bands (e.g., K–8 and 9–12), then at least four assessment videos are needed.

(TECHNIQUES Continued)

To Build and Improve:

Training Videos

- Pre-score additional benchmark videos for missing parts of the rubric, and replace existing examples with better ones. Consider where multiple examples of the same part of a rubric are needed to clarify how it might look in different classrooms, grades, subjects, and so on.

- Consider where rangefinder examples are needed to clarify boundaries between two ratings (e.g., the difference between a low 3 and a high 2).

- Pre-score mini-segments—as short as one minute—that each illustrate key terms in the rubric that may be new to observers or that may be best defined through examples of practice.

- Look to teacher observation results and observer assessment data to determine what additional examples to prioritize for pre-scoring. Ask what examples will most likely support better feedback to improve practice for the most teachers.

Assessment Videos

- Establish an ongoing process to pre-score additional assessment videos to replace problematic ones and to replace ones that must be retired before they get overused (i.e., for assessment integrity reasons).

- Create additional sets of assessment videos to use in periodic checks on observer accuracy (e.g., every year or few months, not just at the end of initial observer training).

- Pre-score videos to use as practice assessments to give observers more opportunities to rate multiple components before their assessment at the end of training. These may include medium-length videos (e.g., 15 minutes).

TIPS

■ Pre-scoring a few examples of high-level performance early on in implementation can help raise observers' expectations during training, especially if the examples are drawn from the local context.

■ A single video clip can be used to exemplify practice for several components of a rubric. But segments from assessment videos should not also be used as training clips. Observers should not be assessed with video they have already seen.

🔅 Putting It into Practice

To Lay the Foundation:

What parts of your of rubric might you prioritize for pre-scoring to help the most teachers improve their practice?

To Build and Improve:

What does your observation and training data suggest about prioritizing new videos to better support teachers and evaluators?

⬇ This item can be downloaded from www.wiley.com/go/betterfeedback

CHAPTER 7

Getting the Right Video to Pre-Score

ESSENTIAL QUESTION

How Will You Get the Right Kind of Video to Pre-Score?

A major challenge of the pre-scoring process is finding enough of the right kind of raw videos of teaching to pre-score. The good news is that changes in technology continue to make it easier and less expensive to capture high-quality video of classroom practice. What once took thousands of dollars of cumbersome equipment can now be accomplished with pocket-sized devices that cost hundreds of dollars—and often with better results. Unfortunately, such advances have yet to produce a plethora of low-cost and easily accessible videos appropriate for pre-scoring. Given that, you will need to invest time in researching possible sources—not just at the outset but on an ongoing basis.

To understand what makes a video appropriate for pre-scoring, consider how it will be used. Annotated segments will serve as models for how to rate performance in a classroom observation. If rating performance in the classroom depends on how students respond, then how students respond must be clear in the video. If observations are meant to evaluate typical lessons in typical classrooms, then the video used for training should not feature highly unusual lessons or teaching methods. Examples of staged teaching are generally not good for modeling how to rate real lessons that unfold in unpredictable ways. Video for pre-scoring should capture authentic teaching clearly enough to evaluate it.

Video for pre-scoring should capture authentic teaching clearly enough to evaluate it.

Don't use video without obtaining consent from all who appear in it. Pre-scored segments that feature real teachers and students are used to illustrate particular performance ratings. Those segments should be shared only in training and with the disclaimer that the ratings apply only to what is featured—not to a teacher's overall ability or to the overall lesson it comes from. Yet it's still easy to see the breach of trust—and legal issues—that can result if videos of teachers who agreed to be recorded are used in ways for which they did not give permission. Likewise, parents may balk—and file lawsuits—if video that features their children is used in training without their consent. (Ask your system's lawyers to review consent forms before using them.)

You need to make sure the right written consent is granted, whether you employ previously recorded videos, record new lessons for pre-scoring, or purchase access to videos from a fee-based provider. Lesson videos recorded as part of the MET Extension project—a continuation of the MET project's study of classroom observations—are available from two such providers: ETS, and the SOE Teaching and Learning Exploratory, a platform created by the University of Michigan School of Education. When purchasing access to such videos, check the terms. You will find it of little use to pre-score video if you can't share it with numerous observers in your training or if you lose access to the video when you expect to use it in upcoming training.

⌕ IN FOCUS:
HOW MUCH RAW VIDEO IS NEEDED?

It's very hard to know ahead of time how many lesson videos will be needed to produce a particular set of pre-scored segments. Often a raw video will include clear-cut examples of just one or two teaching components, but more is possible. (Those with most or all teaching components are best designated as assessment videos.) The yield rate depends largely on video quality and the nature of the teaching captured. A video in which 10 minutes is spent handing out papers might yield an example of low performance on maximizing instructional time but not much else. To find examples of teaching components that show up less often than others also requires reviewing more videos. As a state or district gains experience with pre-scoring, it will learn roughly how many usable segments it tends to get from most lesson videos. This number will likely increase with experience, as school systems get better at identifying raw video appropriate for pre-scoring.

Whether you buy, create, or repurpose video will depend in large part on your available resources. Low-cost options may be needed when you are starting out and before stakeholders have seen the full benefit of pre-scoring video; the focus at that point is to build an understanding of the process while pre-scoring a small number of videos. School systems may also achieve economies of scale by sharing the products of their pre-scoring, if they use the same rubric. Over time, your school system may tap multiple sources as it learns more about what it needs to enhance observer training. With experience, you will find that it also becomes easier to determine which sources are the most dependable in providing video appropriate for pre-scoring.

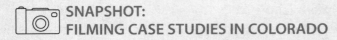

SNAPSHOT:
FILMING CASE STUDIES IN COLORADO

As in other places, Colorado's state evaluation system calls for multiple observations of a teacher over the course of a year. But initially, the state's online platform for sharing pre-scored video featured only teachers recorded at one point in time. To change that, the state department of education has begun filming in the classrooms of teacher volunteers at different points during the school year. Segments from the recorded lessons will be assembled into video case studies that are pre-scored by state-trained master coders. This will allow users of the state's online evaluator-training platform to practice rating instruction based on different observations at different times in the same classroom. Disclaimers will stress that the segments are excerpted to illustrate specific levels of performance and do not represent the overall proficiency of the teacher volunteers.

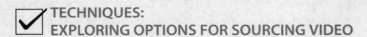

TECHNIQUES:
EXPLORING OPTIONS FOR SOURCING VIDEO

To Lay the Foundation:

- Review existing video from local sources, if any, to see whether it is of sufficient quality and shows the right content, and whether the permissions granted by teachers and parents would allow its use. (It's possible, but difficult, to get new consents on previously recorded video.)

- Consider to what extent local teachers would consent to have their lessons recorded for pre-scoring. (This might require purchasing video equipment or contracting with a videographer.) Make every effort to ensure a positive experience for such teachers so others step forward.

- Look for opportunities to share video across school systems—either by sharing locally recorded lessons or by sharing in the cost of purchasing access to video from a commercial vendor, such as ETS or Teachscape.

- See whether fee-based providers can provide access to a limited number of videos for a minimal cost to build an understanding of the pre-scoring process while producing a starter set to begin training observers.

- Ask school systems with experience pre-scoring what sources have been most useful and cost-efficient for them.

To Build and Improve:

- Determine which of the sources you have used is the most consistent in yielding high-quality segments that add value to your observer training. Continue or expand your use of those sources and consider discontinuing the use of ones that less frequently yield good segments.

- Consider how a mix of sources can better enhance training while building out a video library. It's important for evaluators to learn to rate performance with examples from classrooms that look like those in which they will observe. But using examples of low performance from outside the local context is one way to address teachers' concerns about possibly not looking their best in a segment used in their own district.

- Based on your experience pre-scoring lessons from different grades and subjects, consider whether some subjects are better recorded using different techniques (e.g., is a "roving" camera better for science labs or for small-group guided reading instruction?).

- Determine what grades and subjects are least represented (or not represented at all) in current sources. You can ask school systems with more experience pre-scoring what solutions they have found to similar challenges.

💡 Putting It into Practice

To Lay the Foundation:

What are the most promising sources of video that you might explore for pre-scoring?

🖉

To Build and Improve:

Which sources have been most productive, and how might additional ones address your most pressing needs?

🖉

⬇ This item can be downloaded from www.wiley.com/go/betterfeedback

ESSENTIAL QUESTION

How Will You Pre-Screen Video for Quality and Content?

Whatever the source of video, be sure to pre-screen it. Before considering a video appropriate for pre-scoring, you want to know that someone watching it could determine the performance level based on its content. Assigning someone to make this determination ahead of time saves master coders from struggling with and ultimately rejecting "unscoreable" segments. In a state or school district, where coding is typically done by full-time teachers and administrators, master coders' time is extremely limited; to maximize that time, ask others to "separate the wheat from the chaff." Pre-screeners could be district administrators who know the rubric.

One of the best ways to pre-screen a video is to try to rate it; if an early viewer can't see or hear enough to make a judgment, then neither will the master coders. Pre-screening also can be used to identify the most relevant parts of a video. Master coders can then skip over periods when little is happening, such as during announcements or when students are working individually for extended periods and their work cannot be discerned. (Augmenting video with artifacts, such as lesson plans and student work, can help when video alone isn't capturing critical evidence.) Pre-screeners can also prioritize segments that appear to include high-priority examples needed to build out a video library or those that appear to include examples of multiple teaching components and so may be candidates for an assessment video.

> *In a state or school district, where coding is typically done by full-time teachers and administrators, master coders' time is extremely limited; to maximize that time, ask others to "separate the wheat from the chaff."*

Even with pre-screening, master coders will find that some of the segments they are assigned are problematic. They may realize that the audio is not clear at key points or that important pieces of evidence cannot be discerned. This is especially likely when a pre-scoring process is new. You should give master coders the opportunity to comment on the judgments of pre-screeners and to explain why they think a segment may not be appropriate for pre-scoring. This feedback will improve the process and tools you use for pre-screening going forward.

⚒ TOOL:
DCPS VIDEO-QUALITY CHECKLIST

The District of Columbia Public Schools (DCPS) uses a checklist to pre-screen lesson videos for possible pre-scoring. The tool is meant to determine whether the video provides enough evidence to be scored by a master coder (called an "anchor rater" in DCPS). Items ask, for example, whether an observer could identify the lesson objective and make a judgment about student understanding based on what can be seen and heard. Depending on the answers, a video that's not rejected may be designated as ideal or merely acceptable for pre-scoring. The two tiers allow for prioritizing those most appropriate to pre-scoring and making sure anchor raters know about any issues with the others. For the full checklist see Appendix, page 305.

·💡· Putting It into Practice

To Lay the Foundation:

Who could be assigned the task of pre-screening videos before any are assigned to master coders?

To Build and Improve:

How could your pre-screening process be improved to further maximize master coders' time?

ESSENTIAL QUESTION

How Will You Share Video and Collect Rating Justifications?

Pre-scoring involves a two-way transfer of information. You need to get videos to master coders, and master coders need a way to submit their evidence, rationales, and performance ratings for each segment they review.

You can use readily available tools to do this. You might go with an essentially no-cost option by posting password-protected videos to a Vimeo account or to Google Drive and by having master coders submit their work in a simple table using a word processor or spreadsheet. Fee-based platforms (such as MyLearningPlan's Elevate) allow master coders to watch video, take notes, and align relevant evidence to each part of a rubric—all in the same system.

Whatever system you use, be sure to test it in the context in which it will be used. If master coders will be reviewing videos on school computers, make sure they're not kept from doing so by the kind of blocking software typically installed on such devices. If they will be meeting as a group, make sure the location has sufficient bandwidth to stream videos. It's a waste of time to assign videos for pre-scoring only to find that participants can't review them and the work must be put on hold until a solution is found.

Make sure you ask master coders how they're experiencing the process and what might improve that experience. Your ongoing efforts to refine the sharing of information may include adding new features, systems, and sources of video.

Putting It into Practice

To Lay the Foundation:

What tools for sharing video and written score rationales make the most sense for your system to use when just starting out?

To Build and Improve:

What would make the sharing of video and information with master coders more efficient?

This item can be downloaded from www.wiley.com/go/betterfeedback

CHAPTER 8

Recruiting and Training Master Coders

ESSENTIAL QUESTION

How Will You Recruit Master Coders?

When pre-scoring video, it pays to involve the right people. Master coders (sometimes called "anchor raters" or "master scorers") must be willing to set aside their own ideas of effective teaching and rate the teaching that they see based solely on the rubric. They must be open to changing their judgments when presented with convincing evidence. But they also need to be active participants; they can't just passively defer to others. In addition, a master coder must have the patience and attention to detail to repeatedly review the same video to accurately record the behaviors most relevant to scoring each teaching component. When master coders don't buy into their charge, the result can be unproductive and awkward.

> *Master coders must be open to changing their judgments when presented with convincing evidence. But they also need to be active participants; they can't just passively defer to others.*

Given the learning curve entailed and that new pre-scored video is always needed, master coding should be seen as a long-term commitment. Most master coders are teachers and administrators who pre-score on a part-time basis. A master coder may take three to four hours to review a video individually and another hour to take part in reconciliation. The task can't be done in the middle of typical work days. Often, pre-scoring begins over the summer and continues throughout the school year. Any stipends paid are modest compared to the time required. The biggest motivation to participate is the chance to engage with colleagues in rigorous professional learning that's focused on teaching.

The overarching question when recruiting master coders is "Where will we find the individuals with the best understanding and appreciation of our rubric?" When a rubric is new and there's no cadre of trained observers from which to select the most skilled, the people with the best grasp of the rubric's indicators may be those who helped develop, select, or field test the rubric. As implementation progresses, data become available that can help identify the most accurate observers as potential master coders. As emphasized throughout this book, it helps to start small. You will learn a great deal about what makes for a good master coder from your early attempts to pre-score.

Despite careful recruitment, you may find it necessary to stop working with a master coder. Individuals who consistently dig in their heels and are unable or unwilling to consider alternative views will not be helpful in determining the right performance rating for an instance of teaching. Keep in mind that it takes time for new master coders to get comfortable with the process; they will need reminders when they go beyond what's in a video segment and the rubric in rating performance. But after some time, it may become clear that some lack the right mindset or temperament. They may feel that their expertise or authority is questioned by the process. Or they may strongly disagree with what's in the rubric.

TIPS

- Recruiting individuals whose instructional expertise is well known builds credibility for the overall observation system.

- Consider recruiting master coders who represent a variety of stakeholders, including teachers and school leaders from different regions and contexts within the school system. Master coders often become advocates for the process, replicating the use of video to build a common understanding of effective teaching in their schools and districts.

- In some cases, long-held views of effective teaching may make it difficult for some experienced educators to see instruction solely through the lens of a rubric that's new to them. Look for individuals who are able to adjust.

☑ TECHNIQUES: RECRUITING MASTER CODERS

To Lay the Foundation:

- If observations are already being done, look for those observers who have demonstrated the most skill in applying the rubric correctly.

- Recruit from among teachers and administrators who helped develop, select, or pilot the rubric.

To Build and Improve:

- Retain master coders who demonstrate the ability to work with others to produce clear, evidence-based score justifications. Make sure such individuals feel valued for their work.

- Recruit from among the most accurate observers, based on observer assessment results.

Note: A cadre of master coders should include experts from different subjects, grade bands, and teaching specialties.

⋰̣̇·̣ Putting It into Practice

To Lay the Foundation:

Who in your system has the best grasp of your rubric and would build the most credibility for pre-scoring?

To Build and Improve:

How can you keep your best master coders and find more like them in more places?

⬇ This item can be downloaded from www.wiley.com/go/betterfeedback

ESSENTIAL QUESTION

How Many Master Coders Will You Need?

Several factors drive the number of master coders your school system needs. Two of the biggest are the number of videos you need to pre-score and the amount of time available for pre-scoring them. (Another is the number of subjects and grade bands for which your evaluators will be trained, as each needs its own set of videos.) Also relevant is how many master coders review each video: variations of this are possible, but quality assurance requires that you have more than just one pair of coders rating a segment. (Quality controls are discussed in Chapter 9, "Ensuring the Quality of Pre-Scoring.") The example estimate in Figure 8.1 assumes that two pairs will review each video before it's used for observer training or assessment.

When determining your recruitment needs, consider how much time your master coders have to devote to the process on an ongoing basis. The estimate shown in Figure 8.1 assumes that a master coder will review two videos each month, which might take a total of six to eight hours (including reconciliation discussions). If they can review more each month, then they can pre-score more video over the course of the year (or complete the same number of videos in less time). You should make adjustments according to your available resources and current needs. The hypothetical school system in the example in Figure 8.1 might scale up its process the following year by doubling the number of videos to pre-score—meaning it would need twice as many master coders. Or a state or district just starting out might only have resources for fewer coders, which reduces the number of videos that could be expected to be pre-scored in the same period.

FIGURE 8.1 Factors That Determine Recruitment Needs

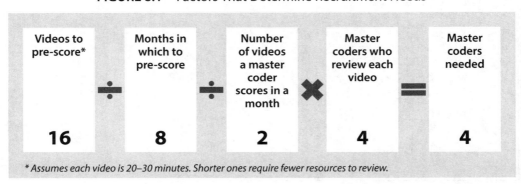

* Assumes each video is 20–30 minutes. Shorter ones require fewer resources to review.

When you are starting out, planning is more of a guessing game. You don't know how quickly your coders will be able to work (although they should get faster with practice). You also don't know how many usable segments of pre-scored video will result from a given set of raw videos of teaching—especially if you're hoping to find specific examples needed in your training. By tracking how long it takes and how much is produced, you'll be better able to plan and improve the process going forward.

Putting It into Practice

To Lay the Foundation:

What's your estimate for each of the factors that determine the number of master coders needed as you start pre-scoring?

To Build and Improve:

In what ways could you better estimate recruitment needs or adjust your process to increase productivity while maintaining quality?

ESSENTIAL QUESTION
How Will You Train Master Coders?

Master coding is a special skill. To be sure, it includes many of the same activities involved in classroom observations carried out for teacher evaluation. Both entail recording evidence and rating practice based on a rubric. But few observers have ever compared notes with others who rated the same teaching after reviewing it repeatedly on video. What's more, master coding a short segment to show one teaching component at one performance level means observers must set aside their knowledge of what happened at other times in the lesson, whereas in classroom observations, an evaluator considers evidence from the whole lesson. Even the most expert observers face a learning curve when they become master coders.

A major goal of training is to help master coders build fluency with the protocol they will follow to review video, rate performance, and prepare score justifications for reconciliation. The protocol will vary depending on the extent of pre-screening that your school system does. Master coders can spend more time rating performance if your pre-screening process identifies which videos may be candidates for assessment videos and which parts of a video can be skipped for lack of relevant content. (See the section "How Will You Pre-Screen Video for Quality and Content?" on page 81.) Possible assessment videos are those in which an extended segment—perhaps 20 minutes or longer—appears to feature examples of most or all of your rubric's components. Regardless, master coders should know what makes for a good assessment video so they can make their own judgments.

The example in Figure 8.2 illustrates a protocol for reviewing a segment that has been identified as a candidate for an assessment video. The protocol begins by identifying instances of specific teaching components and recording detailed evidence with which to determine the performance level of each. The evidence is objective: It might include exact quotes from teachers and students, descriptions of behaviors, or numbers (e.g., how many students responded). Opinions and generalizations—like "the questions were low level" or "the students were on task"—won't help evaluators learn to recognize the right indicators of performance, which is fundamental to ensuring consistent ratings and specific feedback.

FIGURE 8.2   A Master Coding Protocol

Steps	Examples
1. Review the assigned video, and note when examples of particular teaching components are exhibited.	■ In a 22-minute video, an instance of "checking for student understanding" occurs from 3:23 to 9:57. During that time the teacher circulates among students as they multiply fractions, after which she addresses a student's misconception by explaining another way to solve such problems.
2. For each teaching component noted, record evidence needed to determine the performance level.	■ To one student at each table, the teacher says, "What will you do first?" and "Okay. Why?" ■ At 6:39 the teacher says to the class, "Okay everyone, I asked Anthony to talk about something he wasn't sure of." ■ At 7:01 the student says. " The answer I got is smaller than the fractions I multiplied. So it didn't seem right." ■ At 7:12 the teacher says, "Okay, Anthony makes a good point. What's happening when we multiply by a fraction?" ■ At 8:10 the teacher says, "Here's another way to look at it." She draws a 3 X 4 grid on the white board, then says, "Anthony, show us what part of this is 2/3? Great, now what part of that is 3/4? Are we getting smaller or bigger?"
3. Determine the performance level described in the rubric that best matched all the evidence recorded.	■ The evidence aligns with a level 3, of which the rubric says, "the teacher checks for understanding before moving on in a lesson" and "the check for understanding provides information to adjust instruction." ■ It is not a 2, of which the rubric says, "the check for understanding does not provide useful information." ■ Nor is it a 4, of which the rubric says, "the check provided information on most students' understanding." In this segment, the teacher spoke to just one student at each table.
4. Draft a score justification for each teaching component that connects the evidence to the rubric's performance indicators.	■ The teacher's check for understanding provided information to adjust instruction. The teacher checked for understanding by asking one student at each table to solve the problem and explain each step of the solution. ("What will you do first? Okay, why?") At the end the teacher asked a student to explain his confusion to the class ("The answer I got is smaller than the fractions I multipled."), after which she showed a different way to solve such problems (using a rectangular grid).

TRAINING OF MASTER CODERS SHOULD COVER:

- Using the video-sharing system

- Using common forms or templates to record evidence, time stamps, and score justifications

- Following a protocol for coding

- Writing specific and evidence-based score justifications using the rubric's language

- Reaching agreement on scores and justifications in reconciliation with other coders

The second half of the protocol involves determining performance ratings and drafting the rationales for these ratings. For the former, a master coder determines which performance level described in the rubric aligns most with the evidence from the video that's relevant to each teaching component. Rationales for the accurate rating, and for why a higher and/or lower rating would be incorrect, must be clear, concise, grounded in evidence, and written in the language of the rubric. A rationale makes a strong case for a particular rating as the correct way to apply a rubric to a specific instance of teaching. It says, in essence: these are the things in the video that make this the right rating, according to this rubric.

Another focus of your master coder training is reconciliation. Before a video segment is used to train observers, multiple individuals must agree on the ratings and rationales; a single master coder, no matter how expert, is not enough to ensure accurate ratings for examples to be used across a school system to norm how observers apply a rubric. There are variations of reconciliation that you can use. Working in pairs—with two master coders comparing notes after rating individually—can be the simplest approach. It also lessens the tendency for some larger groups to seek consensus rather than to make the best judgment based on the evidence. Whatever structure you use, you should provide guided practice on how to reach agreement so that reconciliation runs smoothly.

How you deliver training to master coders will depend on context and will evolve over time. Geography may limit the extent to which people can be brought together. Webinars and individually completed activities may be used to introduce protocols and video-sharing systems, and for some practice reviewing segments. But a good deal of face-to-face training is recommended when starting out. You are likely to encounter many unforeseen challenges the first time you train a group of master coders. You may discover that your training needs to better clarify when a particular kind of behavior indicates one teaching component versus another or the difference between opinion and objective description when justifying scores. Begin with a small group, and learn from an early round of training before you formalize a process to prepare larger numbers of coders.

The exact content of your training also will depend on the prerequisite knowledge of your participants and how much of the pre-scoring process they'll take on. When a rubric is new to master coders, they will need more time to review its language before attempting to score. If your master coders will recommend whether segments are used as training or assessment videos, then your training should cover that process (by determining whether a longer segment includes enough clear examples of different components to serve as an assessment video). If reconciliation will be done without a facilitator—say, with pairs of master coders discussing on their own to reach agreement—then your training should include practice resolving disagreements and creating coherent justifications.

> *You may discover that your training of master coders needs to better clarify when a particular kind of behavior indicates one teaching component versus another or the difference between opinion and objective description when justifying scores.*

Regardless of content, you will find that facilitated group discussions are especially helpful for training new master coders. Group discussions let them practice justifying their scores with others who have reviewed the same lesson. Pressed by each other, master coders get increasingly more specific in pointing out relevant observed behaviors and in explaining what distinguishes between a rubric's teaching components and performance levels. A good approach is to begin with a facilitator leading whole-group discussion of the same videos, followed by master coders working in smaller groups that more resemble how they'll score video after their training (e.g., with coders reconciling their scores and justifications in pairs).

TIPS

- Whoever leads training should be a highly skilled facilitator. Trainers must be able to guide discussion of segments toward agreement based on evidence, without stepping in to decide what the correct rating should be. When trainers take sides, it doesn't help master coders learn how to weigh evidence and determine a rubric's precise meaning.

- Training works best when it includes review of already pre-scored video. When pre-scoring for the first time, this can be accomplished by asking two to three rubric experts (including the training facilitator, if possible) to rate three to four videos that represent a range of classroom contexts. Even if the facilitator doesn't share the predetermined ratings, pre-scoring makes it easier to guide discussion to the relevant evidence.

- Begin review of video in training with the most clear-cut examples available. These might be of low inference rubric components (i.e., components for which observers don't need evidence from different points in a segment to interpret a teacher's intent or student's response).

- If prolonged discussion fails to move training participants closer to agreement, a facilitator should move to another video. When this happens, it should be noted whether the disagreement seemed due to video quality, some distracting behavior in the lesson, or difficulty interpreting the rubric. Videos deemed problematic should not be assigned for pre-scoring.

- Reconciliation of evidence is needed even if master coders agree on scores but for different reasons. Both the correct score and the correct justification based on the evidence are needed to support observers in understanding how to apply a rubric to different instances of teaching.

⚒ TOOLS FOR MASTER CODING

RIFT Master Coding Worksheet

The Rhode Island state affiliate of the American Federation of Teachers (AFT) created a simple paper template to guide master coders when pre-scoring video. The tool has space for evidence, timestamps, agreed-upon ratings, and reasons why ratings other than the correct one would be not be appropriate. Teachers and administrators who engage in pre-scoring organized by the union complete the form when reviewing video in three-hour work sessions. Review and reconciliation of ratings takes place in pairs. You can find the worksheet on Appendix, page 307. The Rhode Island Federation of Teachers and Health Professionals (RIFT) started pre-scoring video as part of the AFT's Investing in Innovation (i3) grant from the U.S. Department of Education. New York State United Teachers is another participant in the grant and is engaged in pre-scoring.

DCPS Advice for Facilitating Reconciliation

In the District of Columbia Public Schools (DCPS), reconciliation takes place in facilitated phone calls after score justifications are submitted by each pair of master coders (called "anchor raters" in DCPS). Facilitators are central office administrators who lead implementation of the district's classroom observation system. To assist them in bringing raters to agreement, the district developed a short set of facilitation tips (See Appendix, page 308). It includes this advice: begin each session with a reminder of goals and norms (e.g., "be willing to consider evidence from a different perspective"), start with areas of agreement, and summarize apparent disagreements in evidence or interpretation before asking raters to clarify them.

DCPS Guidelines for Score Rationales

DCPS provides its anchor raters with a two-page set of guidelines for drafting score justifications. Included are annotated examples of justifications that meet specific criteria, such as beginning with the language of the rubric when describing evidence and including any specific evidence relevant to determining the performance level. Examples of justifications that don't meet the criteria also are provided. You can find the full set of guidelines on Appendix, page 311.

☑ TECHNIQUES: TRAINING METHODS FOR MASTER CODERS

To Lay the Foundation:

Train a cadre of new master coders using a boot-camp model in which:

- As pre-work, master coders score video segments using the video-sharing system, coding protocol, and template;

- Master coders meet in group sessions to compare scores and score justifications and to reach agreement by reexamining the segment, the recorded evidence, and/or the rubric indicators; and

- Master coders leave the sessions knowing what to expect going forward (e.g., how video will be assigned, how reconciliation will take place).

For a detailed description of master coder boot camps, see the MET project's "What it Looks Like: Master Coding Videos for Observer Training and Assessment," (2013). Seattle, WA. Bill & Melinda Gates Foundation.

To Build and Improve:

Use differentiated training for new and experienced master coders in which:

- Highly skilled and experienced master coders help train in the boot camps that continue for new master coders (e.g., to role-play the process);

- Master coders are given examples of quality score justifications from previous rounds of pre-scoring, with written explanations of why they meet quality criteria; and

- Returning master coders score pre-scored video to make sure they've maintained their accuracy. A refresher is offered for those who need it.

·ϙ· Putting It into Practice

To Lay the Foundation:

Who has deep knowledge of your rubric, has strong facilitation skills, and might be able to lead training of master coders?

To Build and Improve:

Where are the biggest gaps in the knowledge and skills of your master coders, and how might you fill them?

⬇ This item can be downloaded from www.wiley.com/go/betterfeedback

CHAPTER 9

Ensuring the Quality of Pre-Scoring

ESSENTIAL QUESTION

How Will You Check the Work of Master Coders for Quality?

When quality is important, quality controls are essential. No matter how carefully a pair of master coders reviews a video and reaches agreement on ratings, you need additional checks on their work before you use a segment in observer training or assessment. With checks on quality, you have greater confidence that other experts in the rubric could replicate the right ratings. Without these checks, you increase the chance that the videos used in observer training will confuse your evaluators or even lead them to apply your rubric incorrectly. Your quality-control checks also will give you more timely information for improving the process so you don't need to wait until the use of your videos in training reveals problems.

> *Your quality-control checks also will give you more timely information for improving the process so you don't need to wait until the use of your videos in training reveals problems.*

How your school system checks for quality will depend in part on your resources and whether your pre-scoring process is new or well developed. When just starting out, you may not have a sufficient number of master coders available to have them confirm the reconciled ratings for videos that they weren't assigned to pre-score. Instead, you may assign experts in the rubric to review the evidence and rationales agreed upon in reconciliation to make sure they align with the rubric (i.e., do the behaviors described match how the rubric defines performance for the rating given?). Later, you can assign pre-scored segments to additional master coders, or to trained observers, to see whether they produce the same scores.

 TIP

The same master coders should not always take part in reconciliation together. Assignments should regroup master coders periodically to avoid the unconscious tendency to defer based on familiarity.

✓ TECHNIQUES:
ENSURING QUALITY OF PRE-SCORED VIDEO

To Lay the Foundation:

- Remove videos that master coders struggle to score. (But first determine whether the problem is a lack of clarity in part of the rubric or misinterpretation by one master coder.)

- Have additional experts in the rubric review all score justifications to make sure that they align with the rubric criteria—that is, does the evidence cited align to the rubric's criteria for the score given?

To Build and Improve:

- Continue to remove from the process any videos that master coders cannot score.

- Before using videos in training, have them scored by additional master coders or observers to see whether they assign the same scores (this is called "back scoring").

- Assign someone to review existing pre-scored video for potential problems (e.g., distracting behaviors, outdated references or materials).

💡 Putting It into Practice

To Lay the Foundation:

What tools and procedures could you use for quality control as you start a pre-scoring process?

To Build and Improve:

How could additional quality controls tighten up your process and build greater confidence in what's produced?

⬇ This item can be downloaded from www.wiley.com/go/betterfeedback

ESSENTIAL QUESTION

How Will You Keep Track of the Process and Products?

An ongoing process requires ongoing management. You need someone to take responsibility for making sure the activities discussed throughout the previous chapters take place, and according to schedule. That means raw video must be acquired and pre-screened before assignments are made to master coders, and master coders must know when to expect new assignments, when their work is due, and when they need to take part in discussion to reconcile disagreements in scores and score justifications. After reconciled ratings are confirmed, you need someone to make sure the reconciled ratings and evidence—along with the video segments they refer to—are organized and accessible for use in observer training and assessment.

KEY MANAGEMENT TASKS IN PRE-SCORING VIDEO

- Scheduling the process, from pre-screening video and the initial training of master coders through each cycle of master coding, reconciliation, and quality checks

- Communicating expectations and deadlines to all participants

- Assigning video to master coders

- Organizing a catalog of finalized ratings, justifications, and videos for use in observer training and assessment

- Keeping track of who played what role in pre-scoring each video segment, and gathering information about each segment's use in training

- Removing problematic videos from the library, and identifying assessment videos for replacement

Figure 9.1 suggests a general schedule of activities throughout the year. Because most master coders are limited in the number of hours they can devote to pre-scoring, pre-scoring typically takes place in a series of cycles, each lasting perhaps several weeks. The number of cycles will vary depending on your school system's available resources and the number of videos you plan to pre-score in a given year. Some activities may overlap or take place on a rolling basis; pre-screening can be ongoing so long as enough videos are pre-screened so you can assign them to master coders at the start of each cycle. Often, master coder training takes place over the summer when schedules are more flexible.

Maintaining the catalog of videos and ratings produced is important to developing your video library. From the beginning, you should keep records of any segments that your master coders were unable to rate; retire any video where the culprit is video quality rather than a lack of understanding of the rubric among the master coders. When building out a library, knowing which parts of a rubric are already illustrated with examples—and which grades and subjects are represented—can guide your subsequent efforts to fill in the gaps. Keeping track of assessment video usage will help you identify which ones need replacing before overexposure results in assessment-integrity issues.

FIGURE 9.1 An Ongoing Pre-Scoring Process

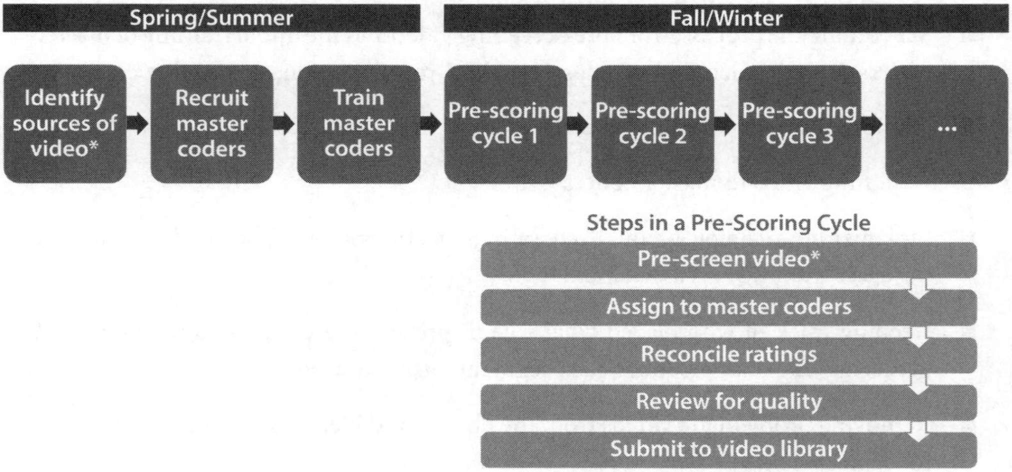

** Identifying and pre-screening videos are ongoing.*

Putting It into Practice

To Lay the Foundation:

Who needs to take part, and when, in the key steps involved in pre-scoring over the course of the year?

To Build and Improve:

How could specific steps of the pre-scoring process over the year be managed differently to improve quality and efficiency?

This item can be downloaded from www.wiley.com/go/betterfeedback

ESSENTIAL QUESTION

How Will You Use Data for Continual Improvement?

Information makes improvement possible. As emphasized repeatedly in this book, your school system's capacity to pre-score video is built through continual improvement. Indeed, the same goes for the capacity to deliver observer training that makes use of pre-scored video, for the capacity to ensure that evaluators are effectively coaching teachers, and for every other capacity required in an observation system that aspires to support great teaching. But whether each attempt to pre-score video is better than the last hinges on whether you collect the right information at the right time, ask the right questions, and make changes when warranted.

Collect data from the beginning. You need to have plans in place from the start of pre-scoring to track information on videos, on participants in the pre-scoring process, and on the videos' subsequent use in training and assessment. Otherwise, you will have no way to know what worked and where you may need to use different processes, tools, or content. You can't leverage the most successful pre-screening practices, or the most successful pre-screeners, if you don't keep track of who pre-screened what videos and how often they succeeded in identifying useful segments. You can't identify the most skilled master coders if you don't keep records of which master coders submitted what ratings for reconciliation.

> *You need to have plans in place from the start of pre-scoring to track information on videos, on participants in the pre-scoring process, and on the videos' subsequent use in training and assessment.*

The list of techniques at the end of this chapter shows the key information you should collect at the beginning of the pre-scoring process and the key questions you should consider at each subsequent stage of implementation. Some of the latter are variations of the prompts included throughout the previous chapters under "To Build and Improve." The main unit of analysis is the video segment. For each completed pre-scored segment, you should be able to call up where it came from, who played what part in pre-scoring it, and how well it served its purpose. As noted, the data include quantitative, categorical, and anecdotal information. As with teaching and learning, improvement of a pre-scoring process requires multiple types of evidence.

Learning by Doing

Knowledge sharing is essential to quality implementation of any new practice, and among promising practices to improve teaching and learning, pre-scoring video is relatively young. This book shares the knowledge of experts involved in pre-scoring for research, assessment, and professional development. But in no way could these pages cover all there is to know or all that might be helpful. Three questions guided what to include:

- What do practitioners most need to know to get started?

- Where are the biggest pitfalls, and how can they be avoided?

- How can practitioners set themselves up for continual improvement?

> *Most of a school system's knowledge about how to pre-score video will be the result of learning by doing. Each activity undertaken as part of the process is an opportunity to better understand what works and where something different is needed.*

The rest must come by experience. Most of a school system's knowledge about how to pre-score video will be the result of learning by doing. Each activity undertaken as part of the process is an opportunity to better understand what works and where something different is needed. States and districts will encounter problems not addressed in this book, and the right solutions will vary by context. Networking with others implementing the process will accelerate this learning.

Pre-scoring video is complex and challenging. But while it takes time to master, the process often hooks participants right from the start. That's because pre-scoring offers the rich opportunity to engage with other professionals in a rigorous analysis of teaching and learning. The great value in sharpening a shared vision of effective teaching quickly becomes apparent.

 TECHNIQUES:
USING DATA TO IMPROVE A PRE-SCORING PROCESS

To Lay the Foundation:

Keep track of the following for each video segment.

From the pre-scoring process:

- **Segment name.** For example, "6th Grade Pollination Lesson: Use of Questioning"

- **Possible use.** Whether as a training video to show one component at one performance level, as an assessment video to practice rating multiple components, or other

(TECHNIQUES Continued)

- **Start and stop times.** When in the lesson video the segment begins and ends; for example, "14:02–17:49"

- **Grade, subject, and topic.** For example, "6th Grade, Science, Pollination"

- **Teacher and school.** For example, "Jane Apple, ABC Middle School"

- **Lesson video.** A name for the longer unscored video from which the segment is excerpted; for example, "6th Grade Pollination Lesson"

- **Video source.** Where the video came from; for example, ETS, recorded by district, or some other

- **Pre-screener.** Who reviewed the raw video ahead of time for quality and, if part of the pre-screening process, predetermined segments for pre-scoring

- **Master coders and ratings.** Names, plus ratings provided by each for each component of teaching

- **Reconciliation results.** Date of discussion and agreed-upon ratings

- **Quality reviewers.** Who did what, and when, to check the work of master coders; for example, "Use of rubric terms checked by John Doe; backscoring performed by Julie Smith"

From use in training/assessment:

- **Trainees' scores.** Scores given by observers in training/assessment for each teaching component and date given

- **Challenges noted.** For example, "Trainees could not hear enough table discussion to collect evidence on checking for student understanding" or "Score justifications from master coders did not cite sufficient evidence for trainees to understand rationale"

- **Strengths noted.** For example, "Clear evidence to help trainees see the difference between questions to push student thinking and questions to check their understanding"

- **Recommendation for continued use.** For same use in training, for different use, or for discontinued use; for example, "Evidence of both high and low performance indicators makes this better for after trainees have been exposed to more clear-cut examples"

To Build and Improve:

Consider the following questions to plan improvements.

- **Which segments worked best and should be reused? Which should be retired or used for a different purpose?** Look for segments that trainees found especially helpful in understanding the rubric and distinctions between score points. Conversely, if many trainees could not reproduce the correct ratings for a segment, review and consider whether the challenge relates to video quality, the presence of conflicting evidence, or clarity of the ratings and justifications produced by the master coders.

- **Which video sources are the most productive?** Determine whether some sources yield more usable and helpful segments than others.

- **Which pre-screeners are the most skilled?** Did the segments that were most successful in training come from particular individuals? If so, consider whether they can do more of the pre-screening and whether they are using techniques that others could use.

- **Which master coders were the most successful?** See which master coders most often submitted ratings that were the same as those determined after reconciliation and quality reviews. See whether some master coders more frequently submitted rationales that were clear, concise, and grounded in evidence and the rubric's terms.

- **Were some teaching components harder to rate correctly than others?** For those that were repeatedly challenging to participants in training, consider whether additional non-video evidence is required (e.g., lesson plans) or whether the footage needs to be captured differently (e.g., with student interviews about what they're learning).

- **Were some grades and subjects harder to score correctly than others?** Look for trends among the least successful segments. Consider whether changes in the nature of the video used in training might address the issue (e.g., with a roving camera operator).

Continue to collect the information listed under "To Lay the Foundation."

Putting It into Practice

To Lay the Foundation:

How could you begin to collect key information to evaluate your pre-scoring process?

To Build and Improve:

What additional information-gathering and analysis would better support your system's continued improvement?

This item can be downloaded from www.wiley.com/go/betterfeedback

PART III

BUILDING THE KNOWLEDGE AND SKILLS FOR OBSERVATION

CHAPTER 10

Knowing the Rubric

ESSENTIAL QUESTION

How Will You Explain Your Instrument?

At the heart of any observation instrument are the criteria for judging the quality of instruction. These criteria, usually organized into rubrics, describe observable indicators of performance for important aspects of teaching. Together, they represent a powerful statement by a community of educators about what signifies effective teaching. Well-constructed rubrics also make it possible for different observers to reach the same judgments about the same teaching. Rubrics also provide the common language for meaningful discussion with teachers on how to improve. At its most basic level, observer training is about developing a shared understanding of how to apply a rubric.

> *At the beginning of training you need to conduct an instrument overview. This will ensure that all observers are reading and understanding the document the same way.*

But before evaluators can learn to observe with a tool, they need to learn their way around it. Rubrics pack a great deal of information into a single document. They have their own structures, terms, and rules. When all evaluators understand these features correctly, they can accurately answer the questions "What am I looking for?" and "How do I judge what I see?" When they don't understand these features, observers will answer those questions differently. At the beginning of training, you need to provide an instrument overview. This will ensure that all observers are reading and understanding the document the same way.

Begin by building buy-in for the instrument. Observers, like teachers, need to see that what they value in teaching is reflected in the observation tool. When asked what characterizes effective teaching, educators cite a common set of themes: high expectations, content knowledge, a focus on individual student needs, and so on. The training activities that you create should prompt observers to connect those themes to the aspects of teaching that are emphasized in your observation instrument. The best way to do this is to craft clear, concise, and resonant messages that emphasize the instrument's research basis and underlying approaches to instruction, and that explain how the tool reflects current imperatives for student learning (e.g., current college and career readiness skills stress innovation, analysis, and synthesis—all supported by teaching that presses students to think and communicate clearly).

At the same time, you must emphasize the purpose of classroom observation. The ultimate goal is to improve teaching, not just to evaluate classroom performance. When the goal is to improve practice, the observer's job becomes to explain why a lesson merited a particular rating, and what changes in teacher performance would merit a higher rating. Ask trainees to reflect on feedback that they personally found helpful, and what made it so. Chances are many will think of specificity as a key ingredient. This puts the focus, from the start, on how a rubric helps evaluators identify specific evidence of performance in a lesson.

To introduce an instrument, training needs to:

- Help observers see that what they value in teaching is reflected in the instrument.

- Clarify how use of a rubric supports fair evaluation and meaningful feedback.

- Explain how a rubric's structure organizes the indicators of teaching performance.

- Point out text features and annotations that clarify how to make judgments.

- Explain how evidence of different indicators is weighed and interpreted in rating.

 ## SNAPSHOTS:
BUILDING OWNERSHIP AND UNDERSTANDING

PUC: Observer training in the Partnerships to Uplift Communities (PUC) charter schools begins not with the rubric, but with the views of effective teaching that trainees bring with them. PUC's training, developed with Teaching Learning Solutions, includes the short group activity that follows to build buy-in for the charter management organization's observation instrument:

1. Each trainee jots down examples of "Effective Teaching" and "Engaged Learning" on sticky notes.

2. Together they group their sticky notes on a wall by common themes.

3. They look for teaching components and indicators in the PUC rubric that match their themes and add the component names to their sticky notes.

4. One trainee reports out on the connections made.

DCPS: At the outset of their observation training, evaluators in District of Columbia Public Schools learn how the nine teaching components in the district's rubric (the

"Teaching and Learning Framework") fall into three categories of practice essential for academic success (see Figure 10.1). As evaluators complete each segment of the DCPS online training program, they are reminded: "Your commitment to consistent application of the TLF rubric ensures quality feedback that promotes teacher growth."

FIGURE 10.1   At-a-Glance View of Components and Themes

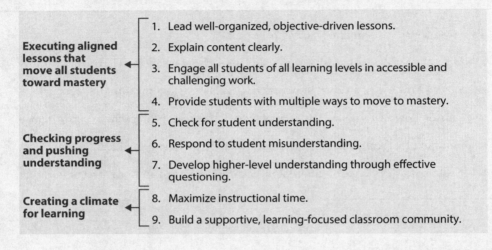

Executing aligned lessons that move all students toward mastery
1. Lead well-organized, objective-driven lessons.
2. Explain content clearly.
3. Engage all students of all learning levels in accessible and challenging work.
4. Provide students with multiple ways to move to mastery.

Checking progress and pushing understanding
5. Check for student understanding.
6. Respond to student misunderstanding.
7. Develop higher-level understanding through effective questioning.

Creating a climate for learning
8. Maximize instructional time.
9. Build a supportive, learning-focused classroom community.

 TIP

Another way to build appreciation for an observation instrument is to have trainees first review a video of high-quality teaching and write down practices they care about. A training leader can then help participants connect those practices to the instrument's teaching components. This strategy can be especially helpful when a common language for instruction is especially lacking in a school system; it allows trainees to connect their own varied terms to those in the rubric, building a shared vocabulary as well as buy-in for the tool.

Explaining a Rubric's Anatomy

To interpret a rubric correctly, you must know what each of its parts is for, and how these parts work together to clarify expectations. Most rubric documents are organized as tables. The use of rows and columns calls more attention to the similarities and differences among the rubric's teaching components.. It's easier to understand the key differences between *proficient* and *exemplary* "checks for student understanding," for example, when the indicators for each rating are next to each other. But you also need to know that "checks for student understanding" is one of the important aspects of teaching to be rated with the rubric, and that the indicators are the look-fors that would signify the performance level for that aspect of a lesson. Figure 10.2 illustrates how to point out these key rubric features.

Make sure everyone in your school system uses the same terms. Different rubrics have different names for each part of their hierarchy: what this book calls a "component," some rubrics

FIGURE 10.2   Rubric Anatomy Lesson

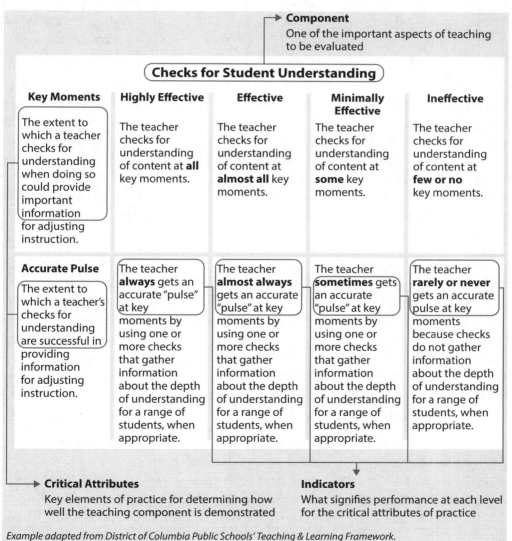

Component
One of the important aspects of teaching to be evaluated

Checks for Student Understanding

Key Moments	Highly Effective	Effective	Minimally Effective	Ineffective
The extent to which a teacher checks for understanding when doing so could provide important information for adjusting instruction.	The teacher checks for understanding of content at **all** key moments.	The teacher checks for understanding of content at **almost all** key moments.	The teacher checks for understanding of content at **some** key moments.	The teacher checks for understanding of content at **few or no** key moments.
Accurate Pulse The extent to which a teacher's checks for understanding are successful in providing information for adjusting instruction.	The teacher **always** gets an accurate "pulse" at key moments by using one or more checks that gather information about the depth of understanding for a range of students, when appropriate.	The teacher **almost always** gets an accurate "pulse" at key moments by using one or more checks that gather information about the depth of understanding for a range of students, when appropriate.	The teacher **sometimes** gets an accurate "pulse" at key moments by using one or more checks that gather information about the depth of understanding for a range of students, when appropriate.	The teacher **rarely or never** gets an accurate pulse at key moments because checks do not gather information about the depth of understanding for a range of students, when appropriate.

Critical Attributes
Key elements of practice for determining how well the teaching component is demonstrated

Indicators
What signifies performance at each level for the critical attributes of practice

Example adapted from District of Columbia Public Schools' Teaching & Learning Framework.

call "standards"; some even use "indicator" for what we call "component," and another different term for what we call "indicator." What matters is that everyone in your school system has the same understanding of the same terms. A common language facilitates learning—for observers and for the teachers they give feedback to—when words mean the same things to different people.

Start at the highest level. Before explaining indicators of performance, show trainees the components, or standards, of teaching that your rubric measures. And for each component, also show trainees the aspects of practice it values. For a component related to establishing a "respectful environment," a rubric might emphasize the quality of interactions between a teacher and students, as well as the quality of interactions among students. A component on promoting a "culture of learning" might stress high expectations and students' pride in their work. Putting all this information on one slide or page helps trainees begin to understand the meaning of each component, and how these components relate to each other.

Next, delve into the role of indicators. The goal at this point is not for the observers to build a deep understanding of each indicator for each component—that comes after an instrument overview—rather, it is for them to see how indicators clarify what needs to be noted in an observation so that the teacher receives an accurate rating and actionable feedback. By describing what's being measured, and by what yardstick, indicators make it possible for different people to note the same things in a lesson, reach the same conclusions about the teacher's demonstrated performance, and have the same understanding about what would elevate that performance.

Use examples to show trainees how a set of indicators helps them know what to look for. As shown in Figure 10.2, one critical attribute of the "checks for student understanding" component might be the extent to which a teacher checked for student understanding at all points in a lesson when incorporating such checks might provide important information about how to proceed with instruction. In this case, an observer would note the number of times in a lesson when a useful check for understanding could have happened, as well as the number of times that one actually did happen. This clear yardstick provides the observer with a basis for objective rating, and a basis for conversation with a teacher about incorporating checks for understanding in more key moments of a lesson.

Different indicators use different yardsticks, and a rubric overview should clarify these for observers. When an indicator uses words such as "always/almost always/sometimes/rarely" to describe different performance levels, it signals that the observer should note the frequency of an action. When words like "all/almost all/some/and few" are used across a set of indicators, it signals that quantity is what matters. For some attributes of a component, what's being measured is more qualitative, such as the clarity of a teacher's explanations or the student investment demonstrated during a lesson. In such cases, the words "generally" or "with some exceptions" might be used to describe different levels of performance. During training, help observers to zero in on such words.

When you call out what's consistently valued throughout the instrument, you help observers understand what tends to characterize different levels of performance. In many rubrics, proficient ratings now call for evidence of constructivist learning, in which students come to their own understanding with the help of the teacher—and the highest ratings require the additional presence of student-driven activities. For this reason, indicators of the same performance levels for different aspects of teaching often use similar terms. Hence, the single term "almost all" may describe evidence of proficient performance for the components "use of questioning," "checks for understanding," and "managing student behavior."

Point out any text features and annotations in the rubric that can help observers understand the critical attributes and indicators of a component. Call attention to any guidelines that help observers interpret quantitative statements; evaluators need to know if, for example, the term "almost always" means between 70 percent and 90 percent of the time. Using short labels and bold text in a rubric, as shown in Figure 10.2, can help observers zero in on, remember, and refer to the key descriptors of performance. Other annotations that might prove helpful to observers include lists of specific practices and behaviors that exemplify particular components, attributes, and indicators (e.g., a teacher circulating around the room during group work as a check for understanding).

Calling Out Rules and Exceptions

Finally, an instrument overview should explain the tool's overall approach toward weighing evidence of different performance indicators to determine a rating. What rating should an observer give, for example, when a teacher checks for understanding only at some key moments (an indicator of ineffective performance), but always does so in a way that produces useful information (indicating highly effective performance)? All observers need to know what to do in such cases to ensure accuracy. Typical rules of thumb include averaging the ratings for each attribute (resulting in "effective" in the just-mentioned example) and considering what the preponderance of evidence suggests.

Observers also should be aware of any exceptions. For example, a school system or instrument developer may emphasize some aspects of practices over others. Another type of exception an observer may encounter is what to do when the preponderance of evidence lies between two ratings. In borderline cases with checks for understanding, for example, the school system or instrument developer may have decided that the effectiveness of the checks outweigh

The goal at this point is not for observers to build a deep understanding of each indicator for each component—that comes after an instrument overview— rather, it is for them to see how indicators clarify what needs to be noted in an observation so that the teacher receives an accurate rating and actionable feedback.

their frequency, because frequent ineffective checks do little to improve student learning. Your instrument overview should give trainees a heads-up that there are exceptions to rules of thumb, if they exist. Otherwise the observers will produce different ratings even if they see the same behaviors.

An instrument overview should also give trainees some practice interpreting the tool. Pointing out a rubric's structure and parts goes only so far. One way you can provide that practice is to ask participants to analyze a component of teaching by identifying its critical attributes and the yardsticks used to measure them, and by suggesting possible practices and behaviors that might indicate performance. Doing this in a facilitated group session allows trainers to hear what participants are taking away and what they're struggling to understand. Online tutorials may use multiple-choice questions (e.g., "What yardstick is used to measure this critical attribute?"); these can also be used to assess the observers' understanding.

SNAPSHOT: RHODE ISLAND'S COMPONENT ANALYSIS ACTIVITY

As part of a rubric overview, the Rhode Island Department of Education includes an activity designed to help evaluators interpret a rubric's content. After explaining the rubric's structure, trainers organize participants into groups and assign each of them one component to analyze. At their tables, trainees review the rubric's language and discuss what's being measured, as well as things they might observe in the classroom that would be relevant to evaluating a lesson on the component. Then each table reports out on their analysis to the larger group. Through the exercise, participants learn how to make sense of a rubric's definitions of practice.

The template and directions in Figure 10.3 are adapted from Rhode Island's process.

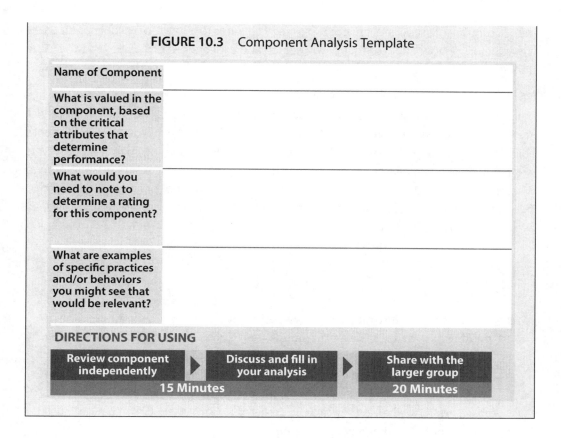

FIGURE 10.3   Component Analysis Template

Name of Component	
What is valued in the component, based on the critical attributes that determine performance?	
What would you need to note to determine a rating for this component?	
What are examples of specific practices and/or behaviors you might see that would be relevant?	

DIRECTIONS FOR USING

Review component independently ▶ Discuss and fill in your analysis ▶ Share with the larger group

15 Minutes   **20 Minutes**

When you plan an instrument overview for the first time, make sure you pilot the explanations and activities with a small number of evaluators. Don't wait until you're actually training observers to learn what important terms and features are not adequately addressed. When you do begin delivering an overview, collect data—in the form of participant surveys, the questions trainees ask, and any noticings by participants as to its effectiveness in clarifying key points—to identify areas for improvement. The extent to which they can read a rubric and answer the questions "What should I be looking for?" and "How will I judge what I see?" will suggest where more clarity is needed.

You'll learn more about what needs changing in an instrument overview as observers are trained on each component in your rubric, and as they begin to carry out observations in the field. You may find that you need additional text features, annotations, or more analysis of rubric components in your overview. Explain any changes to a rubric or guidelines for using it in your follow-up training so that newly trained and experienced observers have the same understanding.

One big caution, however: don't take lightly the implications of making changes to an instrument. Even minor revisions to the instrument may create a need for new training material. Pre-scored video may need rescoring. More important, changes may erode the instrument's ability to measure what's intended. Test any changes before adopting them. Ask observers what they would do differently based on the change to the instrument, and pay attention to what they actually do (e.g., annotating part of a rubric with a list of practices may help clarify what might indicate a particular aspect of teaching, but it also may unintentionally lead evaluators to look for only what's listed).

TIPS

- Don't assume an instrument overview isn't needed because those coming to initial training have had some exposure to the tool. Knowing what aspects of teaching are emphasized by an instrument is not the same as understanding how to locate and correctly interpret the language that can answer the questions "What should I be looking for?" and "How should I judge what I see?" In addition, given most observers' limited time, they can't be expected to learn on their own how to interpret a rubric. The skill must be taught.

- When adding labels to an instrument, make them distinctive. When two sound like the same thing—like "procedures" and "directions"—they may confuse. If it's difficult to capture the key idea of an indicator in two or three words, the indicator might contain too many elements for evaluators to easily assess. Always remember to test such labels with observers to make sure the intended meaning is understood. One way is to ask a small number of observers to think of the kinds of evidence from a lesson that might relate to proposed language.

- Include teachers in the process. As much as your observers need to understand and feel ownership of your observation instrument, your teachers need it more. Get them involved in developing your instrument overview, and make sure they receive their own training on the tool as well.

✓ TECHNIQUES:
EXPLAINING YOUR OBSERVATION INSTRUMENT

To Lay the Foundation:

■ Build buy-in for the instrument with activities that connect its teaching components with aspects of instruction valued by trainees. Also build credibility by summarizing its research basis and underlying approaches to instruction.

■ Point out the rubric structure and key elements with a high-level view of all its components and a close-up view of the elements for one component.

■ Provide opportunity for trainees to practice identifying the critical attributes and descriptors of performance in a rubric's language (e.g., for "checks for student understanding," what's critical is the frequency and effectiveness of the checks).

■ Explain the instrument's general approach toward considering evidence across different indicators to determine overall performance for a component (i.e., if "preponderance of evidence" is the general rule). Also give a heads-up that there may be exceptions to those general approaches (i.e., if some indicators weigh more heavily than others in certain situations).

To Build and Improve:

■ Use input from training participants and any data collected on their ability to read an instrument correctly to identify areas where trainees need more clarity. Options for clarification may include additional text features in the rubric to call out key ideas, annotations to qualify statements or provide examples, or additional opportunities for trainees to analyze the wording for particular components.

■ Make sure any changes to a rubric, or the guidelines for interpreting it, are reflected in both initial training for new evaluators and follow-up training for experienced ones. Build appreciation for the changes by explaining the rationale, how they better support the work of observers and teachers, and how observer input may have led to the changes.

■ Use follow-up training to guide evaluators in analyzing particular parts of a rubric that are the source of common confusions (e.g., by analyzing the difference between two components of teaching that evaluators struggle to distinguish).

Putting It into Practice

To Lay the Foundation:

Review your rubric. What are the key structural features, and how will you communicate them when introducing the instrument to observers and teachers?

To Build and Improve:

How could changes in your rubric overview—in initial or follow-up training—clarify any confusion revealed by feedback from training participants and other data?

This item can be downloaded from www.wiley.com/go/betterfeedback

CHAPTER 11

Collecting Evidence

ESSENTIAL QUESTION

How Will You Teach Evidence Collection?

Evidence is the basis of fair evaluation and meaningful feedback. Evidence is what grounds agreement on the quality of practice, as well as the conversation about how to improve. With concrete evidence, an observer can say, "Let's talk about what happened here, and what could be done differently." When an observer calls attention to specific actions that took place in a lesson, it demystifies the reasons why a specific performance rating is warranted and also provides a clear starting point for discussing how to implement changes. Quality observation depends on quality evidence (see Figure 11.1).

> *For an observer, getting an accurate account of what matters for feedback and evaluation is no small challenge. Even experienced instructional leaders need coaching and practice on collecting evidence before they learn how to rate practice.*

But a lot happens in a few minutes of teaching. It's not just a teacher talking. Teachers and students make statements in response to each other and write things down. They move about the classroom. They use materials and tools. They exhibit body language. Moreover, different students within a classroom act differently, and teachers react differently to different students. For an observer, getting an accurate account of what matters for feedback and evaluation is no small challenge. Even experienced instructional leaders need coaching and practice on collecting evidence before they learn how to rate practice.

But first evaluators need to understand what constitutes evidence. Untrained observers may think evidence is whatever they write down during a lesson. It's not. A piece of evidence is an objective description of something observed in a lesson. It makes no suggestion of quality. An observer's notation of "Lesson objective clearly explained" is not evidence; rather, it is a statement of the observer's interpretation of evidence. Evidence would be the actual statements a teacher made to explain the objective and how students responded. What you've seen at times outside a particular observation also is not evidence that you can use for rating the teaching that you just observed. A good way to illustrate the distinction between evidence and interpretation is with a side-by-side visual that compares the characteristics of each, with examples (see Figure 11.2).

FIGURE 11.1 How Evidence Supports Each Step in Observation

COLLECT	SORT	INTERPRET	PROVIDE FEEDBACK
An observer looks for and records evidence relevant to assessing practice.	**The observer categorizes the evidence by teaching component.**	**The observer finds which indicators of performance best match the evidence.**	**The observer uses evidence to ground discussion with the teacher on improving.**
Evidence might include teacher and student . . .	These might be:	Possible indicators:	An evaluator might use:
▪ questions	▪ Maximizing Instructional Time	▪ For **Proficient,** students should articulate academic expectations.	▪ Questions to prompt teacher reflection
▪ responses	▪ Promoting High Cognitive Engagement	▪ For **Exemplary,** they also must know the difference between work that meets expectations and work that doesn't.	▪ Suggestions of specific practices to employ
▪ behaviors	▪ Clarifying Academic Expectations		▪ Modeling of possible techniques to use
▪ statements			
For example:	*For example:*	*For example:*	*For example:*
T: How will we know if we have good topic sentences?	This teacher-student exchange reflects **Clarifying Academic Expectations,** which refers to how a teacher helps students understand what constitutes quality work (e.g., a quality topic sentence).	This evidence aligns with **Proficient,** because students articulated what makes for a good topic sentence but not the difference between good and weak ones.	An evaluator asks the teacher:
(8 hands go up)			▪ What did students say about good topic sentences?
S1: If it tells you what's important.			▪ How could you also find out if they understand the difference between strong and weak ones?
T: Important about what?			
S2: About the paragraph.			

FIGURE 11.2   Side-by-Side Comparison of Evidence and Interpretation

EVIDENCE IS . . .	INTERPRETATION IS . . .
Nonjudgmental	**Judgmental**
■ Teacher: When a car is accelerating, its speed changes.	■ The teacher's explanation of acceleration was clear.
Specific	**Generalized**
■ 4 of 10 students raised hands.	■ Students were minimally engaged.
■ 2 students had side conversation.	

Types of Evidence

- Direct quotes of teacher and students
- What the teacher and students write on the board
- Description of materials and how they are used
- Descriptions of what happened, in what order
- The number of times something happens

Observers need practice to internalize the distinctions between evidence and interpretation. When training observers, one useful approach you can use is to give them examples of descriptions and statements, and then ask which examples are evidence, which are not, and why. Later, evaluators can practice recording evidence while reviewing a video; then they can compare and discuss their notes with each other. Such videos should be pre-scored so a facilitator knows what evidence there is to capture. Keep in mind that evaluators have a tendency early in their training to focus almost exclusively on what teachers say and do. If they do notice students, they may only notice those students who are working directly with the teacher. Through practice, evaluators will learn to see exchanges, body language, and behavior throughout the entire classroom.

To teach evidence collection, training should:

- Develop an understanding of what is evidence.

- Explain why evidence is essential for accurate evaluation and meaningful feedback.

- Provide opportunities for collecting different types of evidence.

- Suggest techniques for efficient and accurate note taking.

Share with trainees this helpful mantra: "Collect evidence now, interpret later." Explain that evaluators should resist the urge to form judgments about the quality of practice during the teacher observation itself. There's too much to look for, listen for, and write down to try to determine performance at the same time. Moreover, a judgment they make at one point in an observation may color how they view the rest of the lesson, so the only other evidence they note is that which confirms their judgment. Evaluators who stay focused on "just the facts" will appreciate having those facts later when they need to match their evidence to the right indicators of performance.

Another tendency among untrained observers is to script everything. Unsure of what is relevant evidence, they try to transcribe all that is said. But very few people can accurately record 20-plus minutes of live conversation involving 20-plus individuals in the room. Regardless, it's counterproductive. When all your attention is consumed by capturing every word, you have none to spare to notice what people are doing.

Collecting evidence involves filtering the whole classroom scene. This eventually becomes automatic as observers gain a deep understanding of each indicator in the rubric, as they practice rating, and as they carry out observations in the classroom. But you will need to provide some upfront guidance and practice on efficient evidence collection to help trainees master this process.

Your most-skilled observers are a great source of effective evidence collection techniques. When you first develop your evidence collection training, tap the expertise of those observers who demonstrate the most skill at producing accurate and focused notes from classroom visits.

Ask observers to collect different kinds of relevant evidence as they watch videos. Explain that this evidence should include teacher and student statements and behaviors, how often repeated activities take place, how materials are used, and so on. Encourage observers to use shorthand techniques for note taking. This might include "T" for teacher and "S1, S2" for different students; "tick marks" for counting the number of instances of off-task behavior; and making a quick sketch of table arrangements. To guide trainees in collecting multiple types of evidence, you can provide them with templates that have space for "teacher statements/behaviors," "student statements/behaviors," and other key types of evidence.

Your most-skilled observers are a great source of effective evidence collection techniques. When you first develop your evidence collection training, tap the expertise of those observers who demonstrate the most skill at producing accurate and focused notes from classroom visits. Chances are they've developed tricks of the trade you can share with trainees. Over time, you'll discover what else you need to address in your evidence collection training as trainees attempt to collect evidence specific to each teaching component. When you plan your follow-up training for those trainees who have completed the initial program, consider including advanced techniques, such as how to use shorthand codes for common teaching practices (e.g., "TnT" for "turn and talk"). Trainees can adapt these techniques as they develop an approach that works for them.

Q IN FOCUS:
AVOIDING EVIDENCE OVERLOAD

Some new observers try to capture everything they see and hear. This is natural, as they're still learning what's most relevant to the rubric. But it's also unmanageable: no one can record everything that happens in a lesson, and even if one could, the resulting feedback would lose meaning. Some training programs tell observers that if the teacher doesn't refer to something, you don't need to record it (e.g., don't describe an anchor chart on the wall that's not clearly part of the lesson).

Another piece of advice is not to worry about capturing the content of every brief dialogue among students; if several pairs of students do quick "think-pair-shares" at the same point in a lesson, just make sure you write down what was said in some of them. The more practiced observers get, the more automatically they can filter the scene for only what they need.

SNAPSHOT:
PRACTICING EVIDENCE COLLECTION IN MINNEAPOLIS

Minneapolis Public Schools includes an exercise in its initial training of observers that's designed to help participants internalize the distinction between evidence and interpretation.

As shown in Figure 11.3, trainees watch a 10- to 12-minute video and individually record what they think would be evidence of a particular aspect of teaching. As a group, they then create a poster of their evidence. Then they review each piece of evidence and discuss whether it is actually evidence or contains judgment and/or generalizations. When the recorded evidence is determined to be interpretation, the group tries to edit the statement to remove the judgment and add detail (e.g., changing "Teacher effectively probed student understanding" to "Teacher asked students to explain character traits").

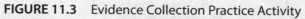

FIGURE 11.3   Evidence Collection Practice Activity

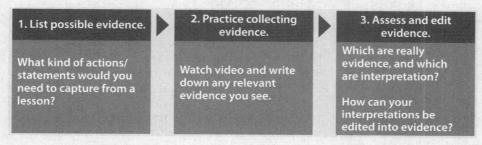

1. List possible evidence.	2. Practice collecting evidence.	3. Assess and edit evidence.
What kind of actions/ statements would you need to capture from a lesson?	Watch video and write down any relevant evidence you see.	Which are really evidence, and which are interpretation? How can your interpretations be edited into evidence?

SNAPSHOT: TEACHING EFFICIENT EVIDENCE COLLECTION IN DCPS

District of Columbia Public Schools includes an overview of evidence collection techniques early in its online program for the initial training of evaluators. (See Figure 11.4 for an excerpt.) As a check for understanding, trainees are given written descriptions of what they might observe during a lesson and then asked which of three techniques would best capture relevant evidence: summarizing anecdotes, coding, or scripting. They then learn which is correct and see an example of how an observer might efficiently capture the evidence using the technique. In another part of the session, trainees watch a video of teaching while captions show in real time what an expert observer would write down. This models how it's possible to capture evidence efficiently, using shorthand, without writing down everything that was observed.

FIGURE 11.4   Evidence Collection Techniques

Technique	What Is Observed	What Gets Written Down
Anecdotes. Brief, objective summaries of what was seen or heard.	At the beginning of the lesson while the teacher is at her desk looking through her papers, 12 students are seated on the carpet talking amongst themselves and 5 are at their desks finishing up a previous activity.	T at desk, 12 Ss on carpet talking, 5 Ss at desks working
Coding. Shorthand symbols or letters to capture common or repetitive classroom practices.	Throughout the lesson the teacher used "1, 2, 3 all eyes on me" 5 times to get the students' attention.	1, 2, 3 all eyes on me √√√√√
Scripting. Direct quotes by teachers or students, which may include use of shorthand for frequently used words.	The teacher is explaining probability. She says, "Probability is the chance that something will happen, or how likely that some event will happen. Who can give me an example of when we use probability?" A student answers, "When we flip a coin?"	**T:** Probability is chance something will happen or how likely event will happen. Who can give example? **S:** When we flip a coin.

TIPS

■ When reviewing video, new evaluators often struggle to turn their attention to things happening in the classroom other than teacher talk. A simple solution is to turn off the video sound. Giving trainees some practice collecting evidence from muted recordings forces them to notice behaviors that might indicate student participation, engagement, and teacher responsiveness.

■ Use time stamps. When collecting evidence from a video, evaluators should note when in the video key exchanges and behaviors took place (e.g., "3:36" to show that something took place at three minutes and 36 seconds into the recording). This makes it easier to go back to parts of the video while discussing the extent to which evaluators were able to accurately note evidence of indicators.

- Collecting evidence from video is different from doing so live. An evaluator in a teacher's classroom can look over students' shoulders to see their work, ask students to explain what they're learning, and walk around the room to get a closer look at materials. Video's great strength is that it allows multiple evaluators to see the same lesson. But you may need to supplement video with other documents relevant to the lesson so that trainees have access to more of the evidence they need. These documents might be lesson plans, student work, or pictures of visuals used in a lesson.

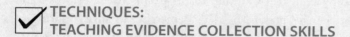

TECHNIQUES:
TEACHING EVIDENCE COLLECTION SKILLS

To Lay the Foundation:

- Lead discussion of how evidence supports trustworthy evaluation and meaningful feedback (e.g., ask trainees for common problems encountered in post-observation discussions with teachers, and how strong evidence could help address them by building a teacher's trust in and understanding of feedback).

- Show side-by-side what distinguishes evidence from interpretation. Provide examples of each and ask trainees to determine which they are.

- Share specific techniques observers may use for efficient coding and note taking (e.g., creating shorthand for frequently heard words or observed behaviors, like "5H" for "five hands" and "bc" for "because").

- Have trainees collect evidence from a video and then compare what they wrote down to the evidence their peers collected and consider to what extent their evidence is specific and free of interpretation.

- Ask experienced evaluators to suggest techniques they use to efficiently record specific and accurate evidence. Share those as examples trainees might want to use.

- Collect sample evidence from all trainees to check their understanding of evidence versus interpretation.

(TECHNIQUES Continued)

To Build and Improve:

- Look for types of evidence that observers often miss; create additional activities that call attention to these, and provide practice collecting them (e.g., create an activity that focuses trainees on differences in students' characteristics if observers are missing evidence of equitable engagement—that is, they aren't noting if teachers respond to students the same way regardless of gender or background).

- Use surveys and other input from training participants to identify parts of evidence collection training that need to be adjusted. Can trainees explain the important role played by evidence? Can they distinguish between evidence and interpretation? If not, changes may be needed. Remember to survey during or immediately after training, and again some months later. Often, it's only after applying a skill in the field that those trained realize how well they were prepared.

⠀Putting It into Practice

To Lay the Foundation:

What activities and resources could you use to develop an understanding of the importance of evidence, what evidence is, and ways to collect it?

To Build and Improve:

In what ways could changes in your evidence collection training address common challenges your observers are encountering, and how could you provide experienced observers with more advanced techniques?

CHAPTER 12

Understanding Bias

ESSENTIAL QUESTION

How Will You Build an Understanding of Bias?

What's your image of an ideal lesson? What's the most important thing to see in the classroom? No two educators will answer in exactly the same way. One might answer "Lots of student talk," and another "Students following procedures." Of course, both are part of effective teaching. But a preference for one aspect of teaching over the other can color an observer's impression of the lesson as a whole. When evaluators who favor "student talk" see lots of it in the classroom, that favorable impression may influence their judgments of other aspects of the same lesson. Without realizing it, they may inflate the ratings they give for the components "classroom management" or "checks for understanding."

Your observer training should cover bias awareness so that observers can identify such preferences. Observers need more than just training on how to recognize evidence for each of a rubric's components and indicators of performance. They also need to understand their own personal tendencies to favor specific aspects of instruction, or to disfavor them, for particular reasons. By understanding these tendencies, observers can be on the lookout for triggers and counter their possible effects on rating. When you realize, for example, that you favor lessons with lots of student talk, you can then ask yourself if your rating of aspects of a lesson unrelated to classroom discussion are being influenced by the amount of student talk you hear.

> *If left unchecked, observers' unconscious tendencies to favor or disfavor something pose a threat to fairness when rating instructional practice.*

Personal preferences that may affect ratings aren't only about instructional methods. Just about anything an evaluator sees or hears in a classroom might trigger a favorable or unfavorable impression. That includes the styles of speech, dress, and backgrounds of teachers and students. In fact, recent research showed district evaluators gave somewhat lower ratings to the same teachers when they were observed teaching classes with more low-income and minority students than when the teachers' classrooms included higher socioeconomic student compositions.[10] If left unchecked, observers' unconscious tendencies to favor or disfavor specific instructional or non-instructional factors can pose a threat to fairness when rating teacher performance.

When training observers to recognize their preferences, you need to show sensitivity. Individuals naturally feel defensive when exploring their biases. Many may question the need for bias awareness training. They may think "I don't have biases," or "I don't need training to know what my biases are." Recognizing these biases can be uncomfortable for observers, and they may feel like it is an admission of fault. But everyone has biases and preferences, and we are unaware of most of them. The goal of training is not to eliminate these biases or even to make a judgment about them. The goal is to help observers identify preferences they need to set aside for the sake of a shared interpretation of effective teaching.

Defining Bias

The best time for you to introduce the subject of bias is early in observers' training. An understanding of bias extends the fundamental notion that evaluations of practice must be based on objective evidence. Explain what bias means, why it matters, and the goal of bias awareness training. In the context of observation, a bias is any preference that might lead an evaluator to rate differently than called for by the rating criteria. The tendency may be to favor or disfavor something. It may relate to aspects of instruction addressed in a rubric, or it may be completely irrelevant to any of a rubric's indicators. It may relate to characteristics of the teacher, students, or classroom environment.

To build an understanding of bias, training should:

■ Describe how different types of bias can influence rating.

■ Provide techniques to help observers identify their personal preferences.

■ Suggest strategies for minimizing the effects of preferences on rating.

Make it clear from the outset that bias is normal. Everyone has biases. They are the natural product of each individual's unique set of experiences. To further make the case for this aspect of training, describe common ways in which observer preferences may affect rating (called "observer effects"). Several of these are shown in the table, "Six Common Observer Effects That Can Bias Ratings." Generally, these effects occur without the observers' knowledge. This discussion will help trainees understand how these biases are likely to occur unless they make a conscious effort to counteract them. Once they understand these common tendencies, observers may be able to recognize when they might exhibit those tendencies themselves.

Six Common Observer Effects That Can Bias Ratings

Effect	Explanation	Example
Familiarity	When prior knowledge of the teacher or students observed causes the observer to be either lenient or overly strict when rating a lesson.	■ An observer "knows," from having been in a teacher's classroom at other times, that a rating should be higher than the lesson observed warrants. Or the observer feels the students are "capable of more" from having seen them at other times.
Halo	When exceptional performance on one aspect of teaching leads the observer to inflate the teacher's ratings on unrelated aspects of teaching.	■ An observer is so impressed with a teacher's use of questioning in a lesson that evidence of ineffective checks for student understanding goes unnoticed.
Fatal Flaw	When low performance on one aspect of teaching colors an observer's impression of other aspects of teaching in a lesson.	■ After a teacher gives students a wrong answer early in the lesson, the observer sees the rest of the lesson in a negative light.
Central Tendency	When observers tend to give undeserved middling ratings rather than using ratings at the high or low end of the scale.	■ Observers inflate low scores to "play it safe," because they lack confidence in their accuracy or their ability to give helpful feedback. ■ Observers' belief that "highly effective" practice is extremely rare leads them to miss it when present.
Consequence	When the perceived stakes attached to the results lead observers to rate inaccurately.	■ An observer inflates the ratings of a teacher believed to be at risk of negative consequences due to low performance.
Drift	When over time observers gradually and unknowingly tend to inflate or deflate their ratings.	■ As time goes by an observer who rated accurately upon completing initial training gradually gives higher ratings in observations. (A group of observers may also "drift together," exhibiting the same tendency to give increasingly higher or lower ratings than warranted.)

Making It Safe

Create an environment in which trainees feel comfortable reflecting on their personal preferences. Training leaders should share examples of their own biases before having trainees think about theirs (e.g., "I realized I favored classrooms with lots of student talk"). Ask participants to first consider preferences they have that relate to other professions (e.g., "If you were choosing a car mechanic, what might you see or hear at the garage that would give you a favorable impression?"). For any group sessions, choose facilitators who can maintain a non-judgmental tone. Consider using outside experts for bias awareness training; this can support more open discussion.

> *Create an environment in which trainees feel comfortable reflecting on their personal preferences. Training leaders should share examples of their own biases before having trainees think about theirs.*

Online or independent activities often work best for this aspect of observer training. Privacy is conducive to honest self-reflection. Trainees need to know that no one will be privy to their responses to prompts, whether administered on paper or online. In this regard, bias awareness training is very different from other parts of observer training. The purpose, in this case, is not to norm everyone's interpretation of a common set of criteria; rather, it's to help observers to better understand their own unique perspectives, which in turn helps them stay true to the common criteria when observing in the classroom.

When using prompts for independent work, include both open-ended and selected-response questions. For the former, ask trainees what they might see in a classroom that could lead them to favor the lesson (e.g., the teacher is well dressed or has especially neat handwriting). Ask the same about unfavorable impressions (e.g., students out of their chairs or speaking in the vernacular). Using selected-response prompts can help identify trainees' preferences for specific instructional methods (e.g., ask trainees to rank a set of practices related to aspects of teaching in the rubric according to how important they feel each practice is to student learning).

Word association exercises are another way to reveal biases. Give trainees a series of words and have them quickly write down the first thing that comes to mind; then have them reflect on each response and note any connotations. Given the word "suit," one person might write "formal" and another "professional"—connoting somewhat different feelings. Association exercises can be helpful in identifying biases related to people's backgrounds. Words like "Southern" will signify different things to different people. Recognizing that one has such associations can be discomforting, but it is critical for accurate evaluation. Activities you can use to build awareness of different types of preferences are in the table, "Ways to Identify Personal Preferences".

Ways to Identify Personal Preferences

Preference Type	Examples	Activities for Self-Reflection
Instructional Methods	■ Favoring lessons that include differentiated instruction regardless of how well other aspects of teaching are demonstrated. ■ Rating lessons more strictly if they include inquiry-based instruction, based on the belief that the method is rarely used effectively.	■ Ask trainees the extent to which they believe specific methods should be used or are difficult to employ (from strongly agree to strongly disagree). ■ Ask them to rank different aspects of effective teaching by how important they feel they are. ■ Have them review their own notes from observations and reflect, "What practices do I particularly attend to?" It helps to do this while also reviewing notes, if any, from co-observers.
Demographics	■ Expecting different levels of practice depending on teachers' racial, ethnic, or geographic backgrounds. ■ Giving higher ratings for responses provided by low socioeconomic status (SES) students than if high SES students gave the same responses. ■ Giving higher or lower ratings if the teacher doesn't share the same background as the students.	■ Ask trainees to consider if they would rate an observed lesson higher or lower if the teacher or students had different backgrounds. ■ Ask them to write down the first thing that comes to mind when shown words to describe people of different demographic backgrounds.
Style	■ Scoring lessons more strictly when the teacher dresses more casually. ■ Scoring lessons more leniently when students are out of their desks.	■ Ask trainees to list things they might see in a classroom that would cause them to think favorably and unfavorably about what they saw. ■ Ask them to write down the first thing that comes to mind when shown words to describe different teaching and personal styles.

Preference Type	Examples	Activities for Self-Reflection
Speech	■ Giving lower ratings when students respond in the vernacular or when teachers make frequent use of certain colloquialisms. ■ Giving higher ratings to a teacher with a British accent.	■ Have them visualize their model classroom and write down what they imagine. ■ Ask trainees to consider if particular styles of speech could make it difficult for them to appreciate what a teacher and students are saying.

A single training module will not reveal all of a person's preferences. The goal of early training on bias awareness is for trainees to build an understanding of how personal preferences may come into play and to identify strategies to address them. Encourage trainees to keep lists of "triggers" and add to it when they recognize new ones. It may take years for an observer to recognize a preference for classrooms that are especially colorful. By noting when their triggers are present, observers can take steps to mitigate their influence on rating teaching practice—say, by taking more time to review evidence they collected and how they aligned it to the rubric, or by asking a colleague to review their collected evidence for possible signs of bias.

Your observer training should revisit the issue of bias as it delves into each component of teaching in your instrument (as we explain in Chapter 14, "Using Criteria for Rating"). Often, you don't realize that you favor, or disfavor, a particular aspect of teaching until you begin collecting and interpreting evidence for it. By introducing the idea of bias ahead of time and building some comfort with the issue, training prepares observers to better recognize their preferences when it matters most. Hence, you should use a general introduction to bias as a prerequisite to learning how to rate.

How you introduce the concept of bias should change as you learn more about the effectiveness of learning activities and the kinds of preferences that most need to be addressed in your school system. Solicit feedback from trainees on how well the training is helping them reveal their preferences and helping them counter any possible effects on rating. Gather input from trainers on common biases they see among observers as they practice collecting evidence and rating. Be alert to comments by trainees that signal they may need specific guidance on avoiding the effects of bias (e.g., comments such as "given the students in the class" when discussing certain teaching components).

TIPS

- Start by using the word "preference," not "bias." To many people, the latter connotes an ethical lapse, when in fact assessment experts merely equate it with a tendency. Beginning the discussion with "preference" helps minimize defensiveness.

- Encourage evaluators to self-monitor for value-laden language. An inclination to say "The teacher should have" or "I would have" may signal a personal preference that could lead to rating in a way that's inconsistent with accurate application of an observation instrument.

✓ TECHNIQUES: BUILDING AN UNDERSTANDING OF BIAS

To Lay the Foundation:

- Make the case for active self-reflection to identify one's own personal and professional preferences. Start with a noncontroversial example of how a preference could affect rating a lesson without the evaluator realizing it, and discuss the consequences to fairness and instructional improvement.

- Make three points: everyone has biases; we can't eliminate them, but we can reduce their impact on rating; awareness of our biases helps us become better observers and provide better feedback.

- Explain common bias factors (e.g., speech and teaching methods) and provide examples of each.

- Ask trainees to independently and anonymously rate the importance of teaching practices related to your rubric and to list things that might cause them to think favorably or unfavorably about a lesson. Encourage them to add to such lists throughout their training and as they observe more classrooms.

To Build and Improve:

- Adjust bias awareness training based on feedback from trainees and trainers on the extent to which the activities helped them to understand the training's importance, helped them to identify their preferences, and helped them take steps to minimize their impact on evaluation.

- Consider augmenting the training with new techniques for minimizing bias that experienced observers have found to be helpful.

- Use observation data, observer assessment results, and feedback from trainers to identify trends that may indicate the need to address certain preferences more specifically (e.g., if trainees make many comments to the effect of "given the students in the class" when classroom composition is not relevant to rating a component of teaching).

Putting It into Practice

To Lay the Foundation:

What would be the best way to introduce bias awareness training in your overall training program for observers?

To Build and Improve:

What do your observation data, assessment results, and feedback from training participants suggest as ways to enhance your bias awareness training?

This item can be downloaded from www.wiley.com/go/betterfeedback

CHAPTER 13

Recognizing Evidence

ESSENTIAL QUESTION

How Will You Develop the Skills to Identify and Sort Relevant Evidence?

Teachers receive meaningful feedback when observers call out examples of what happened in a lesson that relate to important aspects of teaching. Providing a teacher with relevant evidence gives meaning to the judgments of performance and to the teaching practices that might be improved. Without relevant evidence, a teacher is left wondering, "*What do you mean* by 'my students were minimally engaged?'" Moreover, the fairness and accuracy of performance ratings are threatened when observers consider only part of what's relevant, or when they give weight to evidence that's irrelevant.

Understanding an instrument's intended meaning requires observers to think about the instrument's core concepts, and to engage in guided practice in identifying evidence of those concepts at work in actual lessons.

To identify relevant evidence, observers must understand an instrument's meaning. But simply reviewing a rubric's descriptors isn't enough to foster agreement among observers. When reading a set of criteria, most people will arrive at their own ideas of what's most important and what it might look like in practice. Or they'll have only a vague idea, leading them to rely instead on personal preference while evaluating classroom performance or to provide meaningless feedback that is unlikely to be challenged (e.g., "nice questioning"). Understanding an instrument's intended meaning requires observers to think about the instrument's core concepts, as well as to engage in guided practice in identifying evidence of those concepts at work in actual lessons.

You need to build an understanding of relevant evidence before you give trainees practice with rating. To do otherwise will lead to frustration. Imagine if you were told you had rated student engagement incorrectly because you missed a piece of evidence that you never realized was important to rating that aspect of teaching. In observation, rating comes after an observer collects and organizes a body of evidence relevant to the instrument (see Figure 13.1). Your training of evaluators should follow the same sequence.

FIGURE 13.1 Gathering and Sorting Relevant Evidence

An observer goes into an observation knowing what evidence to look and listen for.	During an observation, the observer gathers evidence relevant to the entire rubric.	After the observation the observer sorts the evidence into the right teaching components.
For example:	*For example:*	*For example:*
For Communicating Learning Objectives:	On Board: Students will be able to determine the right formulas for length, area, and volume.	**Communicating Learning Objectives:**
■ What's written on posted objectives	**T:** There are a lot of formulas for measuring shapes. We're going to figure out when to use each one.	On Board: Students will be able to determine the right formulas for length, area, and volume.
■ Teachers and student statements about the objective at the beginning and throughout the lesson	Teacher holds up a box. "What does the volume tell us?"	**T:** There are a lot of formulas for measuring shapes. We're going to figure out when to use each one.
For Checking for Student Understanding:	Five students raise hands.	**T:** So we're going to figure out what formula to use to figure out how much space it takes up.
■ Teacher questions and activities to probe understanding	**T:** Angela?	**Checking for Student Understanding:**
■ Which students respond and how	**S1:** How much it could hold.	Teacher holds up a box. "What does the volumes tell us?"
■ How the teacher follows up on such checks	**T:** Good, so we're going to figure out what formula to use to figure out how much space it takes up.	Five students raise hands.
		T: Angela?
		S1: How much it could hold.
		T: Good...

To develop the skills to identify and sort relevant evidence, training should:

■   Unpack the rubric components to clarify what to look and listen for.

■   Provide for modeling and practice collecting relevant evidence using pre-scored video.

■   Provide for modeling and practice aligning evidence to the right rubric components.

Why Pre-Scored Video Is Essential

Pre-scored video is essential for this part of training (see Figure 13.2). You help observers learn to identify relevant evidence by giving them feedback on their repeated attempts to identify relevant evidence. But you can't give a trainee feedback if you don't know what evidence was in the lesson that the trainee should have captured. An expert observer might try to identify relevant evidence by observing a lesson alongside a trainee and then comparing notes. But if that's the only check on trainees' accuracy, you're putting all your faith in an expert's ability to identify what's relevant, and on the fly. When you use video that has been pre-scored by multiple experts, you can have confidence that the relevant evidence has been identified in a recording that can be reviewed, repeatedly, with lots of trainees.

FIGURE 13.2   Uses for Pre-Scored Video in Observer Training

To clarify what different components of teaching might look like in the classroom (e.g., a check for understanding)

To model evidence collection for specific components and provide feedback on trainees' collection attempts

To allow for practice collecting and sorting evidence to the right components

TYPES OF PRE-SCORED VIDEO FOR USE IN TRAINING

Benchmark	A clear-cut (not borderline) example of one teaching component at one performance level (e.g., a Level 2 for communicating learning objectives). May be 2 to 12 minutes, depending on the component and video quality.
Rangefinder	An example of teaching at the low or high end of a performance level (e.g., a high Level 2 or low Level 3 for communicating lesson objectives). Useful to clarify what makes the difference between two levels for a component. Similar in length to benchmarks.
Mini-Segment	A clear illustration of one concept important to recognizing relevant evidence (e.g., what "a range of students" means in the context of checking for student understanding). Might be 1 minute or shorter.

Understanding how to pre-score video is detailed in this book in Part II: Pre-Scoring Video. This chapter provides guidance on how to use pre-scored video in training, of which there are many variations. Trainees might review multiple video illustrations of a component of teaching before they try to collect evidence themselves. But another option is to go more directly from a discussion of relevant types of evidence to the actual practice of collecting evidence, followed by feedback on their attempts to identify and collect evidence. However you use pre-scored video in your training, it's critical that the pre-scoring process involved quality control checks to ensure that the agreed-upon ratings and rationales for those ratings are based on the rubric's language and observed evidence.

 TIPS ON USING PRE-SCORED VIDEO

- Observers want videos of classrooms that look like the classrooms in which they will observe. A school system that uses pre-scored video from elsewhere may need to augment their training with some examples from its own schools. It can be especially helpful to include examples of high performance in local classrooms. This can have the effect of raising the bar for what observers see as possible in their schools.

- Make sure observers are exposed to video from a range of contexts that reflects the types of classrooms in which they will be observing. For example, evaluators shouldn't be trained only on video from middle school English classes if they'll also be observing other subjects or in high school classrooms. They need to recognize relevant evidence wherever they're asked to evaluate.

Unpacking Rubric Components

Understanding relevant evidence begins not by reviewing videos, but with a close read of the rubric's descriptors. Observers should ask themselves: What is the rubric saying about what's important for this component of teaching? For the component, "communication of learning objectives," what's important might be the clarity of a teacher's explanation and the extent to which the teacher refers back to the objective during the lesson. The observer should next ask: What would I need to write down as evidence of those qualities? To continue the example of communicating lesson objectives, that would include the teacher's actual explanation—verbal and written—and references the teacher or students make back to it.

One way to facilitate this close read extends a process outlined in Chapter 10, "Knowing the Rubric" (see page 123). In that process, trainees learn the general approach for interpreting a rubric by doing a quick component analysis, in which they review the language for one component and write down what seems to be valued (e.g., repeated references to the lesson objective, students' ability to articulate the objective, etc.) and what that might look or sound like in practice. Trainees can use a similar process to unpack each of the rubric's components, by considering what would make for relevant evidence.

 TIPS FOR UNPACKING RUBRIC COMPONENTS

- Use text features to call out the key words in a rubric's descriptors that are most important for determining performance for each component (e.g., "The teacher *refers* to the learning objective").

- Compile lists of evidence that would be relevant to each component's indicators of performance (e.g., for checks for student understanding: teachers' questions or tasks assigned to students to determine mastery of concepts or procedures).

- Augment lists of evidence with examples to further clarify what it might look like (e.g., "A teacher asks students to work out the lowest common denominator at their desks while she circulates"). Make sure to stress that such examples are never exhaustive; otherwise evaluators may narrow their focus to only those practices described.

- Critique trainees' analyses. Evaluators get more precise in their understanding when pressed to cite the rubric language that leads them to make a claim about what they need to look and listen for (e.g., "Where does it say referencing the standard is part of communicating the objective?"). Critiquing analysis may involve multiple-choice questions (e.g., "Which of these might be relevant evidence?"), peer assessment, or self-assessment.

 SNAPSHOT: UNPACKING COMPONENTS OF TEACHING IN ONLINE TRAINING

In the online observer training program developed by District of Columbia Public Schools (DCPS), the module on each component of teaching begins by unpacking the component's core concepts. For example, a critical attribute of checking for student understanding is the extent to which a teacher does such checks at key moments in a lesson. But before observers can collect evidence of this, they need a shared understanding of what is meant by a "key moment." In the DCPS training module, a 10-minute tutorial clarifies what makes for a key moment, and when they typically occur. See Figure 13.3 for an excerpt.

FIGURE 13.3   Unpacking What It Means to *Check for Student Understanding* at *Key Moments*

What is a key moment?

Key moments are critical points in the lesson where the teacher needs to check content understanding.

They should inform the teacher's instruction.

Key moments often occur:

- After introducing a new concept or key term
- Before increasing the complexity of a concept or task
- Before releasing students to independent practice

Source: District of Columbia Public Schools Align Training Platform.

SNAPSHOT: DETERMINING WHAT TO LOOK AND LISTEN FOR IN GROUP TRAINING

Minneapolis Public Schools uses whole- and small-group work to train observers on what evidence to collect for each component of teaching. Designed with Teaching Learning Solutions, the training begins with a whole-group activity in which trainees identify the key words that distinguish the different performance levels for one critical attribute of one component of teaching (see Figure 13.4). Based on those words, trainees suggest what they might see and hear in a lesson that would be relevant. Following discussion, each type of evidence is added to a poster of teacher and student actions. Trainees are then organized into groups of two to four, and each group is assigned their own critical attribute to similarly analyze to create a poster of relevant types of evidence. When done, each small group presents its poster to the whole group for discussion.

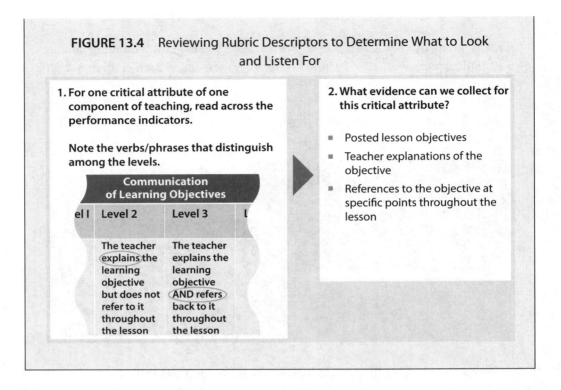

FIGURE 13.4   Reviewing Rubric Descriptors to Determine What to Look and Listen For

1. For one critical attribute of one component of teaching, read across the performance indicators.

   Note the verbs/phrases that distinguish among the levels.

   Communication of Learning Objectives

el I	Level 2	Level 3	L
	The teacher explains the learning objective but does not refer to it throughout the lesson	The teacher explains the learning objective AND refers back to it throughout the lesson	

2. What evidence can we collect for this critical attribute?

   - Posted lesson objectives
   - Teacher explanations of the objective
   - References to the objective at specific points throughout the lesson

Providing Opportunities for Guided Practice

After analyzing rubric components, the next step is to practice collecting relevant evidence for those components. This is what evaluators do while observing in the classroom: they write down things they see and hear that matter for evaluating the lesson. Interpreting that evidence to produce ratings and prepare feedback comes later. Watching the lesson is the only opportunity an evaluator has to record strong evidence. Our memories aren't accurate enough to reconstruct after the fact how many times a teacher responded to student misbehavior, what the teacher did in each instance, and how students reacted.

It takes practice and guidance to learn how to recognize and record relevant evidence in the dynamic and unpredictable environment of the classroom. Chapter 11, "Collecting Evidence," explains how to teach efficient methods for capturing different kinds of evidence. To practice collecting relevant evidence, an observer-in-training applies those skills while attempting to identify all the things that happen during a lesson that relate to the aspects of teaching to be evaluated. During this stage of training, evaluators go from "talking the talk" about what to look and listen for to actually "walking the walk."

Modeling is useful at this point in training. One approach is for an expert observer to review a lesson, or part of one, while typing notes that trainees can see. This can be combined with think-alouds, in which the expert pauses and provides commentary (e.g., "Okay, I need to write down that lesson objective on the board … that was another reference back to the objective, I need to record that."). This can be accomplished online by showing videos with annotated notes for the evidence an observer needs to capture. Whatever the approach, modeling should use pre-scored video to ensure that the evidence trainees see collected is in fact accurately captured and relevant to the component of teaching under discussion.

Of course, you can't really understand how to do something until you actually try it. A trainee might see evidence collection modeled by an expert observer but miss the specificity of the notes that observer took. Or a trainee may focus too much on behaviors similar to those in the lesson used in the model (e.g., if only the teacher referred to the lesson objective in the model observation, a trainee might miss students' references to the objective in other lessons). For each component that observers-in-training will rate, they should practice watching instances of teaching and recording evidence themselves.

> *Modeling should use pre-scored video to ensure that the evidence trainees see collected is in fact accurately captured and relevant to the component of teaching under discussion.*

For such practice to hone their skills, trainees need specific feedback. It's of little help to practice capturing relevant evidence from a lesson if you never learn to what extent you were successful. Again, video used for practice should be pre-scored so that feedback is grounded in good observation practice (see Figure 13.5). A training leader who knows what relevant evidence a video contains can get trainees thinking

FIGURE 13.5   Using Pre-Scored Video for Guided Practice on Collecting Relevant Evidence

1. Trainees review a video of teaching and record evidence relevant to communicating lesson objectives.

2. Trainees compare their evidence to that collected by expert observers from the same lesson.

What of the following did your evidence include?

On Board: Students will be able to determine the right formulas for length, area, and volume.

2:04: T: There are lot of formulas for measuring different shapes. We're going to figure out when to use each one.

6.07: T: So we're going to figure out what formula to use to figure out how much space it takes up.

about what they got right and what they missed. Observers-in-training also need to know when they captured evidence of something important but without enough detail to be meaningful, or when their notes include judgment (e.g., "lesson objective unclear").

⚒ TOOL:
DISTRICT OF COLUMBIA PUBLIC SCHOOLS EVIDENCE COLLECTION TEMPLATE

DCPS provides observers with templates designed to support their collection of relevant evidence. Organized in columns with headings for different types of evidence, these tools help observers keep in mind the kinds of things they should be noting. The example in Figure 13.6, of collecting evidence of checks for student understanding, shows how the columns guide observers to record not just the teacher's prompts, but also students' responses and any subsequent action taken as a result. As shown, an observer may use arrows to indicate connections and sequence when multiple lines of evidence are part of the same conversation. Observers are introduced to these templates as they begin to practice collecting evidence for each component of teaching. See page 314 for a template with space for all of the district's components of teaching. As observers get more proficient, they're able to record evidence directly into the tool during the observation.

FIGURE 13.6   Using a Template to Collect Evidence of Checking for Student Understanding

Questions and Prompts	Student Responses	Teacher Responses
Record all questions and tasks posed to students.	Identify students and their oral, written, and non-verbal response to questions, prompts, and teacher follow-up.	Note teacher response, including follow-up strategies or lack thereof.
T: What does the protagonist do at the end of the story?	S1: He runs away.	T: Do you think he ever came back?
	S1: The author says that he was never to be seen again in that land.	

Training on How to Sort Evidence

Between collecting evidence and rating teacher practice comes another step: sorting. Sorting is the bucketing of evidence according to an instrument's components: it puts all the evidence for the component "communicating learning objectives" into one bucket, all the evidence for "use of questioning" into another, and so on (see Figure 13.7). Sorting produces the sets of evidence an observer will later interpret to rate the observed practice according to each part of a rubric. Sorting also supports meaningful feedback by putting evidence where it belongs, so observers can refer to it when discussing their observations with teachers.

It's important that all observers sort evidence correctly. If a teacher prompt gets sorted to the "use of questioning" component when the prompt really belongs to the "checks for understanding" component, then the ratings for both teaching components will be based on the wrong evidence. When different observers sort differently, they can produce different ratings even though they saw and heard the same thing. More fundamentally, incorrect sorting clearly signals that observers lack a shared understanding of effective teaching.

Sorting presents several challenges. The distinctions between what evidence belongs to which teaching component may not be obvious (is that question a check for understanding or a discussion technique?). Some evidence may belong in more than one bucket; an

FIGURE 13.7   Sorting Evidence of Questioning into the Right Component

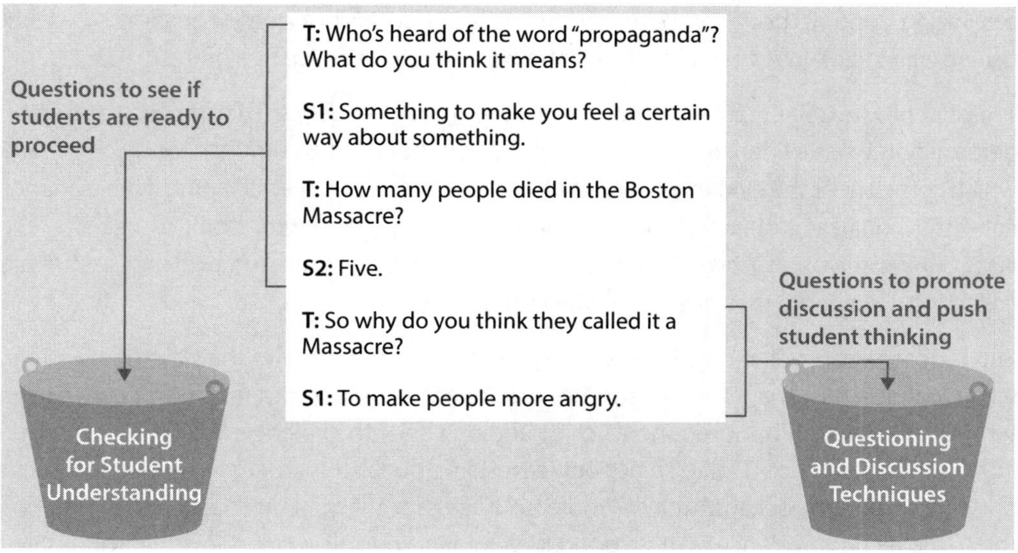

Questions to see if students are ready to proceed

T: Who's heard of the word "propaganda"? What do you think it means?

S1: Something to make you feel a certain way about something.

T: How many people died in the Boston Massacre?

S2: Five.

T: So why do you think they called it a Massacre?

S1: To make people more angry.

Questions to promote discussion and push student thinking

Checking for Student Understanding

Questioning and Discussion Techniques

exchange among students may be evidence of both intellectual engagement and respect and rapport among students. But overuse of the same piece of evidence for multiple components may give it too much weight. Training should clarify an instrument's guidelines for assigning evidence to more than one component and provide opportunities to practice applying them.

As with evidence collection, modeling is a good way to teach sorting. Start with a raw set of notes from an observation and walk through what evidence goes where, and of equal importance, why. Facilitate discussion as you lead a group of trainees through sorting exercises. Point to specific pieces of evidence and ask trainees where they belong. Use examples produced by expert observers so that what's modeled represents correct sorting. This may include pre-scored video with evidence relevant to multiple components of teaching. Give trainees meaningful feedback on their sorting attempts. Like teachers, observers need evidence and explanations to make sense of critiques.

> *Give trainees meaningful feedback on their sorting attempts. Like teachers, observers need evidence and explanations to make sense of critiques.*

Your training should also cover how to use tools to make sorting easier. These tools will depend in part on the observers' level of comfort with technology. You can sort evidence by cutting and pasting with a word processor or with a computer spreadsheet. With the latter, observers can record their notes directly into the tool and assign a number to each piece of evidence, indicating the component to which it belongs—the program's "sorting" function can then reorganize the material into the buckets. Without some tool for organizing content, be it computer- or paper-based, sorting can easily become unwieldy. During training, trainees can use sticky notes to easily recategorize as a group.

Typically, new observers are not sorting while they collect evidence. They are too focused on determining what evidence to record, which makes it difficult to simultaneously determine which component the evidence belongs to. For the novice observer, deciding if the evidence collected signifies high expectations or intellectual engagement, or both, comes after the classroom observation is over. To ask new observers to organize relevant evidence as they are collecting it will more than likely overwhelm them.

But as observers develop greater automaticity in filtering the scene in the classroom for relevant evidence, they may begin to sort by component as they record (e.g., using note-taking templates organized by components or by adding codes to evidence, like "CFU" for "checking for understanding"). Doing so not only saves time but also sharpens the evaluators' focus on what's relevant, because they're more conscious of the particular aspects of teaching they're collecting evidence of. It's a good idea to explain to new observers that this is what they should aspire to after they gain experience observing (see Figure 13.8).

FIGURE 13.8 Efficiency Comes with Expertise

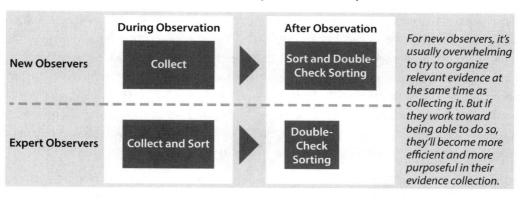

Even experienced evaluators who can sort during an observation must review their work after the observation. What happens later in a lesson may clarify where evidence collected earlier belongs (e.g., only after seeing a behavior more than once may it become clear it's evidence of the component, "classroom rituals and routines"). Moreover, the mantra of "collect evidence now, rate later" should apply regardless of an observer's skill. Ratings are based on the preponderance of evidence from an observation, which can be known only when it's over. While it's impossible to keep judgment from one's mind while observing, evaluators must keep those judgments from affecting what they see, hear, and record as the lesson unfolds.

Q IN FOCUS:
SOME EXAMPLE CODES FOR RECORDING AND SORTING EVIDENCE

- HR = Hands raised

- CR = Choral response

- IR = Individual response

- MU = Misunderstanding

- AAS = Teacher asked another student

- FI = Factually incorrect

- KP = Key point

- IP = Independent practice

- RA = Read aloud

Adjusting Your Training Based on Needs

How you teach observers to recognize relevant evidence will evolve as you learn what's working and what observers are still struggling with. They may need more time to analyze the critical attributes of teaching components that depend more on inference (e.g., what clues are needed to assess the extent to which each part of a lesson moves students toward mastery of objectives). Or they may need to focus more on what distinguishes between two components. When working to expand your library of pre-scored video, you should prioritize your greatest current needs. If many observers find it difficult to collect evidence on cognitive engagement, then you will need additional videos that feature this component.

Observation data and observer assessment results will suggest where your observers need more support. You should periodically review the sorted evidence submitted by evaluators, as this may show trends: components for which strong evidence is often lacking or misplaced. Ask trainees which parts of the training did the most to build their confidence and which didn't, and what they want more of. Do they want feedback on more attempts at evidence collection or on sorting? Should some videos be replaced because they confused more than clarified? Regardless, your follow-up training should reinforce what observers learned in initial training. Recognizing relevant evidence is a skill that needs sharpening.

> *Keep in mind that observers will progress at different paces as they learn to identify and record relevant evidence. Some will be quicker to home in on the salient details in a lesson. Others may need more opportunities for practice.*

Keep in mind that observers will progress at different paces as they learn to identify and record relevant evidence. Some will be quicker to home in on the salient details in a lesson. Others may need more opportunities for practice. You should do some probing to determine why some trainees are struggling so you can provide them with the right support. It may be a matter of note-taking skills, or a tendency to over-focus on some things (e.g., only on teacher talk). Or someone may need a deeper understanding of certain aspects of instruction to recognize when it's happening (e.g., you won't notice use of "academic vocabulary" if you're not clear on what it is).

 TIPS

■ Explain why each component matters to student learning. This builds appreciation for the instrument, and it deepens observers' understanding of what to look for. For example, one reason to communicate learning objectives is to support student self-monitoring; when students understand what they're supposed to learn, they're better able to assess their own progress. With this in mind, an evaluator is a better judge of what would be relevant evidence for communicating learning objectives (e.g., a teacher's question that draws student attention back to a lesson's expected outcomes).

■ Practice what you preach. If your observation instrument emphasizes questioning to push student thinking, then use questioning to push observers' thinking in your training. If checks for understanding are supposed to come at key points in a lesson, then refer to points in your training that include thoughtful checks for understanding. This not only makes use of research-based instructional practice but also reinforces what it is observers should be looking for.

■ If observers use shorthand codes for rubric components, encourage them to all use the same ones. It's confusing in training and in feedback discussions when some observers use "CFU" for check for understanding and others use "CKU."

■ Ask for participant feedback while it's still fresh. A good signal of where training is succeeding is the extent to which trainees feel confident after they've had the chance to compare their own attempts to collect relevant evidence to that of expert observers. Survey this for each component (e.g., "To what extent do you agree: this training helped me recognize evidence for questioning techniques").

SNAPSHOT:
CLARIFYING THE DIFFERENCE BETWEEN SIMILAR COMPONENTS

The Rhode Island Department of Education (RIDE) has used a quick training activity to clarify the difference between teaching components that observers struggle to distinguish. Some observers, for example, had difficulty knowing when an observed behavior related to the "culture of learning" in a classroom or to "student engagement." To call out the key distinctions, RIDE put the rubric language for the two components side by side and asked evaluators to consider how they differed. An excerpt of the exercise is in Figure 13.9. In addition to the critical attributes for each component, RIDE placed the descriptions of "proficient" performance for the two components next to each other. Participants were able to see how "culture of learning" related more to evidence of effort and expectations, while "student engagement" related more to evidence of student thinking.

FIGURE 13.9   Analysis Activity to Clarify the Difference between Two Components

1. Independently review the critical attributes for each component.	2. Discuss with a partner any noted differences in purpose, focus, or emphasis.

Component	Establishing a Culture of Learning	Engaging Students in Learning
Critical Attributes	▪ Expectations are high and supported through verbal and nonverbal behaviors. ▪ Effort and persistence are expected and recognized.	▪ Student enthusiasm, interest, thinking, problem-solving. ▪ Learning tasks that require high-level student thinking and are aligned with lesson objectives.

Noted key differences:

 TECHNIQUES:
TRAINING OBSERVERS TO RECOGNIZE AND SORT RELEVANT EVIDENCE

To Lay the Foundation:

▪ Lead trainees through the process of unpacking the rubric descriptors for each component of teaching. Call out the critical attributes for evaluating each component, and ask trainees to consider what each might look or sound like in the classroom.

- Use text features to call attention to key words in a rubric. Annotate the rubric document with types of evidence and examples relevant to each component.

- Have evaluators practice collecting relevant evidence for each component using pre-scored video; when done, let them compare the evidence they collected to that collected by the expert observers who pre-scored it.

- Provide observers with evidence collection templates to guide them in recording the types of evidence relevant to each component. Give them codes for tagging frequently observed practices (e.g., RTP = classroom routines, transitions, and procedures).

- Model for trainees the process of sorting collected evidence into the right components. Then have them practice sorting and compare their sorting to the work of expert observers.

To Build and Improve:

- To prioritize improvements in training, consider the extent to which observers are able to identify evidence relevant to each component. Look for the source of any confusion: Are observers confounding seemingly similar components? Are they missing key language in a rubric's descriptors, or do they need more practice collecting particular kinds of evidence for some components (e.g., more practice identifying tasks and student statements relevant to cognitive engagement)?

- Replace pre-scored videos that prove problematic (e.g., if they prompt endless debate in training or include overly distracting behaviors). Build out a video library prioritizing those videos that would address observers' greatest current needs, while expanding the range of classrooms featured to reflect the diverse contexts in which evaluators will observe.

- Give experienced observers practice sorting evidence into the right components while they are collecting it. This may include use of additional evidence collection templates.

Putting It into Practice

To Lay the Foundation:

How can you begin to help observers unpack rubric descriptors and provide opportunities to practice collecting and sorting evidence using pre-scored video?

To Build and Improve:

What does feedback from participants, their practice during skill development, and their post-training work suggest about the need for better training on recognizing and sorting relevant evidence?

This item can be downloaded from www.wiley.com/go/betterfeedback

CHAPTER 14

Using Criteria for Rating

ESSENTIAL QUESTION

How Will You Build an Understanding of Accurate Rating?

Accurate ratings are an essential product of any observation system. If classroom observations factor significantly into teachers' performance reviews—as they do practically everywhere—then teachers need to know their ratings represent a true picture of their teaching performance, and not just the particular view of whoever observes them. Moreover, accuracy is critical if school systems are to use observations to measure the success of their efforts to improve teaching and learning. You can't know if your supports for teachers are working without good data on classroom practice.

> *Observers need to take part in guided practice with interpretation. That means they need a primer on a rubric's rules for rating, opportunities to apply those rules to relevant evidence, and feedback that tells what they did correctly and what they need to do differently.*

An observer rates teaching practice by reviewing evidence and finding the rubric indicators that best describe it. That involves interpretation and judgment. Determining if a teacher checked for student understanding at all key moments in a lesson requires the observer to make a judgment about how many moments there were in a lesson that warranted a check for student understanding. The challenge of training is making sure all observers are interpreting and judging classroom performance correctly. When observers' interpretations of a lesson's key moments differ, so will the ratings they give.

Learning to rate instructional practice accurately isn't just a matter of seeing examples—it's not "here's a Level 2, here's a Level 3—now go rate." Observers need guided practice with interpretation of evidence. That means they need a primer on a rubric's rules for rating, opportunities to apply these rules to relevant evidence, and feedback that tells what they did correctly and what they need to do differently. The feedback you give an observer is as much about critiquing the observer's rationale for giving a specific rating as it is about the rating itself. Trainees will find the examples of teaching at different performance levels valuable, but the focus of their learning should be on developing the thought process that helps them accurately rate performance.

Keep in mind, learning to rate begins with learning to identify relevant evidence. To rate a lesson on questioning, you need certain kinds of evidence: teacher prompts, student responses, the extent of student participation, and so on. In this book, we deal with collecting relevant evidence and accurate rating in different sections to fully explain each. But in training, they're inseparable. An observer's understanding of an instrument is best supported when training flows directly from how to collect evidence for a teaching component to guided practice on how to rate teaching practice using that evidence.

To build an understanding of accurate rating, training should include:

■ Close study of the key words that distinguish each performance level that a rubric describes for each component of teaching

■ Practice interpreting and matching evidence for individual components to the right performance levels

■ Practice reviewing and rating whole lessons on all components of teaching

■ Feedback that compares the ratings, evidence, and rationales that trainees produce to those produced by expert observers

 SNAPSHOT:
SCAFFOLDING THE SKILLS TO RATE ACCURATELY
IN DISTRICT OF COLUMBIA PUBLIC SCHOOLS

In District of Columbia Public Schools (DCPS), observers-in-training learn how to rate teaching in a series of modules that all follow the same structure. As shown in Figure 14.1, each module focuses on one component of teaching, progressing from a review of key rubric language and relevant evidence to guided and independent practice rating pre-scored videos. Trainees complete the process for one component before going on to another.

FIGURE 14.1   Structure of Training Modules on Each Teaching Component

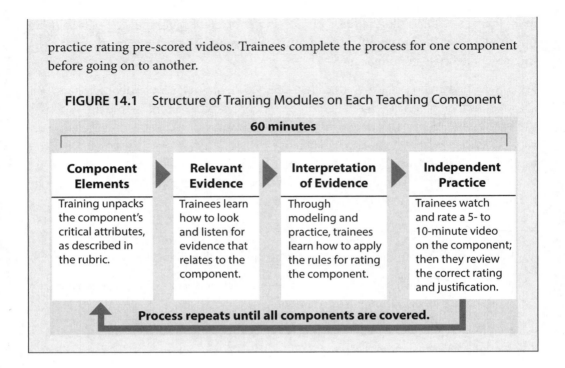

60 minutes

Component Elements	**Relevant Evidence**	**Interpretation of Evidence**	**Independent Practice**
Training unpacks the component's critical attributes, as described in the rubric.	Trainees learn how to look and listen for evidence that relates to the component.	Through modeling and practice, trainees learn how to apply the rules for rating the component.	Trainees watch and rate a 5- to 10-minute video on the component; then they review the correct rating and justification.

Process repeats until all components are covered.

Reviewing the Rules for Rating

The first thing your training needs to cover after relevant evidence are the rules for rating with your system's rubric. A well-crafted rubric spells out what needs to be true for an observer to give a lesson a particular rating for each component of teaching. The rubric says "If both X and Y are true, then the rating is 'proficient,' but if only X or Y is true, it's 'basic.'" Observers who don't follow these rules will produce inaccurate ratings even if they collect all the relevant evidence. This is why new instrument language should be tested with evaluators. If they can pose scenarios for which the rubric's criteria don't point to a clear rating, then the descriptors may need to be refined or annotated.

Rules that apply to all components are best introduced in a rubric overview early in training. These general rules include:

- Definitions of quantitative terms (e.g., if "almost all" means between 70 percent and 90 percent).

- Guidelines for weighing evidence of different performance levels throughout a lesson (e.g., look for the rating that most of the relevant evidence points to).

- What to do when the preponderance of evidence sits between two ratings.

- Similarities in performance indicators across different components (e.g., if proficient levels generally call for evidence of student cognitive engagement).

Your training on how to rate each teaching component should refer back to these general rules as needed. (See page 121 in Chapter 10, "Knowing the Rubric," for more on explaining general rules.) But most of your discussion will be about the rules particular to each component. Call out the important distinctions among the indicators that describe the different performance levels. Highlight key words so trainees can easily see them. Use scenario-based prompts to check for understanding (e.g., "Given these criteria, how would you rate a lesson in which some classroom time is lost to noninstructional activities and students need reminders on how to transition?").

This part of your training may reveal where you need to clarify additional terms. Many rubrics describe some performance indicators using qualifiers like "when appropriate." This language keeps evaluators from robotically applying criteria even when doing so wouldn't make sense. An instrument that stresses the extent to which a teacher provides clear definitions of academic vocabulary might add "when appropriate," because precise definitions aren't needed in the middle of an instructional unit if these were provided earlier in the lesson. Trainees may need guidance on how to interpret such qualifiers.

Training should focus on the process of deciphering the rubric, not on memorizing it.

Make sure also to explain any exceptions to the general rules. An instrument's developers may have decided that if a teacher makes a derogatory remark about students, then the teaching component "supportive tone" is automatically given a low rating, regardless of any other evidence for that aspect of classroom climate. In certain cases, some critical attributes also may weigh more heavily than others when determining borderline situations. An example would be if the *effectiveness* of a teacher's checks for students' understanding counts more than the *frequency* of such checks when the preponderance of evidence lies between two ratings.

The point of reviewing the rules is not for observers to memorize them. Rating a lesson isn't like refereeing a game in sports; observers should avoid making judgments as they watch a lesson—they should focus instead on collecting evidence. When they later review their evidence, they should have the rubric in hand. Certainly, over time observers get quicker at locating the descriptors that best match the evidence they've collected and sorted. But training should focus on the process of deciphering the rubric, not on memorizing it.

TIP

Start with expected performance. If a rating of a 3 out of a total of 4 represents "proficient" or "effective" practice in your rubric, then explain what constitutes a rating of 3 before explaining what would merit a higher and lower score. You may need to spend more time on the difference between adjacent ratings in the middle—say, between 2s and 3s—which are often the hardest to distinguish for observers.

Minimizing Bias When Rating

When training observers to rate, it's important to revisit the issue of bias. You should make sure trainees have a general understanding of bias, and of ways to avoid it, before you delve into how to collect evidence for each component of teaching. (For more on this, see Chapter 12, "Understanding Bias.") But it's when trainees begin rating performance that their personal preferences are most likely to be revealed—if they're looking for them. Bias at this point is often a matter of an observer giving too much weight to an attribute of practice the observer feels is especially important. Or an observer may factor in evidence that isn't relevant out of a sense that it should be.

Remember, a preference can bias interpretation in either direction. This preference may cause an observer to favor or disfavor an attribute, usually unintentionally. An observer who favors student-led discussion may unconsciously discount the fact that the content of a discussion was low-quality (a "halo" effect). Another observer may be so turned off when teachers fail to resolve student confusion that it affects the rating of other, unrelated aspects of teaching (a "fatal flaw" effect). A bias is any observer tendency that leads them to give ratings in a way that's inconsistent with the rubric's rules.

You can incorporate several bias awareness strategies into your training on how to rate:

- A training leader provides examples of typical preferences that may come into play when rating each component (e.g., for classroom environment, colorful decorations or a teacher sitting at her desk; for student engagement, lots of project-based work, regardless of purpose or quality).

- Ask trainees what kinds of biases might affect an observer's rating of a particular component. Another way is to ask what evidence might lead someone to rate the component higher or lower than it should be.

- Encourage observers to compile lists of their preferences as they consider each component, and to add to them as they move on to practice rating lessons they observe. They should ask themselves: Am I rating based solely on the rubric's criteria, and if not, is it due to a preference?

> *It's when trainees begin rating performance that their personal preferences are most likely to be revealed—if they're looking for them.*

As with every skill involved in observation, learning to minimize bias takes practice.

Whenever you discuss bias, make sure you stress that preferences are natural, and that everyone has them. Bias awareness is not about admitting some personal fault. It's about building self-awareness so that observers can be as accurate as possible when rating. Often observer preferences are related to aspects of teaching that are valued in the rubric; it's just that unchecked, those preferences cause observers to give less consideration to evidence of other aspects of teaching. Even so, people are reluctant to profess their biases, so don't pressure trainees to reveal theirs to others. What matters is that each observer recognizes his or her own biases.

 TIP

Although you shouldn't force trainees to reveal their biases, you can ask them if training was successful. Survey observers about the extent to which training made them more aware of their biases so they could monitor them while rating performance. The responses will help you assess whether this aspect of training is working or needs changes.

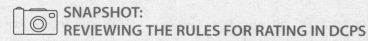 SNAPSHOT:
REVIEWING THE RULES FOR RATING IN DCPS

DCPS observers learn how to interpret evidence by first reviewing the key distinctions among performance levels. For each teaching component, the district's online training modules unpack the indicators of performance by calling out the key descriptors and how they change from one performance level to the next. Simple graphics are used to reinforce the differences (see the example in Figure 14.2). After reviewing the rules for rating a component, trainees apply those rules to evidence in guided practice.

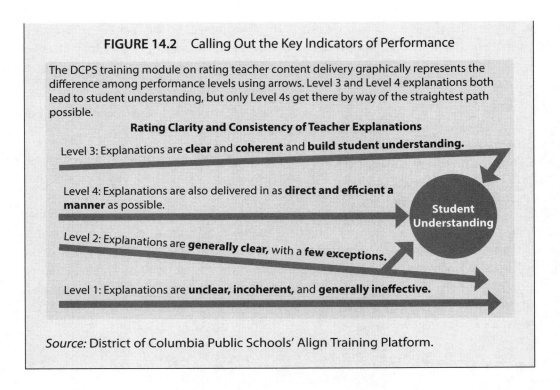

FIGURE 14.2   Calling Out the Key Indicators of Performance

The DCPS training module on rating teacher content delivery graphically represents the difference among performance levels using arrows. Level 3 and Level 4 explanations both lead to student understanding, but only Level 4s get there by way of the straightest path possible.

Rating Clarity and Consistency of Teacher Explanations

Level 3: Explanations are **clear** and **coherent** and **build student understanding.**

Level 4: Explanations are also delivered in as **direct and efficient a manner** as possible.

Level 2: Explanations are **generally clear,** with a **few exceptions.**

Level 1: Explanations are **unclear, incoherent,** and **generally ineffective.**

Student Understanding

Source: District of Columbia Public Schools' Align Training Platform.

Practicing with Pre-Scored Video

To really understand the rules for rating a component of teaching, you need practice applying these rules to evidence. Two observers may agree on the most important language that distinguishes a "basic" rating from "proficient," but they may still have different ideas of the kinds of evidence that would best align with each. What one person thinks of as a "generally clear" explanation of content or a "precise definition" of vocabulary may be different from what another thinks. The only way to norm their understanding is to connect those words to actual examples.

Pre-scored video is the foundation of this part of training. You can't learn to rate accurately without examples of rating that are accurate. Observers need to see how expert observers interpret and match evidence to the appropriate performance levels, and they need to compare that work to their own. You can't do this with live observations and have full confidence that trainees are consistently getting normed to an accurate interpretation of the relevant evidence. (For more on how to pre-score video, see Part II: Pre-Scoring Video.)

Your training will likely include different types of pre-scored video. You can best support understanding of what it looks like when most of the evidence points to a specific performance rating by using "benchmark" videos that each show a clear example of one component of teaching at one performance level. "Rangefinders" that show teacher performance at the high or low end of one rating can clarify what observers should do in borderline cases, or they may be used for advanced practice. Using very short clips—perhaps one minute—can help you illustrate specific ideas that may be new or challenging for evaluators (e.g., what "academic vocabulary" looks like in a lesson).

Your use of pre-scored video during training should include modeling as well as practice. A training leader can model the rating process by playing a benchmark video, collecting relevant evidence, and then thinking aloud as he or she applies the component's rules for rating the observed instruction. Trainees can then practice doing the same process themselves. But it's critical that you follow this practice with feedback. It won't help trainees to practice rating if they never find out to what extent they were successful. It's not fair to evaluators, or to the teachers they'll evaluate, to leave them in the dark as to their level of accuracy.

The feedback you give trainees should include the correct rating, the correct evidence, and the correct rationale (see Figure 14.3). When they miss the mark, trainees need to know why. Did they miss a key piece of evidence, or did they collect all the relevant evidence but misinterpret the rules for rating? Did professional preferences or bias come into play? Knowing where they went wrong is key to observers getting it right the next time. This includes knowing when they got the right rating for the wrong reasons. In such cases, knowing only that they got the right final answer can validate their misinterpretation of how to apply the instrument.

Seeing the evidence and rationale that trainees used to determine their ratings also is much more helpful to a training leader than just knowing how far off the observers' ratings were. As with students, getting inside the heads of observers is central to determining how to resolve

FIGURE 14.3   Feedback on Practice Rating of Pre-Scored Video

For Rating Questioning Techniques on Cognitive Demand	
Rating You Gave	Highly Effective
Correct Rating	Effective
Evidence for Correct Rating from Video	▪ 14:02 "What tools would a scientist use?" ▪ 16:58 "What would a butterfly do?" ▪ 17:59 "How is the pollen going to come off the flower and go to another?"
Rationale for Correct Rating	Most of the questions the teacher asks are open in nature and engage students in deeper thinking and further discussion.
Why Your Rating Is Too High	The teacher's questions do not also provide students an opportunity to demonstrate reasoning or to formulate their own questions.

their confusion. A too-low rating for the component, "use of questioning," might be given because observers counted questions a teacher asked that were really checks for student understanding and not meant to push student thinking. With that information, a trainer can go back and clarify for trainees when a question would be relevant to one component versus the other.

> *The feedback you give trainees should include the correct rating, the correct evidence, and the correct rationale. When they miss the mark, trainees need to know why.*

Although pre-scored video is essential for training, it's helpful to begin their practice rating components of teaching with examples of written evidence. Do this by giving trainees the evidence from a lesson for one component of teaching and then asking them to apply the instrument's rules for rating that component. A training leader should press trainees to justify the ratings they give by asking them how their evidence aligns with the key ideas in the rubric's descriptors of performance. When trainees can't justify the ratings they gave, they should be open to the possibility that the correct rating is not the one they initially chose.

TIP

Make sure that trainees rate individually first when they practice. When a group rates together, group dynamics often influence the interpretation. Only after each evaluator reviews and rates individually should a group hear each person's judgment, and the evidence and rationale for it.

SNAPSHOT: GUIDED PRACTICE IN DCPS

The online modules in the DCPS observer training program employ a strategy of gradual release to independent practice. After unpacking a component's key elements and descriptors of performance levels, the system has trainees review short pre-scored videos—typically around 10 minutes—and then answer a series of questions relevant to rating the segment (see an example in Figure 14.4). Correct answers are then provided, along with the evidence from the video to support them. This models the kinds of questions observers need to ask themselves when rating each component.

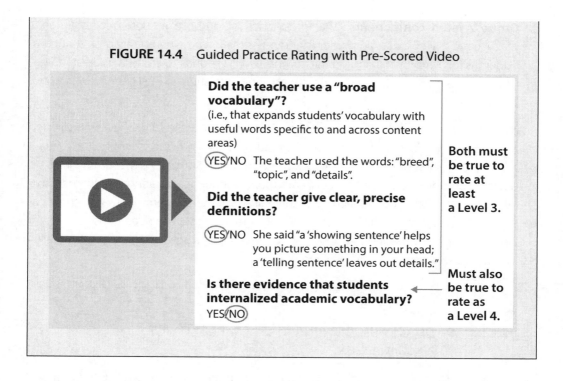

FIGURE 14.4   Guided Practice Rating with Pre-Scored Video

Did the teacher use a "broad vocabulary"?
(i.e., that expands students' vocabulary with useful words specific to and across content areas)

YES/NO   The teacher used the words: "breed", "topic", and "details".

Did the teacher give clear, precise definitions?

YES/NO   She said "a 'showing sentence' helps you picture something in your head; a 'telling sentence' leaves out details."

Both must be true to rate at least a Level 3.

Is there evidence that students internalized academic vocabulary?
YES/NO

Must also be true to rate as a Level 4.

Developing the Skill to Rate Multiple Components

After trainees practice rating individual components of teaching, they need practice rating these components together. Collecting and interpreting evidence from a lesson on all components is different from doing so for just one. An observer must pay attention to, and accurately record, all relevant evidence—not only the evidence needed to evaluate one aspect of teaching. Sorting that evidence into the right indicators also involves far more decisions than rating a single component. Doing all this while maintaining awareness of one's personal preferences is complicated, to say the least.

Here are some ways to scaffold the skill to rate all components:

Increase the complexity gradually. Going directly from rating single components individually to rating all of them simultaneously can overload new observers. A more manageable alternative is to go from rating one component to rating two or three at the same time before having trainees attempt to evaluate lessons on all parts of a rubric.

Start with the components that require the least inference. This means those for which performance can be determined based on what's directly observable. For example, most indicators for classroom management are readily apparent, such as the number of times a teacher responds to off-task behavior.

Group related components. The importance of purpose in determining when a practice is a "check for student understanding" is reinforced when training on that component is followed by training on the component, "responds to student understanding". Like students, evaluators learn by comparing and contrasting, and by connecting to prior knowledge.

Again, using pre-scored video is a must for practicing this skill. Make sure to review the sorted evidence that trainees used to determine their ratings. Look for evidence that's not where it belongs, components of teaching that lack sufficient evidence, or evidence that shows up in so many components that it has a disproportionate influence in rating the entire lesson. This should help inform your reteaching of the skill and, if the problems recur, any enhancements you need to make in this aspect of training. It may be that you need to use a different sequence, grouping, or pacing of the content to help trainees develop the ability to rate full lessons on all the components of teaching.

 SNAPSHOT:
GRADUALLY INCREASING THE COMPLEXITY OF
TRAINING IN DCPS

DCPS organizes observer training into a series of units that each cover three of the nine components in the district's observation instrument. These three "spirals," as DCPS calls them, are shown in Figure 14.5. Their grouping reflects two key strategies:

■ **Training goes from the least challenging components to the most.** The first spiral deals with the clarity of teacher explanations and with student behavior, which require little in the way of inference. The second spiral deals with responding to student understanding, which requires more diagnosis by the teacher. The last spiral involves the teacher's judgment of when and how to use appropriate differentiation.

■ **Training builds gradually toward rating all components in stages.** Within each spiral, trainees first learn to collect and interpret relevant evidence for three components individually; then they practice rating on all three components in the spiral. This gives trainees at least three opportunities to attempt rating multiple components before the end of their initial training, when they rate a video on all nine components in the district's observation instrument.

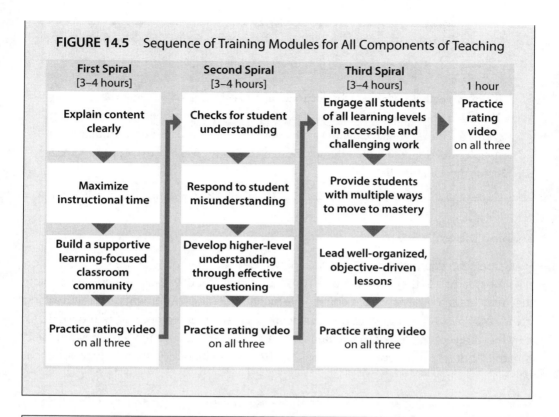

FIGURE 14.5   Sequence of Training Modules for All Components of Teaching

First Spiral [3–4 hours]	Second Spiral [3–4 hours]	Third Spiral [3–4 hours]	1 hour
Explain content clearly	Checks for student understanding	Engage all students of all learning levels in accessible and challenging work	Practice rating video on all three
Maximize instructional time	Respond to student misunderstanding	Provide students with multiple ways to move to mastery	
Build a supportive learning-focused classroom community	Develop higher-level understanding through effective questioning	Lead well-organized, objective-driven lessons	
Practice rating video on all three	Practice rating video on all three	Practice rating video on all three	

TOOL: PARTNERSHIPS TO UPLIFT COMMUNITIES EVIDENCE RECORD RUBRIC

The Partnerships to Uplift Communities (PUC) charter school network has defined a set of criteria for determining an observer's proficiency in collecting, sorting, and interpreting evidence for all components in its observation instrument. The evidence an observer provides after rating a pre-scored video is judged on three qualities:

- The amount of objective evidence for each component;

- The alignment of evidence to the right components; and

- The absence of common problems, such as biased or vague statements, generalizations, or overreliance on the same evidence for multiple components.

PUC uses this "Evidence Record Rubric" adapted from a tool developed by Teaching Learning Solutions to certify if individuals possess sufficient skill to observe and rate teaching on their own. See the Appendix, page 318, for the complete tool.

🛠 TOOL:
TOP 10 PRINCIPLES OF TRUE SCORING

A list of important reminders for accurate rating is given to observers in schools participating in The College Ready Promise, an initiative to support effective teaching in a group of charter management organizations. The tool is based on a similar set of principles developed for the Literacy Design Collaborative. See the Appendix, page 320, for the complete list.

Keeping the Skills Sharp

Evaluators who complete your initial training will get better at many of the key observation skills they learned as they carry out observations in the field. But without periodic renorming, they may gradually deviate from correct interpretation of the instrument. Without realizing it, they may allow their rating to be influenced by criteria that are not part of the rubric. Or they may neglect to consider key criteria that are in the rubric. This tendency toward "drift" is natural, but you must counter it to ensure that observations continue to produce accurate information.

Your follow-up training should reinforce the skills required for accurate rating. This training should involve additional opportunities for rating pre-scored video and for participants to compare their evidence and rating rationales to the correct ones. Your reinforcement of these skills should also address common challenges that your observers may have. It may be that evaluators are struggling to determine when the evidence supports a rating of "highly effective" for some components; if so, your follow-up training might include a refresher on the key distinctions among performance levels, and practice with short clips that reinforce the contrast between "highly effective" and "effective" performance.

Your follow-up training is also the time you should address how to rate less common situations. Your initial training should focus on what evaluators are most likely to encounter; there's too much to absorb and process to cover more topics. Only in later trainings should you devote any time, for example, to what observers should do in the unusual case in which students show evidence of correctly internalizing academic vocabulary that the teacher defined incorrectly (the answer might be to choose the lower of two ratings because of the importance of providing students with correct definitions). After mastering the basics, observers can learn the nuances.

SNAPSHOT:
FOLLOW-UP TRAINING IN CHICAGO PUBLIC SCHOOLS

After completing their initial training, principals in the first year of the Chicago Public Schools' Excellence in Teaching Project came together for monthly Professional Learning Community (PLC) sessions. Each three-hour session included a series of activities meant to build participants' observation skills while keeping them normed to a correct interpretation of evidence using the district's observation instrument. Figure 14.6 shows a series of learning stations that principals could rotate through at a PLC meeting. As shown, principals reviewed and rated video together; they also brought evidence from their own observations (without teachers' names) to discuss with their peers.

FIGURE 14.6   PLC Learning Stations

Station 1	Station 2	Station 3
Watch a video clip, record and sort evidence, and discuss how to determine ratings.	Review written evidence from observations at your school and discuss how to rate it correctly.	Meet with an expert observer to discuss any challenges (e.g., note taking, sorting evidence, etc.).

TOOL:
RHODE ISLAND'S CALIBRATION SESSION PROTOCOL

The Rhode Island Department of Education (RIDE) has developed a process for periodically norming observers' interpretations of an observation instrument. Outlined in Figure 14.7, the process is described in a set of protocols RIDE has distributed throughout the state. The department suggests that "calibration sessions" using the process take place multiple times a year among observers in the same school, and at least once a year among observers across a district. Variations of the protocol are provided for norming with the use of video and with live lessons, and for use of the process for professional learning among teachers. It's important to note that prior to taking part in calibration sessions, observers have participated in initial training, so they have a foundation in their instrument, experience collecting evidence, and practice with interpretation and rating. See the Appendix, page 322, for the complete protocol.

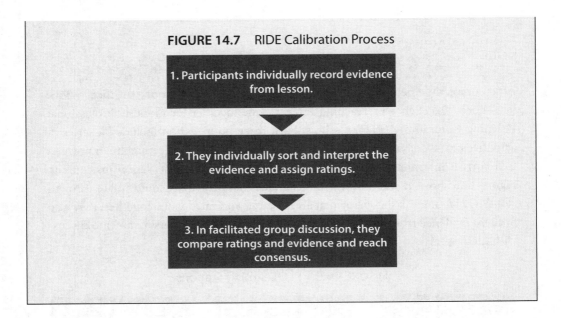

FIGURE 14.7   RIDE Calibration Process

1. Participants individually record evidence from lesson.

2. They individually sort and interpret the evidence and assign ratings.

3. In facilitated group discussion, they compare ratings and evidence and reach consensus.

Where to Start and How to Build

If your state or district is in the early stages of implementing observations, you may find that there is limited content available to train observers how to rate accurately. It might take years to develop a library of pre-scored video that includes multiple examples and practice videos that cover every component and performance level in an observation instrument. Indeed, it takes time just to develop the capacity to pre-score video to the point where you have sufficient confidence in the ratings and rationales produced by your pre-scoring process. If there isn't an existing training program for the observation instrument you've adopted, you will need to start from scratch.

But where to start? Look for the most common situations where observers need the most help distinguishing one performance level from the next. They may find it less challenging to identify evidence of the lowest level of performance for classroom management than it is to distinguish between "basic" and "proficient" use of questioning, for example. Aside from some novices, few teachers are truly ineffective at managing their classrooms. Asking a group of evaluators to try rating several lessons with your observation instrument can reveal where the need for video examples and other content is greatest.

From then on, your rule of thumb is "What are the next biggest areas of need?" Are observers struggling to rate particular components, even with all the relevant evidence? If so, your training may need to call greater attention to the difference between adjacent levels, and/or provide observers additional practice with videos that demonstrate these levels. If observers assign ratings that are all over the place when practicing with a particular video, then the video itself may need replacing, or repurposing if it is more appropriate for advanced training or other uses. (For more, see page 228 in Chapter 17, "Collecting and Using Data from Training".)

Make sure that your training conveys a supportive tone. You're not questioning participants' competence; you're giving them what they need so they can confidently provide teachers with accurate ratings and meaningful feedback.

Learning to rate accurately can be a source of anxiety for many evaluators at first. It's the part of training that can feel most like assessment. Sooner or later, you find out you gave a wrong rating. To reduce anxiety and defensiveness, make sure that your training conveys a supportive tone. You're not questioning participants' competence; you're giving them what they need so they can confidently provide teachers with accurate ratings and meaningful feedback. For an instructional leader, it's hard to imagine more valuable professional development.

✔ TECHNIQUES: BUILDING AN UNDERSTANDING OF ACCURATE RATING

To Lay the Foundation:

- If existing training isn't available, prioritize content development based on the most common situations in which evaluators are likely to struggle to rate accurately (e.g., distinguishing between the middle performance levels of instructional components related to cognitive engagement). To determine this, ask a group of evaluators to rate a series of lessons using your rubric.

- For each component in the rubric, point out the key terms that distinguish among different performance levels. Check for evaluators' understanding by posing scenarios and asking which would be the correct rating. Also, make sure evaluators understand what is meant by such qualifiers as "when appropriate," "generally," and "sometimes."

- Model the process of rating based on evidence using written examples and pre-scored video.

- Provide opportunities for trainees to review and rate pre-scored video. Make sure they get feedback not just on whether they got the correct performance levels, but also on their ability to collect the relevant evidence and provide the correct rationale for the rating.

(TECHNIQUES Continued)

To Build and Improve:

- Enhance and refine initial training on how to rate accurately based on participant input and available data on evaluators' strengths and areas of greatest needs. Consider replacing example videos for which trainees produced wildly different ratings.

- Build out a video library of examples and practice videos with multiple examples, from different contexts, that cover additional parts of the observation instrument. A library should be expanded until evaluators demonstrate sufficient accuracy in rating all parts of a rubric.

- Begin regular follow-up training in which evaluators get feedback on their attempts to rate additional pre-scored video. Include follow-up training refreshers on aspects of rating that evaluators continue to struggle with. Also include guidance on how to rate when the evidence from a lesson presents a less common, more nuanced situation.

- Provide additional opportunities to practice rating for evaluators who request it or who need it, as shown by their rating of practice videos.

- Consider "auditing" evaluators' rating rationales as another way to identify common needs to address in initial and follow-up training.

Putting It into Practice

To Lay the Foundation:

What content and training activities would you need to get started norming observers to the correct way of rating with your rubric?

To Build and Improve:

How can your initial and follow-up training address what you see as your next biggest areas of need in helping evaluators to rate accurately?

This item can be downloaded from www.wiley.com/go/betterfeedback

CHAPTER 15

Coaching Teachers

ESSENTIAL QUESTION

How Will You Build a Shared Vision of Effective Feedback?

We've all been there: as feedback, you get advice that's so vague as to be meaningless (e.g., "utilize multiple strategies to increase engagement" or "find ways to reach all learners"). As an educator, you want better ways to help your students succeed, but what you're told leaves you confused. When this is the norm for feedback, a school system has missed one of the biggest opportunities to improve teaching and learning. It's a huge waste to invest all the effort required to ensure accurate observations if the resulting feedback doesn't lead to professional growth and a change in practice. Indeed poor feedback not only frustrates teachers, it also makes them wary of the whole purpose of evaluation—and its validity.

Effective feedback is specific, practical, and focused on improvement. A teacher should leave the feedback conversation with a clear idea of how to put a strategy into immediate use.

> *Whether a post-observation conference succeeds depends greatly on what happens before it takes place. Like a good lesson, good feedback takes forethought and planning.*

That idea might be a specific plan for how to use an anchor chart to emphasize key points in an upcoming lesson. Or it could be a set of follow-up questions to ask students to push their thinking in an ongoing unit on animal classifications. The specificity of suggestions can make the difference between feedback that feels like judgment and feedback that feels helpful. More important, it makes change in practice possible.

Few principals and other instructional leaders have experienced this kind of feedback. Certainly they've engaged in discussion about why teaching might or might not be working in a particular classroom. But for the most part, they haven't had the chance to really practice applying a consistent set of ideas about what makes feedback effective. To ensure that all teachers benefit from feedback that incorporates these ideas, observers will need explicit training on giving effective feedback. A school system shouldn't leave to chance whether or not feedback is successful. You need to proactively develop a shared vision of what effective feedback looks like.

When many people think of feedback, they naturally picture the post-observation conference. This is where the rubber meets the road in an observation system, and the quality and content of those conferences determine to a great degree both the extent to which teachers trust their evaluations and whether they act on them. But whether a post-observation conference succeeds depends greatly on what happens before it takes place. Just as a good lesson depends on good planning, a powerful feedback session requires considerable forethought. Indeed, helping observers prepare for the feedback session may be the most important aspect of feedback training.

To build a shared vision of effective feedback, training should:

■ Include protocols that support practical, specific, and improvement-focused post-observation conferences.

■ Provide guidance on how to help teachers implement specific techniques in the classroom.

■ Explain ways to maintain a supportive tone, and to adjust feedback for different teachers.

■ Provide opportunities to practice employing the elements of effective feedback.

Keep in mind that the ability to develop effective teaching depends on the ability to identify it. The training required to provide effective feedback includes everything that's needed to identify effective teaching.

The value of feedback training goes far beyond what it does for formal evaluation. When your principals and other instructional leaders understand how to prepare for and deliver effective feedback, they will improve the effectiveness of their informal interactions with teachers as well. For every observation that factors into teachers' annual performance review, teachers will engage in many more discussions with their school leaders based on classroom visits for which there are no stakes. When all these formal and informal conversations are specific, practical, and focused on improvement, the cumulative positive effect on teaching and learning can be significant.

Keep in mind that the ability to develop effective teaching depends on the ability to identify it. An observer who can recognize the relevant evidence of performance in a classroom can use

FIGURE 15.1 From Observation to Action Planning and Follow-Up

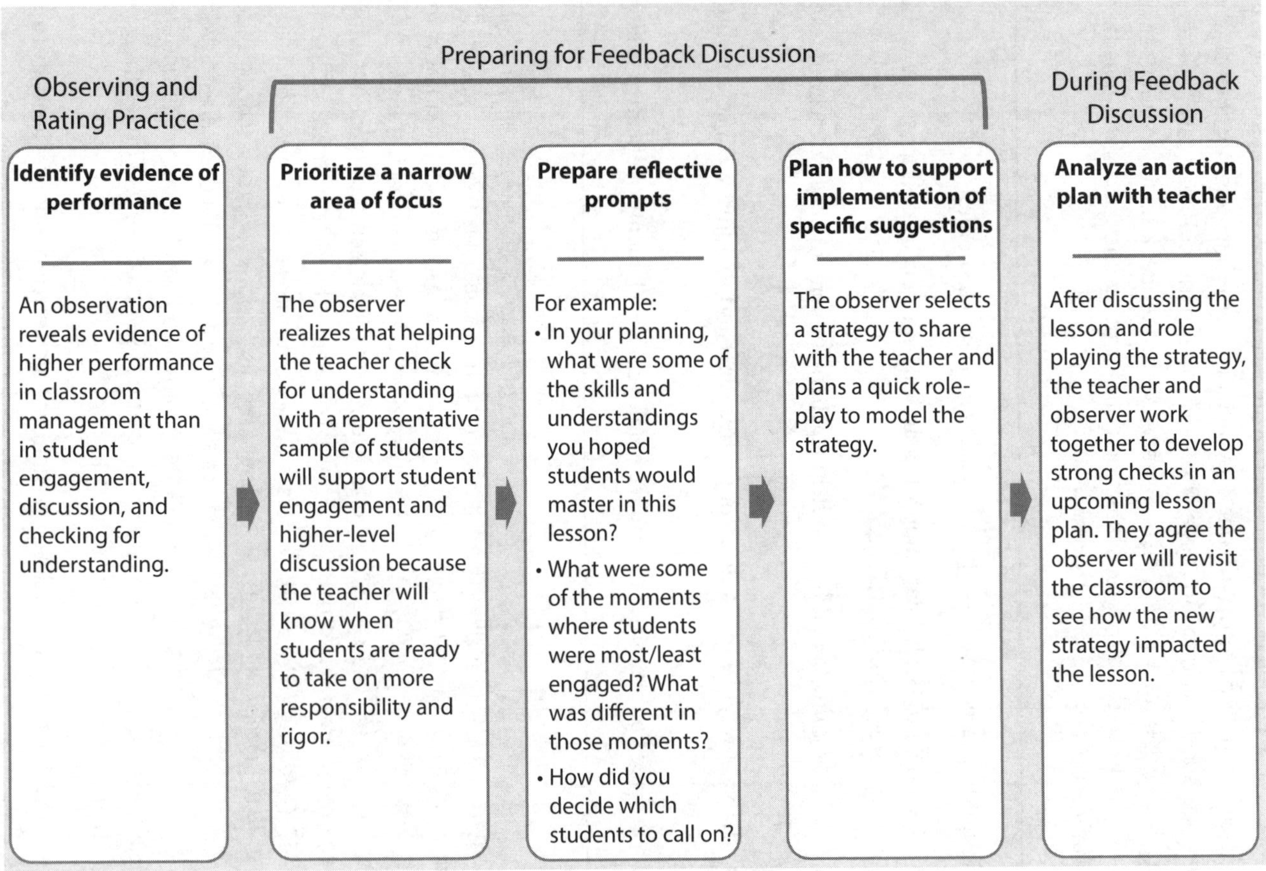

Observing and Rating Practice

Preparing for Feedback Discussion

During Feedback Discussion

Identify evidence of performance

An observation reveals evidence of higher performance in classroom management than in student engagement, discussion, and checking for understanding.

Prioritize a narrow area of focus

The observer realizes that helping the teacher check for understanding with a representative sample of students will support student engagement and higher-level discussion because the teacher will know when students are ready to take on more responsibility and rigor.

Prepare reflective prompts

For example:
• In your planning, what were some of the skills and understandings you hoped students would master in this lesson?
• What were some of the moments where students were most/least engaged? What was different in those moments?
• How did you decide which students to call on?

Plan how to support implementation of specific suggestions

The observer selects a strategy to share with the teacher and plans a quick role-play to model the strategy.

Analyze an action plan with teacher

After discussing the lesson and role playing the strategy, the teacher and observer work together to develop strong checks in an upcoming lesson plan. They agree the observer will revisit the classroom to see how the new strategy impacted the lesson.

that evidence to anchor conversations with a teacher about improving performance. But an observer who struggles to point out the most important parts of what happened in a lesson will find it hard to offer concrete feedback—or worse, will give an inaccurate assessment of a teacher's practice. The training required to provide effective feedback includes everything that's needed to identify effective teaching.

Starting with a Shared Definition

Before jumping into the mechanics of providing feedback, it's important to agree on what feedback is—and what it isn't. Some evaluators may think the ratings produced by observations are feedback, or that those ratings become feedback when backed by evidence. But evaluation alone isn't reason enough for an observation system. The resources required to produce accurate ratings are too great to justify these observation systems as simply a means to identify the small portion of teachers whose significant underperformance might put them at risk of dismissal. The much larger benefit of observations will come from their potential to support all teachers in transforming their practice.

Principals and other observers need to hear this message consistently. If not, then many will naturally view observation through the lens of traditional performance reviews, which were more about assigning ratings than changing practice—and that will set the tone for the feedback they give. Early on in your implementation of an observation system, you should bring stakeholders together to create a common definition of feedback that gets repeated early and often throughout your feedback training. Evaluators' feedback needs to help teachers understand not only their current level of practice, but also how to elevate it.

 SNAPSHOT:
MINNESOTA DEPARTMENT OF EDUCATION'S VISION OF
EFFECTIVE FEEDBACK

To guide district leaders in planning new teacher evaluation systems, the Minnesota Department of Education asked representatives of stakeholder groups to craft a common vision of effective feedback. The group produced a set of characteristics that define feedback and outlined a set of practices that need to be part of feedback for it to be effective. The brief document is meant to spur local system leaders to develop their own agreement on what they mean by effective feedback.

Minnesota's Vision Document for Effective Feedback

Feedback is . . .	Practices associated with providing feedback:
■ Sharing and communication of evidence (evidence-based conversations) ■ Collaborative conversations or dialogue ■ Focused on strengths, growth areas, development of next actionable steps, and available resources ■ Ongoing conversations (follow-up) versus a single event ■ Clear and concrete so that teachers understand the feedback ■ Timely ■ Consistent evidence aligned to a standard (rubric) ■ "Judgment" that is honest, fair, evidence-based, and aligned with the tool (rubric) ■ Nested within other goals or activities such as student impact, teacher individual growth goal, schoolwide goal, district goal ■ Distinguishes between performance levels (growth)	■ Coaching conversation that moves teacher practice forward ■ Time for teacher self-reflection prior to providing feedback ■ Data shared prior to providing feedback ■ Transparent on criteria and processes used ■ Documented and occurs face-to-face ■ Discussion based on teacher need and observer role ■ Share students' "voice" as supported by evidence ■ Pre- and post-observation conferences, as appropriate for the type of observation being conducted ■ Owned by the teacher and facilitated by the observer and includes next steps that both people believe in ■ Opportunity to practice

Promoting the Basics with Protocols

To be effective, feedback must overcome psychological barriers. As the Carnegie Foundation for the Advancement of Teaching points out, the same fight-or-flight response we have to physical threats kicks in when we perceive feedback as threatening.[11] When all we see are demands, we're not in a frame of mind for reflection or considering new ways of doing our work. But, adds Carnegie, when demands come with commensurate resources—including the necessary knowledge and external support to fulfill them—we're more likely to see feedback as an "invigorating challenge" to which our creativity and thoughtfulness can be brought to bear.

One of the most straightforward ways to promote feedback that feels supportive is with protocols for post-observation conferences. A good protocol helps observers avoid common pitfalls, like starting off with what a teacher did poorly (which only heightens the perception of threat) and overwhelming a teacher with too much information (out of the mistaken belief that more is better). It also ensures some measure of predictability to the post-observation conferences. When teachers know what to expect, they're less likely to fear these conferences, especially if what they come to expect is feedback that helps them become a more successful teacher.

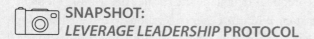

SNAPSHOT:
LEVERAGE LEADERSHIP PROTOCOL

In his book *Leverage Leadership*, Paul Bambrick-Santoyo presents a protocol for post-observation conferences that resemble work sessions more than performance reviews. Although guided by the observer, the conference has the teacher and observer working together to analyze what happened in a lesson as it relates to a specific aspect of teaching and planning specific ways to do things differently. A key feature is that in the conference itself, the two parties co-plan how to implement a "bite-sized" change in the classroom—something observable that can be accomplished within a week. The protocol is explained in detail in the book's second chapter, "Observation and Feedback." Narrated videos of the protocol in action are at www.uncommonschools.org (search for "Six Steps to Effective Feedback").

FIGURE 15.2 *Leverage Leadership* Protocol for Post-Observation Conferences

1. Praise	Call out observed evidence of things done well.
2. Probe	For an area for improvement, ask why it's important or how the teacher tried to address it in the lesson.
3. Identify Problem and Action Step	Examine what happened in the lesson that's relevant to the focus area; agree on a technique that the teacher can try in the next week.
4. Practice	Role-play or simulate how to apply the technique in the classroom.
5. Plan Ahead	Design or revise an upcoming lesson to implement the technique.
6. Set Timeline for Follow-Up	Agree on when the teacher will complete the action step and when the evaluator will check in to provide additional support.

Q   **IN FOCUS:**
PROVIDING WRITTEN FEEDBACK

While a post-observation conference typically focuses on one or two areas for improvement, written feedback that's part of formal evaluation should include evidence for every component of teaching for which a rating is given. Understanding the rationale for every rating builds trust in the process and contributes to a shared vision of effective teaching. But even with written feedback, it's possible to engage teachers in self-analysis. One technique is to include the rubric's descriptors for all of the possible performance levels along with the observer's rationale and evidence for each rating. This prompts the teacher to compare what was observed with the criteria for each performance level, much the same way an observer does. As a result, the teacher can see which level best matches the observed evidence and what the teacher would need to demonstrate for a higher rating.

To better understand a protocol, an observer needs to see it in action. A blank template leaves much to the imagination. Without clarification with concrete examples, an observer may envision areas for improvement that are too broad or action steps that are too vague. Videos of post-observation conferences can be especially helpful if reviewed through the lens of a set of criteria for judging the extent to which the discussion followed the protocol (e.g., does the feedback include action steps that offer a clear picture of what they would look like in the classroom?).

Reviewing examples of written feedback can also clarify expectations for each element in a protocol. It's easier, in many ways, to see what's meant by specific qualities of effective feedback when reading examples rather than watching them. The written word allows more time to process. An effective approach is for a training leader to first call out the specific elements of effective feedback in one written example, and then have trainees try to identify and judge the same elements in other examples, including examples of written feedback that the trainees themselves have prepared. Good feedback training gets observers in the habit of self-assessment.

TOOL:
RHODE ISLAND'S FEEDBACK QUALITY REVIEW TOOL

The Rhode Island Department of Education (RIDE) uses a feedback quality review tool to help evaluators understand five qualities of effective feedback: prioritized, specific, actionable, supportive, and timely. Before introducing the tool, training leaders from RIDE clarify each quality with specific examples (see Figure 15.3). Training participants then review samples of written feedback that they've prepared using the quality review tool, which includes questions like "Are specific examples from the observation cited throughout the feedback?" and "Is the feedback feasible to implement successfully in the near future?" See the Appendix, page 327, for the full set of questions.

FIGURE 15.3   Clarifying the Qualities of Effective Feedback with Examples

Targets **specific** area to encourage teacher to continue practice	**Reinforcement** **Managing Classroom Procedures**
Justifies praise with **specific** evidence from the lesson	Students are well aware of the routines and procedures in the classroom. **When you signaled you were starting the lesson, the classroom helpers retrieved the materials needed for the class and distributed them seamlessly.**
Prioritizes one area for improvement	**Constructive Feedback** **Questioning and Discussion Techniques**
Justifies judgment based on **specific** evidence observed	**Almost all questions asked of students were low-level knowledge or comprehension ones** that did not require them to explain their thinking or cite specific examples.
Suggests **actionable** next steps for the immediate future	Challenge students to think critically and engage in discussion with their peers. To do this, **prepare questions that require higher-order thinking such as analyzing, synthesizing, or evaluating** when prepping your lesson. In addition, **have students explain their answers and allow them to challenge each other's** responses to promote dialogue.
Supports improvement with resources and strategies	**See attached article on Bloom's Taxonomy** for guidance on creating questions. **Ask yourself: "How do I create opportunities for students to think critically?"**

Unpacking the Preparation Process

By themselves, protocols for post-observation conferences can go only so far to improve the effectiveness of feedback. For all teachers to receive consistently high-quality feedback, observers need guidance on how to prepare for those discussions. A good deal of strategic thinking needs to happen between the time an observer determines the ratings from an observation and when that observer walks into the conference with the teacher. Planning requires a deep understanding of each element of effective feedback, which comes from guidance, examples, and practice.

Prioritizing Areas of Focus

The first step in preparing feedback is for an observer to prioritize areas of focus to discuss with the teacher. A post-observation conference that covers multiple aspects of teaching won't allow for the kind of analysis and action planning that transforms practice. It also works against the self-efficacy that feedback needs to build. It's deflating to receive a laundry list of suggested improvements. What's motivating is the prospect of achieving a specific goal in a short period of time.

An area of focus needs to be narrow. An entire component of teaching is too broad. For example, the teaching component "use of questioning" includes too many critical attributes to address in a short period of time. Examples of useful areas of focus would include increasing the degree to which all students in a class participate in answering questions, or greater use of cognitively demanding questions that push students' thinking. Such a narrow focus lets a teacher and observer plan how to implement the kind of specific suggestions that can quickly make a noticeable difference in the classroom.

There is no one rule for determining the best area of focus in every situation. Rather, training should build the habit of considering relevant factors. These include:

The clarity of evidence collected. The better teachers understand what specific behaviors from their lesson observers are referring to, the better able they are to analyze what happened and plan ways to do things differently. Among all the possible areas for improvement from an observation, some will have more clear evidence than others.

What's attainable given the teacher's skill level. Some practices are trickier than others. A teacher's lesson might rate poorly on aspects of use of questioning and classroom management. But increasing the rigor of questioning can be more challenging than improving the efficiency of transitions. Look for the most likely "quick win" for a particular teacher.

The likelihood of driving improvement in multiple areas. Improvement in one area of practice often drives improvement in one or more other areas. When teachers learn to better communicate lesson objectives, they also better understand what students need to learn in a lesson. This understanding, in turn, often has a positive impact on the learning activities they plan, and subsequently on the level of student engagement in the classroom.

Note that the area of focus that makes the most sense may or may not be one of the aspects of teaching for which a teacher received the lowest ratings. An evaluator might determine that improving a somewhat more developed practice would have a greater impact on teaching and learning.

> *It's deflating to receive a laundry list of suggested improvements. What's motivating is the prospect of achieving a specific goal in a short period of time.*

One of the best ways to train your observers to prioritize is to prompt them to defend their choices. You can accomplish this in a group by having observers individually review evidence from a lesson—either written or on video—and then report to the group the areas of focus they picked and their rationales for picking them. Doing so forces participants to self-assess while considering if alternatives might get more bang for the buck. The point is not to reach precise agreement. There's no way to know for sure which improvement will have the maximum impact. What matters most is that your observers gain practice in thinking strategically about identifying areas of focus.

Preparing Reflective Prompts

Feedback should sharpen teachers' abilities to analyze their own practice. For that to happen, teachers need to be meaningfully engaged in the feedback conversation. Simply telling teachers what to do differently doesn't help them better understand the relationship between their teaching and student learning. This is why reflective prompts are a mainstay of teacher feedback. Such prompts ask teachers to consider how they approach their craft and what might improve it. In this way, feedback more resembles the mentoring approach known as "cognitive coaching," in which a mentor helps others learn how to become more effective by building a habit of disciplined self-reflection.

Crafting prompts that guide teachers in this kind of thinking is hard. A recent content analysis of principal-led post-observation conferences in Chicago found that only 10 percent of questions asked required deep reflection about instructional practice.[12] Nearly two-thirds of the questions principals asked required little response from teachers—often just a single word or an affirmation of the principal's perception. For all teachers to benefit from post-observation conferences, principals and other observers need training on how to prepare reflective prompts.

> *Teachers need to be meaningfully engaged in the feedback conversation. Simply telling teachers what to do differently doesn't help them better understand the relationship between their teaching and student learning.*

High-quality prompting guides people to particular understandings. In a post-observation conference, the most productive understandings for teachers are of specific opportunities in their teaching to enhance student learning. An overarching question to guide observers in prompt writing is: What can you ask that will draw a teacher's attention to what happened in a lesson that reveals the opportunity to enhance instruction? What questions, for example, might draw a teacher's attention to how he checked for student understanding at a particular point, and see that he had an opportunity to better probe the depth of that understanding?

Observers' prompts should use the language of the observation rubric. If the words "depth of understanding" describe an aspect of teaching in the tool, then the observer should use those exact words in the prompt designed to call a teacher's attention to his practice in that area. This builds the shared understanding of the expectations that the rubric embodies and reinforces the relevance of the feedback. When an observer frames a prompt by first referring to the relevant critical attributes of effective practice from the rubric, then it further sets the stage for a teacher's self-assessment. It also depersonalizes the feedback: this isn't one person's opinion of another; it's two people looking at expectations and evidence.

But providing observers with criteria won't by itself help them to produce effective prompts. They need guided practice, which may include:

Analysis of strong and weak prompts. Given a set of criteria for prompt writing, trainees can review written examples and determine to what extent they meet those criteria. Do they ask a teacher to consider his or her specific goals, to what extent those goals were met, and why?

Practice in using question stems. Provide trainees with a list of ways to begin a reflective prompt, and have them pick one after they've determined an area of focus. Generic stems that promote critical thinking, sometimes called "meditational stems," can help evaluators develop questions that encourage analysis of specific strategies.

Self and peer assessment. Participants can bring to training prompts they've prepared based on classroom visits, to review on their own or share with others. In reviewing, they can look for ways to improve them (e.g., incorporating rubric language, citing specific instances from a lesson, etc.).

Group prompt writing and review. A trainer can lead a group of observers through preparing targeted prompts for a teacher after they've watched him or her in a video. Another approach is for trainees to review prompts based on a video of teaching they've seen and consider how to improve them.

IN FOCUS:
MEDIATIONAL COACHING STEMS TO PROMPT TEACHER REFLECTION

- What's another way you might . . .?

- What would it look like if . . .?

- What do you think would happen if . . .?

- What sort of impact do you think . . .?

- How did you decide . . .?

- What criteria do you use to . . .?

- What might you see happening in your classroom if . . .?

Source: ETS

Those who manage and support observers can do them a big favor by creating prompt banks. This organizes high-quality prompt examples by specific aspects of teaching. An observer who has prioritized the teaching component "smooth transitions" for feedback can then find examples of well-written prompts for that aspect of teaching. Typically, observers need to tailor these prompt examples to draw attention to the specific evidence they collected from the lesson they've just observed. But it's immensely helpful for them to see how others have included sufficient framing, details, and focus in similar situations. A prompt bank may start with just a few examples and grow as training and feedback activities produce more.

SNAPSHOT:
SAMPLE REFLECTION AND PLANNING QUESTIONS

A master educator with District of Columbia Public Schools (DCPS), Matt Radigan, prepared a set of example prompts for each component of teaching in the system's observation instrument. Evaluators are given these examples to consider as they develop prompts based on their own observations. The table presents an excerpt from the list of examples.

Explain content clearly	**Reflect on observed lesson**: When you compare your explanations to what your students then did independently, what were some of the similarities/differences?
	Planning future lessons: If you were to start referencing a "key points chart" in your lesson, how do you think your students would respond to this?
Check for student understanding	**Reflect on observed lesson**: When you reflect on the observation, what student behaviors most helped you gauge their understanding?
	Planning future lessons: If you were to consider using think-pair-shares, whiteboards, or equity sticks with your students, what systems or expectations would you need to develop with your class?

Identifying "Bite-Sized" Suggestions

To be supportive, feedback must include more than prompts crafted to promote self-reflection. The onus for identifying techniques to improve teaching shouldn't rest only on the teacher. Observers need to bring something to the table. If the focus of feedback is on writing better lesson objectives, the observer should come with a handful of very specific and practical techniques for doing so. This is what allows for the most productive part of the feedback conversation: working out how teachers can apply new strategies in their own instruction. A teacher who leaves a post-observation conference with something of value is much more likely to view observation in a positive light.

For this to happen consistently, observers must understand what makes for a helpful suggestion. An evaluator who says "You should probe more deeply for student understanding" will

A teacher who leaves a post-observation conference with something of value is much more likely to view observation in a positive light.

leave teachers scratching their heads. Expert observers use the term "bite-sized" to describe the suggestions they bring to the table. These suggestions should be implementable in the immediate future (e.g., in an upcoming lesson). It should also be clear to teachers what the outcome will look like when they have implemented the suggestions. A bite-sized action step might be "when students give examples in response to a check for understanding, ask them to explain why the examples are correct."

Evaluators learn to hone bite-sized suggestions by critiquing and revising examples. Training may involve reviewing short videos of instruction and then reading written recommendations for the teacher. Trainees should consider the extent to which the suggestion is concrete and could be accomplished by the teacher within the next few days. Revising suggestions that are vague, rely on buzzwords, or represent too significant a lift builds evaluators' capacity to assess and improve their own work. Your training should also provide multiple examples of high-quality suggestions.

Another powerful way to support your observers is to compile a catalog of good suggestions organized by the aspects of teaching defined in your observation instrument. Like a bank of reflective prompts, this gives your observers a base to start with as they consider suggestions for a particular teacher. Your catalog of suggestions may include links to relevant articles, video clips, and information on who in your school system has related expertise. It's hard to overstate how much your evaluators will appreciate having ready access to a set of practical suggestions to provide teachers.

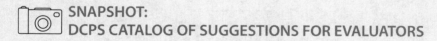 **SNAPSHOT:**
DCPS CATALOG OF SUGGESTIONS FOR EVALUATORS

DCPS collected suggestions from observers and other instructional experts in the school system to create a catalog of specific suggestions for each aspect of teaching in the DCPS observation instrument. As shown in Figure 15.4, each entry includes straightforward ideas for techniques to move a teacher's performance from one level to the next, as well as suggestions for how to practice those techniques with the teacher during the feedback conference.

FIGURE 15.4   Excerpt from the DPCS Suggestion Catalog for One Aspect of Teaching

Emphasis of Key Points in a Lesson		
Level 2 indicator that describes teacher's *current* practice	Techniques to move to Levels 3 and 4	
	"Bite-sized" recommendations	Ways to practice with teacher
The teacher **sometimes** emphasizes key points when necessary, such that **students are sometimes unclear** about the main ideas of the content.	**Script key points.** Script the most important ideas prior to the lesson to ensure consistent delivery. **Draw attention to key points.** Clearly signal key points by writing the points on the board, pointing to pre-written words, or asking students to capture important notes. **Display content.** Use an anchor chart or other visual to capture key points. Repeatedly return to the chart throughout the lesson to emphasize how classwork addresses these points. **Level 4 Suggestion:** **Sentence stems.** Stage moments in the lesson where students discuss the key points covered up to that point in the lesson. Provide students with sentence stems such as "The most important idea is . . ." and "If I taught this to someone else I would . . ." to support their conversation.	**Plan.** Ask the teacher to bring the plan for an upcoming lesson to your meeting. Work together to list the key pieces of information students must master to be successful in the lesson. Plan how those points will be emphasized and/or create an anchor chart to display the key points. **Model.** Role-play a brief explanation of content using signals or an anchor chart to emphasize the key points. Have the teacher practice explaining the same content with similar signals or chart.

Ensuring That Feedback Is Well-Received

A post-observation protocol that begins with the teacher's areas of strength and includes reflective prompts can go a long way toward increasing the teacher's receptivity to feedback. But many other factors affect how a teacher perceives a feedback conversation—including an observer's body language, word choice, and demonstrated regard for the teacher's view. Your observer training should build awareness of such factors and provide opportunities for observers to hone their feedback skills. This helps observers avoid unnecessary mistakes, like using overly formal seating arrangements, using accusatory language, or failing to maintain eye contact.

Discourage observers from answering their own questions in a feedback conversation. We learn best when we arrive at our own conclusions. Observers may be tempted to answer a reflective question for a teacher who's initially stumped, but doing so won't build that teacher's capacity to analyze his or her own instruction. Observers would do better to ask a narrower question that leads the teacher closer to a response (e.g., "When students give examples of reptiles, how could they show they understand what makes an animal a reptile?"). Ultimately, an observer may need to give an answer, but only after repeated attempts to draw one from the teacher.

Also, encourage observers to share the work of action planning with teachers. An observer should bring concrete suggestions to the feedback conversation, but determining how those suggestions are applied in the teacher's classroom should be a collaborative effort. A teacher isn't going to benefit from an observer's rewriting the objective for an upcoming lesson as much as from writing her own lesson objective with someone's guidance. A guided practice approach to action planning also gives observers a better sense of the extent to which teachers understand their guidance, so it may be adjusted if needed. An observer might think she's clearly delivered bite-sized feedback, but the teacher may have an entirely different understanding of what's been suggested.

Your observer training should cover the importance of adjusting feedback based on a teacher's disposition and level of expertise. Feedback to a teacher who's defensive will look different from feedback to a teacher who's accepting of constructive criticism. A teacher who's overwhelmed may need an observer to call extra attention to small victories and express confidence that "you can do this." During your training, pose different scenarios to observers and have them discuss strategies to address each scenario. Tap experienced observers with strong track records of supporting teacher growth to share their techniques for handling different situations.

 IN FOCUS:
WAYS TO INCREASE RECEPTIVITY

Start with goals and agenda. Clarify that what's to come is meant to help the teacher (e.g., "I want to point out some things that went well, go over some areas I think we can work on, and see how I can help you try some ideas I have.").

Ask what the teacher thought went well. This signals your interest in their views and brings to mind things they feel good about.

Avoid accusatory language. Instead of "What you didn't do was," say "What you can also do in that situation is . . ."

Use plural forms. Instead of "Why did you do X?" ask "What might be some of the reasons you did X?" This reduces the perception that the observer is looking for one right answer.

Use positive presuppositions. Begin questions with an acknowledgment, like "Based on past successful experiences . . .," or "As an experienced educator . . ."

Shift the focus to students. Instead of "Your lesson objective needed a clear outcome," say "The students seemed to have difficulty saying what they would be able to do."

Maintain eye contact, nod. Show you're listening, interested, and thinking about what the teacher is saying.

Consider seating arrangements. Sitting across from a teacher may imply confrontation. Sitting side by side can enhance the sense of collaboration.

Don't read from a script. A post-observation conference should be professional, but conversational. Bring talking points and observation notes to refer to but memorize key questions.

TOOL:
HILLSBOROUGH COUNTY'S POST-OBSERVATION ASSESSMENT CHECKLIST

As a final step in their initial observation training, observers in Hillsborough County Public Schools in Florida are assessed on their ability to lead a post-observation conference. Training leaders sit in on conferences led by trainees and use a checklist to rate their performance in five areas: setting the tone, eliciting teacher reflection, communicating feedback, co-planning next steps, and summarizing feedback in writing. A trainee's score is based on reviews from two such conferences. See the Appendix, page 328, for the full set of elements in the checklist.

TIPS

■ Teach pacing. It's essential that observers get through all the steps in a conference protocol in the time they have with a teacher. By learning pacing, they can avoid the situation in which they identify an area for improvement but run out of time before they've planned a solution with the teacher. Encourage evaluators to practice running through entire conferences. Make sure observers know, and adhere to, your system's guidelines for how long conferences should be; teachers will rightfully balk if their colleagues get much more attention than they do.

■ If training involves practice delivering feedback in actual post-observation conferences, keep in mind that the presence of the observer's assessor may affect the discussion. Some teachers may not feel as open to express themselves in such a situation.

Building Capacity for Feedback Training

Ensuring that teachers are provided with feedback should be part of your observer training program from its first iteration. This increases the chance that the teachers' initial experience with a new observation system feels—and actually is—supportive. From the beginning, states and school districts should ensure that observers are provided protocols for post-observation conferences, as well as annotated examples of what constitutes strong and weak feedback. Also, states and school districts should make sure observers understand the system's definition of feedback as a vehicle to transform teaching, and not simply the justification of performance ratings.

To ensure sufficient consistency and a higher level of quality of feedback, your school system will need to go into greater depth on how to prepare for a feedback conversation. Provide your observers with guidelines and opportunities to practice identifying areas of focus, preparing reflective prompts, and coming up with suggested action steps. After your evaluators understand the general approach toward preparing for and facilitating a post-observation conference, they should get follow-up training on tailoring the approach to more specific scenarios (e.g., less engaged teachers, highly skilled ones, etc.).

One of your greatest resources will be your instructional coaches with the most expertise. From their experience, they can provide examples of reflective prompts, "bite-sized" suggestions to give teachers, and tips on engaging different personality types. A profitable investment would be to assign someone the task of collecting, curating, and organizing this valuable knowledge. Your school system also should consider tapping outside experts, such as the New Teaching Center at the University of California-Santa Cruz, Uncommon Schools, and Teaching Learning Solutions, among others, to advise on training topics and activities, and possibly to deliver some feedback training until more local capacity is built.

You should also conduct surveys to inform your decisions about how to enhance training and support on providing feedback. Ask your principals and other observers how well the training is meeting their needs and what they need more of. Do they find role-plays useful, or do they want more opportunities to review videos of conferences? For which parts of the planning process do they need more support in order to feel confident? Survey your teachers to find out how the feedback they are receiving aligns with the vision you're trying to make real. If teachers say feedback is focused but not helpful, then observers may need better guidance on identifying suggestions for teachers.

> *There's considerable anxiety on both sides of the feedback conversation. Teachers are apprehensive about an evaluation system that's no longer perfunctory. Meanwhile, school administrators worry about conflict, challenges to their authority, and their own ability to identify and develop effective teaching.*

Know that there's considerable anxiety on both sides of the feedback conversation. Teachers are apprehensive about an evaluation system that's no longer perfunctory. They're thinking first and foremost about how their results will cast them. Meanwhile, school administrators worry about conflict, challenges to their authority, and their own ability to identify and develop effective teaching. Your feedback training must work to alleviate both parties' anxieties, while still maintaining expectations. While much about providing feedback is technical—prioritizing areas of focus, preparing reflective prompts—a major goal is to build everyone's confidence in the process.

The good news is that most school leaders and others who observe teachers are highly appreciative of feedback training. They want to be more effective in supporting teacher growth. Observers know their stock rises with any teacher who experiences success from feedback they have provided. No one knows better than a school leader that performance ratings, by themselves, will have at best a marginal positive impact on teaching and learning. Feedback training helps them get something highly valuable from their ability to identify effective teaching.

 TIP

One way to gauge the quality of feedback training is to audit evaluators' written feedback. To do so, a school system periodically collects examples of feedback from a sampling of evaluators and has it reviewed against clear criteria. This may suggest, for instance, that evaluators need more guidance on drawing attention to specific evidence from an observation in their feedback.

IN FOCUS:
INCORPORATING VIDEO IN THE FEEDBACK CONVERSATION

The advent of high-quality, low-cost video technology has opened up new avenues for providing feedback to teachers on their practice. With video, the post-observation conference is grounded in a recording of what actually happened in the lesson, not just in the teacher's and observer's notes and recollections. The analysis that takes place resembles the video-based post-game analyses that sports teams engage in. The most powerful feedback is that which builds the habit of self-analysis. Video lends itself especially well to this because teachers get the chance to see more clearly how students respond to them.

But post-game analysis doesn't typically involve rewatching the entire game; it's focused on a few key plays. Likewise, a post-observation conference might zero in on a few one- to two-minute clips that capture clear evidence for areas of reinforcement and improvement. For each clip, an evaluator needs to go into a conference ready to guide the teacher to the specific behaviors relevant to the component of teaching to be discussed. Prompting teachers to look for relevant evidence in a video of themselves makes them better observers of their own practice.

Another use of video in feedback is for demonstration. An evaluator may have a teacher review a clip of another teacher's practice to show how a similar situation was handled differently. Again, review of such clips should be guided by prompts that call attention to specific behaviors (e.g., "How did she use a follow-up question to make sure students were ready to move on?"). Conversation may then shift to how the teacher receiving the feedback could apply a similar technique. If pre-scored videos are used in this way, make sure that videos made available for the purpose are not at the same time being used for observer assessment, which would compromise the assessment results.

Despite the benefits, video-based feedback is rare. Some teachers are self-conscious about being recorded and may be worried about how the video will be used. With recording also comes the cost of equipment and the need to train people how to use it (although equipment costs keep coming down). Video also doesn't fully mimic observation in a live classroom. You can't step into a video and ask a student to explain what he's working on. Drawbacks aside, video offers a significant opportunity for close study of what happens in a lesson.

Where video feedback is planned, it should be introduced gradually, and first with teachers and observers especially interested in piloting the approach. This also allows time to work out the kinks while learning how to produce and edit video of sufficient quality to use in feedback—and how to integrate clips into a feedback protocol. Sharing a few positive early experiences and providing training on how to achieve similar success should draw more interest.

 SNAPSHOT:
VIDEO-BASED COACHING IN MyTeachingPartner

Video figures prominently in feedback provided via MyTeachingPartner (MTP), the teacher-coaching program created by experts at the University of Virginia Curry School of Education. Participating teachers are paired with MTP-trained coaches, who facilitate a series of eight to ten coaching cycles over the course of a year. Each cycle begins when the teacher submits a video of him/herself engaged in teaching, out of which the coach picks three segments, each approximately one minute long. These segments are then shared with the teacher, along with carefully crafted prompts that call attention to specific student-teacher interactions in each clip. Discussion of these clips provides the springboard to plan changes going forward, which are captured in subsequent videos. (See Figure 15.5.)

FIGURE 15.5   Types of Video Segments Used in MyTeachingPartner's Coaching Cycles

Nice Work	Consider This	Making the Most
Builds self-efficacy by calling attention to positive aspects of a teacher's actions	Improves a teacher's ability to analyze the impact of his or her actions on student learning	Pushes a teacher to critically examine his or her practice in one area of instruction
As you watch this clip, what do you notice that you do or say?	In this clip, what does the boy in the front row do that shows you he needs your support? What criteria did you use to gauge when to move on?	What things do you notice that your students say or do that shows that the cognitive demands of these activities rest primarily with them?

✓ TECHNIQUES:
BUILDING A SHARED VISION OF EFFECTIVE FEEDBACK

To Lay the Foundation:

- Convene stakeholders to draft an agreed-upon statement defining effective feedback—a statement that drives consistent messaging to teachers and principals as well as the skills to address in feedback training.

- Provide evaluators with protocols and criteria for post-observation conferences that promote a supportive tone, teacher reflection, and co-planning of action steps.

- Create opportunities for trainees to critique and suggest improvements to examples of feedback using videos or role-playing.

- Enlist experienced instructional coaches with a strong track record of supporting teacher growth in suggesting techniques and tips to share with trainees.

To Build and Improve:

- Give in-depth guidance on each step in the process of planning a post-observation conference, including prioritizing areas of focus, preparing reflective prompts, and identifying suggestions for teachers to use in their teaching. For each, provide strong and weak examples, plus opportunities to practice preparing.

- Survey principals and other observers on the extent to which they feel prepared to execute each step in the process of preparing and delivering feedback. Survey teachers on the extent to which the feedback they receive meets agreed-upon criteria for effectiveness. Use results from both to target training areas for enhancement.

- In follow-up training, discuss with evaluators how to adjust feedback for different situations (e.g., for highly skilled teachers, for reticent ones).

- Compile high-quality reflective prompts and suggested teaching techniques for each part of the observation instrument so that evaluators have a resource to go to for inspiration.

- Consider a pilot of video-based feedback in which post-observation conferences are grounded in review of selected parts of a recording of the teacher's lesson.

☀ Putting It into Practice

To Lay the Foundation:

Who would you enlist and what resources would you need to establish and spread a clear vision of effective feedback in your system?

To Build and Improve:

What additional resources and learning activities would address the areas in which you see observers needing the most support to increase the effectiveness of their feedback?

⬇ This item can be downloaded from www.wiley.com/go/betterfeedback

CHAPTER 16

Organizing a Training Program

ESSENTIAL QUESTION

How Will You Organize Training?

Successful teaching depends on sequencing, pacing, and coverage. Certainly, a lesson's activities are critical. But even the most thoughtfully constructed activities will fall short if students lack the necessary prerequisite knowledge, the lesson moves too quickly, students lack opportunities to practice, or the class doesn't revisit what's learned. So it is with observer training. In Chapters 10–15, we detailed the learning activities that can build the skills needed to identify and develop effective teaching. But to be effective, those activities must be organized in a way that sets up a group of trainees for success.

The task of organizing an overall training program is complex. Meanwhile, the number of qualified trainers available will limit the number of people you can train in person at any one time. The use of online or independent work can help, but typically such training is supplemented with some face-to-face sessions—to begin training, to check for understanding, and to resolve confusion. Even if training is entirely online, you still need to make sure trainees have time to complete it in a pace conducive to learning.

> *On the one hand, there's a lot to cover. On the other, trainees have busy schedules, and their opportunities to engage in training for extended periods are often limited.*

Solving this organizational puzzle requires knowing how much time you need, when it's good to pause in training and when it's not, and what opportunities people have in their schedules to take part in training. You also need to plan early and thoughtfully. It's very hard to add to change a training schedule after the school year begins. You don't want to find yourself tied to a schedule that leaves critical gaps in skill development or leaves observers overwhelmed.

Organizing Initial Training

There's no way around it: initial observer training takes a lot of time. How much time depends on many factors, especially trainees' prior knowledge and expertise, and the complexity of an observation instrument (i.e., it takes longer to learn how to rate with a rubric with more indicators). It can easily take 30 hours to train the minimum prerequisites and core skills needed to rate with sufficient accuracy and provide meaningful feedback. That number may cause sticker shock, but remember that the effect of a cadre of well-trained observers is multiplied over the many teachers they support.

The first few sessions of your initial training shouldn't be spread out over an extended time period. The best time for trainees to learn how to identify relevant evidence is soon after they learn the rubric's structure. The best time for observers to learn how to prepare meaningful feedback is soon after they learn to rate accurately. If too much time elapses between these lessons, then trainees will need significant review. For in-person training, a good rule is: don't break for more than a couple of days until trainees are rating multiple components. If your initial training is online, make sure trainees don't take several weeks to complete the first modules.

But don't rush things, either. You don't learn to juggle by picking up three balls; first you learn how to toss and catch one, then you add another, and finally a third. You need to take a similar approach for trainees to learn the cognitively challenging task of observation. We explained how to increase complexity gradually in this book's chapter on training to rate accurately (see page 177 in Chapter 14, "Using Criteria for Rating"). Trainees gain confidence and competence when you start with the easiest-to-rate components and have observers practice rating two or three components before rating them all. When planning your trainees' initial training, build in frequent small "wins," so trainees can see themselves gaining mastery.

Figure 16.1 is an example sequence and schedule for initial training that uses group sessions for the first few sessions. In two consecutive days, trainees learn the prerequisites and begin to practice collecting, interpreting, and rating evidence for a small number of teaching

FIGURE 16.1   Sequencing the Elements of Initial Training

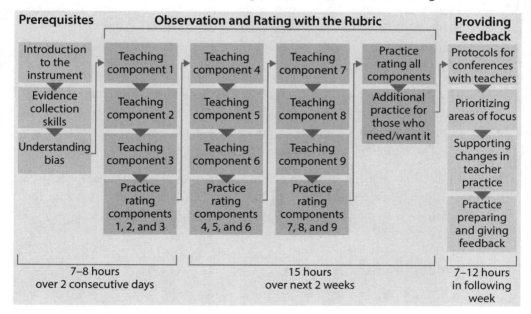

components. This familiarizes them with the process so they can practice on their own until they learn more components. In the same example, subsequent sessions could be conducted face-to-face or be completed independently. The latter has the advantage of reducing the need for trainers, and it lets trainees complete their work when they're able.

The good news is that, in most cases, you need to do initial training only once for each observer. You don't need to find 30 hours in their schedules every year. It's also easier to make the argument for adding professional development days to the schedules of new observers; their success going forward depends on strong initial training. Make sure to deliver that message when working with others in your system to find enough time. Don't start off by just asking for 30 hours; explain what you need to do with those hours, and why it's important.

Once you know your blocks of time for initial training, map out the elements. You can do this on a large wall calendar using different-colored sticky notes for the prerequisites, core observation skills, and feedback training. You may need to move elements around several times to frontload the hours, limit the breaks in training, and allow trainees to develop their competencies in stages as we've suggested. Remember also to allow opportunities for additional independent practice for those who need or want it before moving on to more complex activities—and before any kind of assessment of their skills.

 TIPS

- Even if observers are familiar with an observation instrument, don't assume an overview is unnecessary. Observers need more than just a superficial appreciation of a tool; they all need the same understanding of its structure and meaning. People familiar with an instrument may still think differently about its organization, instructional emphasis, and use.

- Allow trainees to take an assessment of their skills soon after they complete their initial training. This is when they generally feel most confident. If they do poorly, you can reteach them and provide more practice opportunities while there's still plenty of time in the year to observe.

- If you use independent or online sessions, keep in mind that trainees will lose focus if they work by themselves for too long. Schedules should allow enough time for people to complete a training program in a manageable period.

Planning for Follow-Up Training

Observers are never done with training. Their initial training should provide enough guidance and practice to ensure their basic proficiency in rating and providing feedback. But this training can't help observers fully develop the skills to efficiently and accurately respond to every situation they might encounter. In addition, their interpretations of a rubric will drift over time if they don't periodically check their work against that of expert observers using pre-scored video. They also need follow-up training whenever changes are made to an observation instrument to make sure everyone's on the same page.

Observers' follow-up training should reinforce and extend their core observation skills. That means they need guided practice collecting and rating evidence for all rubric components. It also means they need guided practice preparing and delivering feedback to teachers based on evidence they collected from a lesson. The extension of skills should focus on particular challenges observers are experiencing and strategies to use in more specific situations. Follow-up training might revisit two teaching components that they are struggling to distinguish, for example, or explain ways to tailor their feedback for highly accomplished teachers.

You may need several hours over the course of a year for follow-up training. Because all experienced observers need follow-up training every year, chances are you'll need to work within the time that's currently available for their professional development. Adding the equivalent of a full day of training to the yearly schedules of every principal and observer in a school system is likely harder than finding things on their current schedules that could be removed without a negative impact on teaching and learning. To plan follow-up training, you'll need to assess what else is on people's plates.

> *The extension of skills should focus on particular challenges observers are experiencing and strategies to use in more specific situations.*

Unlike initial training, follow-up training works best when it is distributed over a period of months. Having multiple sessions during the year is better for maintaining accuracy and building new skills than a schedule in which experienced observers come together once a year. A schedule with more frequent sessions also lets you more quickly respond to any challenges observers are encountering in their work. To keep training at a manageable size—with not much more than 25 participants if it is held in person—you'll probably need to offer multiple times for each session. An example is in Figure 16.2. Of course, this isn't an issue with online or independent work. But with independent work, you still need to make sure observers have time to complete it according to expected schedules.

 TIP

Some observers respond better than others to practice with video. Although all observers should be trained with pre-scored video, including some practice observing live classrooms can be helpful for many trainees.

FIGURE 16.2   Sample Follow-Up Training Schedule

All experienced observers complete one fall and one spring training.

Fall Training	**Spring Training**
Guided practice observing and rating	Guided practice observing and rating
Guided practice preparing and giving feedback	Guided practice preparing and giving feedback
Common observation challenges and advanced skills	Common observation challenges and advanced skills
One 3-hour session offered two times in October and November	One 3-hour session offered two times in February and March

In the beginning, you'll need to plan a sequence and schedule with much less than perfect information. You'll lose a year of implementation if you wait until every session is designed and tested before asking for and blocking off time on people's calendars. Estimate how much time you need by thinking through the key activities for each element of training detailed in this book. If you're much under 30 hours, rethink your assumptions. Communicate to stakeholders and senior system leadership that data collected from the first year of training may indicate more time should be allocated the following year.

After a first iteration of initial and follow-up training, you should have better information with which to plan. Remember, there's no rule that says it takes the same amount of time to learn every skill. You may find that trainees are quickly able to identify and rate evidence for certain teaching components, but that others require repeated guided practice with different pre-scored videos. There's also no rule that says all observers learn at the same pace; in fact, as a rule they don't. As you build on an initial iteration of training, look for more ways to give each observer the training he or she needs to become proficient.

 TIP

Make sure your principal managers (sometimes called instructional leadership directors) are on board. Often they have control over how principals spend their time. They need to emphasize the importance of follow-up training and continually check to make sure the principals they support take part in it. This is especially important when observer training is new; over time, principals see more clearly its value to their work and need less incentive to take part.

✓ TECHNIQUES: ORGANIZING TRAINING

To Lay the Foundation:

- Estimate how much time it will take for each element of initial training. Add up the amount of time needed to cover the prerequisites and how to collect evidence for and rate the first few components of teaching in your instrument. Consider this the minimum time you need in consecutive days for the beginning of initial training. If the rest of initial training can't happen in consecutive days, it should take place in no more than a couple of weeks.

- When working with district leaders to get the time for initial training, make sure to communicate all that needs to happen in that training and its importance to developing instructional leadership and better teaching across the system.

- Sequence the elements of initial training to ensure the prerequisites are covered before guided practice on how to observe and rate components of teaching. Start with the components that require the least inference (that can be rated solely on directly observable indicators). Increase the complexity gradually, and build in opportunities for trainees to experience success before each transition to more challenging tasks.

- Plan for each experienced observer to receive follow-up training at more than one point during the year. At each point, make sure to include enough time for guided practice observing and rating pre-scored video, guided practice preparing effective feedback, and advanced training that addresses common observer challenges and how to handle more specific situations.

To Build and Improve:

- Consider changes in how you sequence and schedule initial and follow-up training based on participant surveys and informal discussions. Did observers need more time for some topics and activities than others? Does training need to cover additional topics at key points to better ensure success with what follows? Would training build confidence and competence more effectively with a different sequence of topics, or with different or additional points at which to pause and practice?

(TECHNIQUES Continued)

■   Consider changes in how you schedule follow-up training, based on participant input and observation data. For example, would more frequent sessions reduce the extent of drift in ratings over the course of the year?

■   If more than minor changes are made to an instrument, then more than the usual follow-up training may be needed to get observers fully aligned to the new expectations.

■   Look for ways to make more use of independent work, including online training and opportunities for additional practice, to ease the logistical challenges of relying on in-person training.

■   Use positive participant feedback and data on successful outcomes when making the case for additional time and for maintaining a successful schedule. Expect that training will take more time than you first thought, and don't take it as a given that support for effective training will continue without efforts to cultivate it.

◌ Putting It into Practice

To Lay the Foundation:

For initial training and follow-up training, list the elements you need to include in each, estimate the time they'll take, and group those elements based on the guidance in this section.

To Build and Improve:

How could your training schedule change to more effectively build and maintain observers' proficiency to rate accurately and provide meaningful feedback?

PART IV

USING DATA TO IMPROVE TRAINING AND SUPPORT OF OBSERVERS

CHAPTER 17

Collecting and Using Data from Training

ESSENTIAL QUESTION

How Will You Use Information to Improve Training?

Improvement requires study. You adapt best practice for your own context, learn from the results, and make changes as needed. Then you do it again. In this way, your training program's second iteration should produce better results than its first, and its third better than its second. But for this to happen, you need data. Without information that connects results to techniques, your attempts to improve are little more than guesswork. Hence, the repeated refrain in this book about training elements evolving over time as a school system gains a better understanding of the needs of its teachers and observers.

Collecting and analyzing information for continuous improvement has to be a coordinated effort. Making sure you gather what you need to know takes forethought. A data management system needs to be set up to organize your data and look for trends. Someone with the time and expertise to do so needs to be in charge of reviewing data from multiple sources and forming hypotheses about what's going on. Once you've begun training observers, it's too late to think about how you'll know if your training is successful. An information management strategy needs to be baked into training from the beginning.

An information management strategy needs to be baked into training from the beginning.

What You Need to Know (and How to Know It)

To improve your observation training, you need data about every step in the process, not just observation ratings (see Figure 17.1). Observation entails the full range of knowledge and skills discussed in the previous chapters. If all you know is the extent to which trainees are picking the correct ratings, you don't know why. Underneath any rating a trainee provides—correct or incorrect—lies a host of possible misconceptions, from misunderstandings about what constitutes evidence to confusion about the rules for rating. Information on how trainees are thinking tells you what needs clarifying, and where new training materials or activities may be needed.

It takes multiple sources of data, collected at different touch points, to identify a training program's strengths and areas for improvement. Among the key ones:

Checks for Understanding: The training around each piece of the knowledge and skills entailed in observation should include checks for understanding. As with teaching, training shouldn't proceed to a new idea until it's determined that trainees have grasped the idea just covered. This might involve asking which of several statements represents evidence, or asking what ratings would be given for different scenarios. Results from these checks should be recorded.

Evidence Reviews: Use of relevant evidence is the basis of accurate rating and meaningful feedback. Looking at trainees' evidence from an observation can reveal if they understand the descriptive nature of evidence, if they know what's relevant to each teaching component, and whether they can capture it. Seeing how they justify their ratings with evidence tells you whether they're correctly interpreting an instrument's rules for doing so. Assign someone to this task.

Feedback Reviews: Make sure to collect data on the effectiveness of feedback training. If you don't, feedback won't improve. Use your criteria for quality feedback to review examples of trainees' written feedback and to judge their skills in role-plays of post-observation conferences, or while practicing with teachers. This will suggest if training is really making clear what it means to provide feedback that's meaningful and actionable. Also, survey teachers about the extent to which they're receiving quality feedback from observations.

Practice Rating: If observers can't rate accurately, something needs to be addressed. As we've said throughout this book, the only way to know this is to see if trainees can review videos of teaching and reproduce the ratings that expert observers have determined to be correct through pre-scoring. Where trainees are most off the mark, it sends a signal to "dig here" to figure out why. The issue could be with who is being trained, but if the problem is widespread, the training has failed.

Participant Surveys: Opinions matter. When trainees feel confident to do something, it's a good indication of their training's success. Indeed, given the anxiousness about observations in many places—among observers and teachers alike—confidence is itself an important objective. Ask participants how prepared they feel, and what would make them more so, at the end of sessions, at the end of training programs, and after they've put their skills to use in the field.

Interviews and Focus Groups: The best way to get inside people's heads is to talk to them. This can be especially helpful in trying to uncover the root cause of confusion. Why did so many trainees see all the examples of differentiated instruction in a lesson, and yet still assign the wrong rating? Are they misinterpreting key words in the rubric? Was there something about a particular video that led to such a wide range of ratings for one component?

FIGURE 17.1   Data to Collect to Improve Training

What You Need to Know

To what extent can trainees . . .

Understand what constitutes evidence? Including its descriptive nature and various types (e.g., quotes, tallies, anecdotes)

Identify evidence relevant to the observation instrument? Do they know what to look and listen for?

Sort evidence into the relevant components of teaching? (e.g., when a question is a discussion technique versus a check for understanding)

Apply the rules for rating? Can they assign the correct ratings, for the right reasons, without bias?

Coach teachers to change their practice? Can they provide specific, practical, and improvement-focused feedback?

Ways to Know It

- Checks for Understanding
- Evidence Reviews
- Feedback Reviews
- Practice Rating
- Participant Surveys
- Focus Groups and Interviews

Whenever you collect information, note the relevant skills, training sessions, trainers, and materials (see Figure 17.2). This will let you zero in on potential sources of a problem—and potential solutions. You may learn, for example, that sessions run by some training leaders leave trainees confused about the difference between two related teaching components; if so, the training leaders who succeeded in building the right understanding may have techniques to share with the others. Alternatively, if trainees struggle to rate a teaching component only when viewing a particular video, that video might need to be replaced.

 TIPS

- Use the practices in your rubric to assess training facilitation. The techniques and strategies emphasized in observation instruments aren't only appropriate for teaching students; they apply to adult learning as well. Ask trainees to what extent their training reflected rigorous thinking, participant engagement, and quality checks for understanding.

- Collect trainees' questions. A training leader should make note of what's being asked in training, and pass that on to whoever is in charge of improving training. Common questions can reveal concepts and skills that need to be better addressed.

FIGURE 17.2 Organizing Data from a Practice Video

Data from practice rating should be organized to identify two things: the components of teaching that most trainees struggled to rate accurately and which trainees struggled to rate accurately across multiple components. When inaccuracy is limited to a few individuals, the best response may be additional training. But if many trainees are off the mark, a closer look at the relevant training activities, trainers, videos, and other materials may be needed.

Practice Video: # 361_Middle School Math Lesson

Trainee	Training session	Trainer	Classroom Procedures Correct Rating: 3		Discussion Techniques Correct Rating: 2		Check for Understanding Correct Rating: 3	Each trainee's results across all components		
			Trainee's rating	Diff from correct	Trainee's rating	Diff from correct	Trainee's rating	% correct	% off by 1	% off >1
M. Rojas	5/16/15	Berger	3	0	3	+1	3	50%	25%	25%
B. Pham	5/16/15	Berger	2	−1	1	−1	2	37.5%	37.5%	25%
H. Stone	6/21/15	Weis	4	+1	4	+2	3	12.5%	37.5%	50%
T. Jones	6/21/15	Henry	2	−1	2	0	2	75%	12.5%	12.5%
Results for each component across all trainees	% trainees correct		45%		39%		52%			
	% trainees off by 1		38%		28%		38%			
	% trainees off >1		18%		33%		20%			

Peeling the Onion

Practice rating of pre-scored video is especially helpful in suggesting where your training is successful and where improvement may be needed. After all, a major goal of training is for observers to be able to rate accurately. If many trainees are off the mark in rating a particular teaching component, that's a good indication that training is failing to clarify something. Also telling are the patterns in the incorrect ratings given. When ratings are all over the place, trainees may have resorted to guessing because they're not seeing the evidence clearly. When ratings are all too high or too low, they may be misinterpreting the rules for rating.

Look for three qualities when reviewing evidence:

Objectivity: Is it generally descriptive, free of biased statements, and not vague or inferential?

Relevance: Is all the evidence the trainee provided relevant to the teaching component it was used to rate?

Sufficiency: Is all the relevant evidence from the observed lesson included so that nothing is missing?

The trends you notice in the data may point to confusion among observers about what evidence belongs with a particular teaching component, or the types of evidence to which observers need to be more attuned. If observers produced inaccurate ratings using all relevant evidence, then the next question is how they understood the distinctions among performance levels. One way to find out is by reviewing observers' written rationales to see what connections they made between their collected evidence and the rubric language for the ratings they gave. Another way is by asking a group of trainees to explain their thought process. The table that follows outlines how to determine the underlying causes of different patterns in the data.

Analyzing Results from Practice Rating of Pre-Scored Video

Patterns from Rating Component	What Might Be Going On	How You Could Tell	What You Might Do About It
Trainees are mostly accurate. (Most get the right rating, or close to it.)	■ Training has probably given them a solid understanding of how to rate this component.	■ Spot check their evidence to make sure they didn't miss or misinterpret anything.	■ If a spot check confirms understandings and trainees are accurate when rating other videos on the same component, continue training for this component unchanged.

Patterns from Rating Component	What Might Be Going On	How You Could Tell	What You Might Do About It
Trainees are mostly inaccurate but consistent. (Most pick the same wrong rating.)	■ Trainees may share one or more misunderstandings about the relevant evidence for this component or how to apply the rating rules. ■ They may be reluctant to assign the lowest or highest scores. ■ It's also possible the expert observers who pre-scored the video missed something. Or a video may contain overly distracting behavior.	■ Review the evidence from a representative sample of trainees to look for common errors. ■ Review the video to see if it contains evidence relevant to the component not cited in pre-scoring. ■ See if trainees' results from rating other videos show similar patterns.	■ Revise training for the component to address any common sources of confusion. ■ Place a greater emphasis on what distinguishes between two adjacent ratings. Train all trainers to implement the change as intended. ■ If no confusion is found, and trainees are able to rate other videos accurately, have the problematic video pre-scored by another group of expert observers to see if they determine a different rating.
Trainees are mostly inaccurate and inconsistent. (Their ratings are all over the place.)	■ Trainees may be guessing, possibly because there's not enough clear evidence in the video to rate it. ■ Or trainees may lack an overall understanding of how to use the instrument, and so are relying on personal preferences.	■ Determine whether trainees are similarly inconsistent in rating other components. ■ Interview a group of trainees and review a representative sample of the evidence they used to rate the component. ■ Ask other expert observers to rate the video to see if it's ratable.	■ If trainees seem to lack a general understanding of what is evidence and how to rate with the instrument, then beef up training on these fundamentals. ■ If the confusion is isolated to rating this video, consider replacing it (or using it for more advanced practice). Keep in mind evidence for some components may need to be captured differently (with student interviews or examples of student work, for example).

TOOL:
DISTRICT OF COLUMBIA PUBLIC SCHOOLS WRITTEN FEEDBACK RUBRIC

District of Columbia Public Schools (DCPS) created a rubric to assess an observer's use of evidence in providing written feedback. The instrument rates feedback on the extent to which each rubric component (called "Teach Standards" in DCPS) is addressed with relevant evidence and specific suggestions to help the teacher improve classroom practice. Also judged is the clarity and professionalism of the writing. See page 331, for the complete tool, and for an example of written feedback.

It's important to consider multiple possibilities when observers rate inaccurately. What does it mean if lots of observers fail to reproduce the ratings determined to be correct by the expert observers involved in pre-scoring? Is it the fault of the training or the video, or even the rubric if it's yet untested? Is the video poor quality, or just not a good example for new observers to use in practice rating (including too many nuanced examples of performance)? Did the pre-scoring process fail to determine the correct ratings? Ratings based on a single video aren't sufficient to say where the problem really lies.

There are too many possible scenarios to suggest in these pages what each one means, how you can tell, and what to do about it. What matters is having the right information and the right approach toward investigating. If something matters to the quality of observation, collect data on it. When the results are off for large numbers of your trainees, assume there's a deficiency in training and peel the onion to find it. But don't make conclusions based on a single piece or type of data. Review evidence and talk to your training participants to understand what's not getting through, and then try something different.

TIP

Consider changes to an instrument only after all other potential problems have been investigated. If observers initially struggle to rate accurately, it's tempting to eliminate what seem to be the instrument's most problematic elements. But doing so could mean you're no longer capturing all the aspects of teaching that are important to student learning. Even minor changes in a rubric's language may cause observers to interpret its indicators in unintended ways. Find out if changes in training can address an issue before revisiting a rubric's components and language. Know that it takes time for an observation system to stabilize; even quality training doesn't produce optimal results the first time around.

☑ TECHNIQUES: USING INFORMATION TO IMPROVE TRAINING

To Lay the Foundation:

■ Assign someone the task of identifying all the data you need to collect during and after training to judge its effectiveness and how you'll collect it. This should include multiple sources and data on evidence collection skills, on identifying evidence relevant to the rubric, on rating accuracy, and on feedback skills. Ideally this should be done as you plan your initial round of observer training.

■ Make sure plans to collect each piece of data include recording of the relevant skills, training sessions, trainers, and materials (including videos used).

■ Establish criteria for reviewing the evidence that trainees collect and use to rate lessons and for the feedback they provide in written exercises, role-plays, and practice. Make sure those who review these artifacts know how to do so consistently.

■ Set up a spreadsheet for organizing results from practice rating of pre-scored video so you can identify trends among trainees and their ability to rate each component of teaching.

To Build and Improve:

■ Review collected data from multiple sources to identify the roots of confusions and skill deficiencies. Keep in mind the issue may be with the training activities, the trainer, or the materials. Confirm your hypotheses by talking with trainees.

■ Also look for pockets of success, like the trainer who succeeds in developing a skill or understanding that others have not. Another example would be identifying the qualities of videos that worked best in training.

■ Test changes in training with small groups of observers to see if they address the issue before you incorporate them into your program.

■ Make sure any changes to training are implemented with consistency. This may involve creating standardized materials (worksheets, presentations, etc.) and training the trainers.

■ Consider changes to your surveys and criteria for reviewing evidence and feedback if these reviews aren't telling you what you need to know.

☀️ Putting It into Practice

To Lay the Foundation:

What information do you need to start collecting to improve your training, and what are multiple ways you can collect it?

To Build and Improve:

What does your review of data tell you should be your top priorities for improving training?

⬇ This item can be downloaded from www.wiley.com/go/betterfeedback

CHAPTER 18

Assessing Observers to Ensure and Improve Quality

ESSENTIAL QUESTION

How Will You Know When Observers Are Ready, and What Will You Do If They're Not?

Imagine that you have invested considerable resources in training observers, only to see your observers go into classrooms and produce results that just aren't credible. Maybe the ratings seem drastically inflated, or widely inconsistent among observers. Or maybe your teachers report they aren't getting specific and helpful feedback from your observers. Whatever the signs, you can clearly see that your observation system isn't providing your teachers, administrators, or system leaders with the trustworthy and useful information they need to improve teaching and student learning.

Only with observer assessment can you learn the extent to which your group of observers has developed the shared understanding of effective teaching and feedback for which you're striving.

Maybe you don't need to imagine such a scenario because you've experienced it already.

Fortunately, you can minimize the chance of this happening—or happening again, if it has already—while at the same time gathering the data you need to continually improve your observation system's overall performance. You do this through observer assessment. When you assess observers after their initial training, you learn who's ready, and who needs additional support before they can carry out trustworthy observations in the classroom. When observers demonstrate sufficient proficiency, it builds confidence—among teachers, school system leaders, and observers themselves—in the ratings and feedback they produce (see Figure 18.1).

WHY OBSERVER ASSESSMENT IS ESSENTIAL

- It tells you if those you've trained are ready to do what you've trained them to do.

- It tells you who needs additional support to become ready to carry out observations.

- It tells you where you need to do a better job preparing observers.

FIGURE 18.1 How Observer Assessment Supports Quality

Your observer assessment also provides you with critical information for evaluating your training program. In Chapter 17, "Collecting and Using Data from Training," we explained the importance of collecting information from training to improve it. It's also essential to monitor the ongoing work of your observers, to make sure they maintain their skills and carry out observations in the classroom appropriately (as we discuss in Chapter 19, "Monitoring Your Observation System"). But only with observer assessment can you learn the extent to which your group of observers has developed the shared understanding of effective teaching and feedback for which you're striving.

To be sure, observer assessment raises many challenges—some technical, others social-emotional, and some political. The chief technical challenge is developing an assessment that reliably tells you what you need to know. Assessment results are of no value for improvement if they're unreliable, if the assessment materials are low quality, or if the knowledge and skills they measure don't support your goals for observation. Another big technical challenge is determining a performance standard for observers that advances your efforts to improve teaching and learning.

The non-technical challenges relate to the perceived risks of assessment. No one likes being assessed, especially when stakes are attached. Many administrators and other observers have a strong reaction to assessment. They think, "I've been doing my job for years, why do I need to pass an assessment now?" School system leaders also face a political challenge when well-regarded principals and instructional leaders fail to demonstrate proficiency. When large numbers of observers fail, system leaders feel pressure to lower their standards for observer proficiency, which threatens reliability.

These challenges can be mitigated, however—and they must be, for observations to be fair and meaningful for teachers, while at the same time providing accurate information for improving instruction. A trustworthy observer assessment is the result of careful planning, design, piloting, review of data, and ongoing refinement. Many of the ingredients are the same as needed for trustworthy observations: clear and relevant criteria, objective evidence, and efforts to ensure consistency in judgements. Hence you'll find that our advice on assessment echoes much of what we covered in the previous chapters.

Addressing the non-technical challenges is a matter of change management. The key is being clear about the purpose of your assessment, while proactively planning ways to help your observers succeed. All stakeholders need to understand what's going to happen—what the assessment will entail, and what will be the consequences for themselves and the school system—and why this needs to happen. The right response when observers fail is to demonstrate your commitment to better observer training and support. You may also need to look at your process for selecting school leaders to ensure that new hires have the foundational instructional skills. But lowering your expectations for observers only denies teachers the feedback and support they need to improve their practice.

In the following pages we first address the big questions related to observer assessment:

- What are your goals for observer assessment, and how do they inform what you measure?

- What types of assessment are best for your context?

- What should be your guiding principle in setting performance standards?

Then we delve into the options for measuring each of the skills an observer needs—from evidence collection and sorting, to interpretation, and providing rating feedback. We finish with advice on appropriate ways to respond when observers miss the mark, and on how to build trust in your assessment over time.

Ideally, assessment is part of your observation system from the beginning. This sets an expectation early in the process for demonstrated mastery. It also forces a fundamental conversation among your stakeholders about what your observers need to know and be able to do—and why—and who bears responsibility for making sure they can do it. Doing this up front drives more purposeful decision-making throughout your system.

But even where an observation system has existed without quality assessment, the assessment conversation can serve as a powerful force for greater alignment. The same goes for school systems that already have some form of observer assessment, but may be missing important pieces. Whatever your stage of implementation, you need to take stock of how you ensure quality, and work toward doing a better job. (See Figure 18.1.)

Clarifying Goals for Observer Assessment

Before getting into the mechanics of observer assessment, consider the purpose of such an assessment. Your understanding of how assessment advances your overall goals for observations will determine, to a great degree, what you assess, how you assess it, and how you interpret and use the results. To consider the purpose, step back and recall where you are, and where you want to be, with regards to teaching and learning.

In the introduction to this book, we provided data suggesting that the vast majority of teaching—perhaps 90 percent—is rated between a 2 and a 3 on a 4-point scale. Improving teaching and learning for the vast majority of classrooms will take more than an observer accurately identifying a teacher's practice on a rubric. If you're a teacher, it's not very helpful to know your rating for the teaching component "checks for understanding" was rated a 2. You need to know why you received that rating, and what to do to improve your rating on that teaching component. Did you transition to more complex parts of the lesson without determining if students were ready? Did you rely only on student volunteers to check understanding? Or was it something else that affected the rating? It's very hard to improve if you don't know with specificity what you could do better.

Given the goal of changing teacher practice—as well as rating accurately—throughout this book, we've presented a four-stage process for quality observation:

1. **Collect** Record objective evidence from a lesson that's pertinent to the rubric;

2. **Sort** Categorize collected evidence by the relevant rubric components;

3. **Interpret** Apply the rubric's rating criteria to the sorted evidence to determine a set of ratings; and

4. **Provide Feedback** Identify specific opportunities for improving practice, and follow up.

Accurate rating is part of the mix. You can't improve teaching without good data on teaching. Observers who rate inaccurately may lead a school system to invest professional development dollars in areas of instructional practice that don't represent actual needs. Observers must be able to tell the difference between effective and ineffective practice. But observers also need to be able to help *change* practice. Think of it this way: an Olympic judge need only know how to score an athlete's performance; an Olympic coach must be able to analyze and assess performance *and* help elevate it. Accuracy and effective feedback are both essential.

> *Observers must be able to tell the difference between effective and ineffective practice. But observers also need to be able to help change practice.*

Knowing what's essential for quality observations is key to identifying your assessment needs. Assessment design begins with the question, "What claims do I want to be able to make, based on my assessment?" To ensure accuracy and effective feedback, what claims must you be able to make about what observers know and are able to do? Answering that question will lead you to the next two questions: What do you need to measure to make those claims, and then how can you measure it? (See Figure 18.2.)

Here's why this matters: You can't make a claim that an assessment wasn't designed to help you make. You can't claim that your observers are able to prepare actionable feedback if your assessment measures only their ability to rate accurately. You can't even claim that observers know how to collect and sort objective evidence if all you know is that they can produce accurate ratings; they might just be good guessers, or they might not be able to justify a set of ratings with strong evidence. What you want to avoid is saying that your observers are ready to do what they need to do, when they're actually not. The way you will know if they are ready to do the job is through assessment.

When you start with the question "What claims do I want to be able to make?" you also wind up with an assessment that tells you where you need to do a better job training and supporting your observers. If all you know is that a group of observers can't rate accurately on the teaching component "checks for understanding," there's little you can do about it. Maybe they don't recognize the points in a lesson when student understanding should be checked—or if they do, maybe they don't realize that the teacher needs to check for understanding at all such moments for a lesson to receive a rating of 4. To know what the problem is, so you can address it, you need to assess observers on their ability to identify, sort, and interpret evidence.[13]

Considering Different Assessment Types

Assessment is a matter of capturing evidence to support the claims you want to make. The tasks and activities you use to capture that evidence may vary. As educators know well, assessments take different forms. Some are paper and pencil, others are computer-based. Some rely on selected-response items, others on constructed responses. Each type of assessment has benefits for particular uses and contexts, and each has its own implications for implementation. Knowing these is important as you think about the specific tasks your assessment should include.

There are two general approaches to assessment. One is to directly measure what observers actually do (e.g., assessing evidence collection by having observers collect evidence from a lesson). The other is to use an indirect, or "proxy" measure. A proxy for evidence collection might include asking observers to review a list of statements and identify which statements represent relevant evidence. This doesn't replicate what observers do in the classroom, but it could capture evidence to support claims about observers' evidence collection skills. The evidence from a proxy isn't as strong as that from a direct measure of the same thing.

FIGURE 18.2 Identifying Assessment Needs

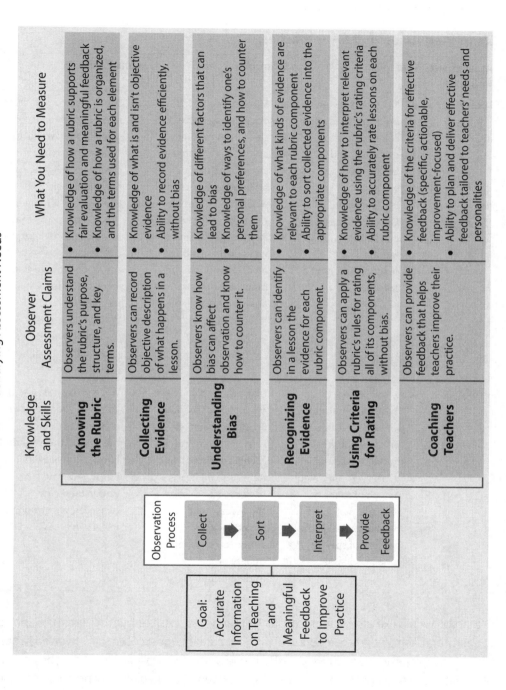

Knowledge and Skills	Observer Assessment Claims	What You Need to Measure
Knowing the Rubric	Observers understand the rubric's purpose, structure, and key terms.	• Knowledge of how a rubric supports fair evaluation and meaningful feedback • Knowledge of how a rubric is organized, and the terms used for each element
Collecting Evidence	Observers can record objective description of what happens in a lesson.	• Knowledge of what is and isn't objective evidence • Ability to record evidence efficiently, without bias
Understanding Bias	Observers know how bias can affect observation and know how to counter it.	• Knowledge of different factors that can lead to bias • Knowledge of ways to identify one's personal preferences, and how to counter them
Recognizing Evidence	Observers can identify in a lesson the evidence for each rubric component.	• Knowledge of what kinds of evidence are relevant to each rubric component • Ability to sort collected evidence into the appropriate components
Using Criteria for Rating	Observers can apply a rubric's rules for rating all of its components, without bias.	• Knowledge of how to interpret relevant evidence using the rubric's rating criteria • Ability to accurately rate lessons on each rubric component
Coaching Teachers	Observers can provide feedback that helps teachers improve their practice.	• Knowledge of the criteria for effective feedback (specific, actionable, improvement-focused) • Ability to plan and deliver effective feedback tailored to teachers' needs and personalities

Observation Process

Collect → Sort → Interpret → Provide Feedback

Goal: Accurate Information on Teaching and Meaningful Feedback to Improve Practice

But you may find that a proxy makes the most sense to use when a direct measure would be cost-prohibitive or require too many resources.

Comparing Assessment Approaches

Assessment Approach	Examples	Strengths	Considerations
Direct	■ Observers review pre-scored video to collect and sort evidence, and use it to rate, as they would in an observation. ■ Observers prepare and deliver feedback to a teacher, based on a lesson.	■ Mimics the observation process. ■ Developing a direct approach can forge a shared understanding among trainers as to what good observation practice looks like. ■ Reviewing the kind of work observers do in an observation helps pinpoint strengths and areas for improvement.	■ Do you have a sufficient number of people, with sufficient expertise, to review and score observers' evidence and their feedback? ■ Can you implement a process to ensure that scoring is consistent, so different reviewers give the same score to the same evidence and feedback? ■ Will it help you understand why observers are struggling in certain areas?
Proxy	■ Observers get written descriptions of evidence and are asked what the rating would be. ■ Observers are asked which of four examples of feedback meets the criteria of specific and actionable.	■ May require minimal resources for scoring. ■ Scoring of selected-response items can be highly consistent. Such items also make it easier to standardize the assessment experience, which supports consistent quality of implementation.	■ Will a proxy measure give you, and your observers, confidence that it's measuring the intended knowledge or skill? ■ Will it help you understand why observers are struggling in certain areas?

Often, you would like assessment to be as "authentic" as possible, but there are pros and cons to each approach. With the exception of rating accurately, most of the skills involved in observation require performance-based tasks, if you want to measure them directly. In actual observations, when observers collect and sort evidence, and when they prepare and deliver feedback, they're not selecting from a short list of possible options; they're filtering an enormous amount of information in the classroom so they can organize and interpret what's relevant. That bears little resemblance to answering true-or-false or multiple-choice items.

But for you to score your observers' collected, sorted, and interpreted evidence—and to do it consistently—takes a good deal of effort and expertise. The scores your observers receive on their ability to collect and sort evidence should be the same no matter who reviews their work. That means you need to develop a common set of criteria and to norm a group of reviewers on how to apply them to your observers' work. Doing so can be valuable; it can forge a shared understanding of good observation practice among those who train and support observers. But it takes time and care—and enough people—to assess evidence reliably.

Other considerations relate to use of technology. Somehow you need to share information with observers—videos, instructions, questions, templates to complete, and so on—and they need a way to submit their work back to you. Moreover, this needs to be done in a way that ensures the integrity of the results. You need to know that the work someone submits is actually theirs, and that person needs to know that any resulting judgments are actually based on their work, and not someone else's.

A growing number of tools exist to facilitate this sharing. Many are the same that can be used to develop observer training (see Chapter 3, "Deciding on Training Delivery Methods"). The more advanced tools let you organize videos and other media and collect written evidence and selected-response answers, all on the same platform. Some produce detailed reports—on, say, the frequency of incorrect ratings given for each rubric component, and how far off they were.

But much of the same can be accomplished using more readily available tools, like Google Drive, Microsoft Word, and Excel. When developing an assessment for the first time, it's a good idea to stick with the most basic features and the most flexible tools. After you've established that your assessment tasks are both viable and a good measure of what you need to know, you can hardwire your assessment process into a more sophisticated system that lets you do more with the data it gathers.

To weigh different assessment methods, ask yourself what constraints you face. For example:

- Is your school system geographically spread out, making it hard for your observers to come to one place for training and assessment?

- How big is your pool of potential reviewers, and how much time could they devote to scoring evidence and feedback?

- How robust and reliable is your Wi-Fi in the places where your observers might complete their assessments?

■ How many observers do you expect to assess each year? Keep in mind the need to score retakes for those who don't initially pass, and the need to reassess observers each year—not just after their initial training—to make sure they maintain their proficiency.

Your constraints needn't preclude you from using certain approaches toward assessment. But they may need to be addressed for you to pursue a particular course. If you want your assessment to be as authentic as possible, but you have just two staff members who might review evidence, you may need to expand your pool of reviewers. If you are in a geographically diverse system in which only one location has the reliable Wi-Fi to handle lots of simultaneous video streaming, you may need to upgrade your technology or provide USB flash drives of videos for other locations to use.

Of course, none of your decisions around assessment methods are either-or. Nor are they permanent. Your observer assessment may include a combination of selected-response items that test observers' understanding of certain ideas combined with constructed-response activities that closely resemble your classroom observation process. Your school system also might rely more heavily on one approach at first, and then shift to another as it builds capacity and you learn what works well and what doesn't.

> *What matters most is whether or not the tasks and activities in your assessment capture sufficient evidence to support the claims you need to make about what your observers know and are able to do. If not, you're just assessing for assessment's sake.*

But don't let the issues of logistics or convenience override the need for quality. An assessment that includes only selected-response items might be easy to administer and score, but it may not advance your goals. What matters most is whether or not the tasks and activities in your assessment capture sufficient evidence to support the claims you need to make about what your observers know and are able to do. If not, you're just assessing for assessment's sake.

TIP

Your planning should keep in mind how much time it takes your observers to complete an assessment. An assessment that covers all the skills referenced in this chapter may take two or more hours. Allow for the fact that some observers will take a lot more time than others to complete the same assessment.

SNAPSHOT:
STRIVING FOR AUTHENTIC OBSERVER ASSESSMENT IN MINNEAPOLIS

Observers in Minneapolis Public Schools must demonstrate proficiency on an assessment that seeks to mimic, as much as possible, the observation process. After completing three days of initial training, they return to the training center to review pre-scored video and submit their organized evidence and ratings via computer. As shown in Figure 18.3 observers' accuracy is determined by comparing their ratings to the ones determined to be correct by those who pre-scored the video. To evaluate observers' use of evidence, observation trainers normed in a review process go over each observer's submitted work. Those who aren't successful on the first try are given follow-up training, then retake the assessment.

FIGURE 18.3   Assessing Use of Evidence and Rating Proficiency in MPS

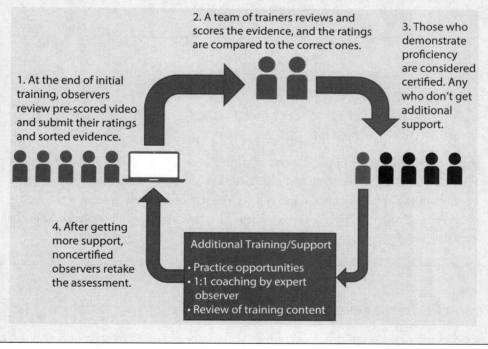

Q **IN FOCUS:**
A RULE OF THUMB FOR RELIABILITY

Whatever approaches you use, take steps to ensure reliability. An assessment isn't reliable just because different reviewers give the same score to the same response, or because it uses selected-response items that are easy to score with consistency.

A reliable assessment gives a reliable indication of an observer's performance. An observer should perform similarly on similar items that measure the same thing. For example, an observer who rates with sufficient accuracy on one video should do similarly on another video that assesses the same skills. If not, the results from one or both are not a good indication of the observer's ability to rate.

As a rule, include at least two items—preferably more—for each skill and aspect of observation knowledge that you measure. If rating a teacher's checks for understanding is part of your assessment, include at least two similar items that assess it. A single attempt to do something is not a reliable measure of someone's ability to do it.

 SNAPSHOT:
ENSURING RELIABILITY IN DISTRICT OF COLUMBIA PUBLIC SCHOOLS

After completing their initial observer training, evaluators in District of Columbia Public Schools (DCPS) review and rate at least two videos on all nine teaching components in the system's observation rubric. The use of multiple videos in the DCPS observer assessment increases the confidence that the results can reliably indicate an evaluator's ability to apply the rubric as intended.

Setting Performance Standards

How good is good enough? How well should your observers perform on your assessment to be considered ready to carry out observations in the classroom? If ever there was a thorny question about assessment, this is it. Where you set the bar will determine which observers pass and which do not. Sooner or later some of your principals or instructional leaders will find they didn't make the cut. Just knowing there's a bar will be a source of some stress. Wouldn't it be easier to not set a performance standard?

It would be easier. It would also undermine your objectives. By setting a performance standard, you ensure that those who carry out observations are equipped to accurately assess teaching and to provide meaningful feedback. Without such a standard, some observers—likely many—will produce inaccurate information on teaching and give feedback that's ineffective, or even counterproductive. That doesn't advance your aim of improving teaching and student learning. Nor does it build trust.

A big part of why we resist performance standards is that we see them *only* as cut-off scores. We think, "They might not pass!" Instead, we should ask ourselves, "How can we help them meet a standard that's going to advance our goals?" Responsibility for meeting a standard shouldn't rest primarily with your observers. Those who train, support, and manage your observers need to take ownership of the results of their own efforts. If your observers aren't meeting your standards, then your training and support need to change. That's how systemic improvement happens.

So back to the question: "How good is good enough?" There's no single answer. Different skills and knowledge call for different definitions of proficiency. What it means to rate a lesson with sufficient accuracy is described differently than what it means to have sufficient knowledge of relevant evidence. We explain ways to articulate performance standards for different measures in the pages that follow. But we can't say what that standard should be for every variation of every measure.

What we can offer is a guiding principle: set your standards based on what's going to advance your goals for teaching and learning. That's different from what you think your observers can do, or what you think will avoid negative consequences for teachers and school leaders. If your goal is better teaching and learning, then you need a set of standards that ensures observers are able to provide useful information and meaningful feedback for changing teacher practice.

To see this principle at work, think about your standards for rating accurately. One approach, used in some school systems, is to require observers to demonstrate they can correctly determine an overall rating for a lesson. An observer gives a set of ratings for each teaching component in a rubric, and if these ratings average to a score close to the lesson's actual average, that's considered accurate. This standard for rating seeks to minimize the chance of mischaracterizing the quality of a teacher's lesson.

But this standard doesn't do much for improving practice. Look at the example in Figure 18.4 of an observer's results from rating an assessment video. The observer's average rating for the lesson is about the same as the average of the correct set of ratings. If that were the only standard for accuracy, this observer would pass. He or she accurately characterized the lesson as a whole; the overall result for the lesson as a whole will not unfairly affect a teacher's summative evaluation.

FIGURE 18.4   Being Accurate on Average Isn't Enough

Rubric Component	Observer's rating	Correct rating
Creating an environment of respect and rapport	3	3
Establishing a culture of learning	2	3
Managing classroom procedures	1	3
Managing student behavior	2	4
Communicating with students	4	2
Using questioning and discussion techniques	3	2
Engaging students in learning	3	3
Using assessment in instruction	3	2
Average rating across all components	**2.625**	**2.750**

Lowest ratings given by observer

Lowest actual ratings for the lesson

Only 2 matches

Average scores about the same

Note: For simplicity, this example shows only an observer's attempt to rate each rubric component once. One attempt at rating is not a reliable indication of an observer's ability, nor does it speak to an observer's other skills (e.g., evidence collection). For assessment, multiple attempts at multiple skills are needed.

> *If your goal is better teaching and learning, then you need a set of standards that ensures observers are able to provide useful information and meaningful feedback for changing teacher practice.*

And yet this observer was off the mark for most of the rubric components. In fact, he or she saw weakness in teaching components where there were really strengths, and strengths where there were really weaknesses. This lesson was strongest in areas related to the classroom management, and left room for improvement when it came to assessing student understanding and pushing it to higher levels. But the observer saw the opposite. The resulting feedback will be counterproductive, and will provide inaccurate data for system leaders on the needs of teachers.

Clearly, a standard for accuracy that supports positive change must go beyond accuracy on average. It needs to set expectations for accuracy in rating the individual components of teaching. We will discuss this later in the chapter. The more important point is that when you consider performance standards you should start by asking what will advance your goal of improving teaching and student learning. To help improve teaching, observers must be able to identify, correctly, specific opportunities for improvement.

 TIP

Setting standards for exceptional performance—and not just for minimally proficient—can help you identify highly skilled observers who might serve as observer trainers or coaches.

IN FOCUS:
USING MULTIPLE PERFORMANCE STANDARDS

Deciding "How good is good enough?" also raises the question of how to account for different competencies. Should you expect proficiency on multiple skills, or combine results into a single number so that excelling in one compensates for low performance in others?

Do what advances your objectives. What are the competencies that observers need so they can help improve teaching and learning? Are there any for which lack of ability could be offset by exceptional ability elsewhere, so they're still able to provide trustworthy information and meaningful feedback?

For example, would it help improve teaching to have observers who can rate very accurately, but cannot use evidence to justify their ratings? Or conversely, observers who are great at collecting and organizing evidence, but consistently get the ratings wrong?

Given the goal of positive change in teachers' practice, an observer assessment should include multiple performance standards. You need to say how good is good enough for evidence collection and sorting, rating, and feedback skills.

SNAPSHOT:
PARTNERSHIPS TO UPLIFT COMMUNITIES' USE
OF MULTIPLE PERFORMANCE STANDARDS

The Partnerships to Uplift Communities (PUC) Charter Schools requires that observers meet multiple performance standards. At the end of their initial training, and at least once each subsequent year, they review pre-scored video as part of a certification process. To be considered fully certified, observers need to meet performance standards in each of three areas: evidence collection, evidence "alignment" or sorting, and rating accuracy. When observers don't initially meet one or more of the standards, PUC uses that information to provide the follow-up training needed to help them become fully certified.

Skill	Performance Standard
Evidence Collection	Three or four facts recorded for most indicators. Evidence is free of inference or bias.
Evidence Alignment	Evidence is sorted to the right indicators.
Rating Accuracy	At least 70 percent matches with correct ratings *and* average rating varies by no more than 0.225 from correct average.

TIP

Give observers only their results, not the correct answers. During training and practice they should get the chance to know what the ratings should have been, or how they should have responded. But doing so with assessment compromises the integrity of the measure—at least if the same form of the assessment will be used with other observers.

Measuring Observer Knowledge and Skills

The activities that you can use to measure observation proficiency are largely the same as those used for training. How you have trainees practice, and how you check their understanding, is also how you can assess their knowledge and skills. Various approaches to practice and checks for understanding are described in detail throughout Part III, "Building the Knowledge and Skills for Observation." Here we briefly recap some of those activities and explain how to use them in assessment.

The specific approaches you choose to use will depend on the capacities and considerations previously discussed. But one nonnegotiable requirement is the use of pre-scored video. To make claims about someone's ability to do something correctly, you need to know with confidence what is the correct way to do it. If you're going to assess the extent to which an observer collected, sorted, and interpreted evidence correctly, you need to compare that person's work with work you know to be correct. You can do that successfully only by using pre-scored video.

Measuring Evidence Collection and Sorting

A direct measure of someone's ability to collect and sort evidence would mimic what an observer does during and after an observation. The task would have them review and take notes on a lesson video and then organize their notes according to the rubric's components (see Figure 18.5). Scoring their work would involve comparing their sorted evidence to the sorted evidence produced by the expert observers who pre-scored the video. (For more on how to pre-score video, see Part II, "Pre-Scoring Video.")

Scoring evidence is tricky, however. It's not just a matter of determining the degree to which an observer identified the same evidence, and assigned it to the same rubric components, as did those who pre-scored the video. Constructed-response scoring isn't so precise. When scoring a student's written response in a standardized test, you're not just looking for one or even a handful of possible right answers. You're looking for a response that meets certain criteria.

FIGURE 18.5   Measuring Evidence Collection and Sorting with Pre-Scored Video

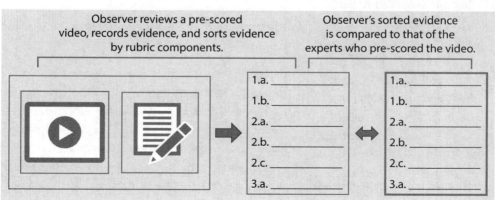

A set of criteria that supports the goal of changing teacher practice will include multiple dimensions. Meaningful feedback depends on evidence that's clear, relevant, and sufficient. It doesn't help teachers when observers give vague generalizations, off-topic advice, and poorly supported assessments of their teaching practice. Criteria that include multiple dimensions also help you target your follow-up training and support for observers who don't initially meet your standards for performance.

But how clear, how relevant, and how sufficient should evidence be? Again, consider what's going to advance your goals for teaching and learning. It doesn't help a teacher if an observer fails to provide any evidence for a rubric component when a lesson actually included multiple relevant teaching behaviors and actions that the observer could have used as evidence. But if the observer gives some relevant evidence for a component when some existed—even if there was more evidence in the lesson—it might very well support meaningful feedback that enables improvements in practice.

Whatever standards for proficiency you establish, your assessment system should tell you more than just who meets it and who doesn't. You also need to know who meaningfully exceeded the standard and, for the underperformers, how much they missed the mark. This lets you do a much better job determining who needs additional support, as well as how much and what type, to clear the performance bar that has been set. Your assessment system should also identify exceptional performers whose practice may warrant a closer look for possible ways to elevate the practice of others.

This calls for a rubric that describes different levels of observer performance, much as an observation rubric does. You need to clarify, for example, what it means for an observer's evidence to be proficient, somewhat below proficient, far below proficient, or significantly above proficient. Scoring is then accomplished by reviewing an observer's evidence in light of this criteria and the sorted evidence of the expert observers who took part in the pre-scoring process.

> *Meaningful feedback depends on evidence that's clear, relevant, and sufficient. It doesn't help teachers when observers give vague generalizations, off-topic advice, and poorly supported assessments of their teaching practice.*

Before making claims about observers' use of evidence, make sure all reviewers can apply your criteria as intended. Just handing them a rubric and saying "Go score" will likely result in inaccurate information about observers' proficiencies and bad decisions about who's ready to carry out observations in the classroom. As a test, give different reviewers the same evidence and see how they score it. You should address any differences in interpretation that are revealed with discussion and additional practice.

> ### TOOL:
> ### MPS RUBRIC FOR RATING USE OF EVIDENCE
>
> In Minneapolis Public Schools an observer's use of evidence is evaluated against a rubric that describes four levels of performance for three aspects of the skill: objectivity, sorting (or "alignment," as it is called in MPS), and sufficiency (the extent to which an observer captured relevant evidence that was present in the lesson). For example, objectivity is rated on a scale of 1 to 4 based in part on whether an observer's submitted evidence included frequent, occasional, very few, or no statements of opinion. District leaders based their evidence rubric on one developed by Teaching Learning Solutions. See the Appendix, page 337, for the complete rubric.

Of course, you can also assess the use of evidence in more straightforward (if less direct) ways. Selected-response items can be crafted to suggest whether observers understand what is and isn't relevant evidence and what constitutes sufficient evidence (see Figure 18.6). This might entail true/false or multiple-choice questions. The questions might use short statements or longer passages (e.g., "Given this description of part of a lesson, which of the following is evidence of use of questioning?").

The challenge with proxy measures is making sure they really do indicate what you want to know. Are observers who answer correctly actually better at the skill you care about than observers who answer incorrectly? To test your proxies, you should collect data from more

FIGURE 18.6   Selected-Response Items for Measuring Use of Evidence

Indicate which statements are evidence and which are opinion		
E	O	
		Students were minimally engaged
		Teacher: "What do you think 'republic' means?"
		Students understood the directions
		Lesson pacing was appropriate
		4 of 10 students raised hands
		Teacher: "When a car accelerates, its speed changes."

Indicate which is evidence for Checks for Student Understanding (CFU) and which is for Questioning and Discussion Techniques (QDT)		
CFU	QDT	
		Teacher: "Who's heard of the word 'propaganda'? What do you think it means?"
		Teacher: "How many people died in the Boston Massacre?"
		Teacher: "So why do you think they called it a massacre?"

direct measures and compare them. Do observers who sort evidence correctly also do well on multiple-choice items meant to test their sorting ability? Do those who sort poorly do worse on such items? If not, the items need rethinking and revision.

Measuring Interpretation Skills

Remember that observers must interpret their sorted evidence before they can assign a set of ratings. This involves judgments as to how the rating criteria apply to the lesson observed. To rate a lesson on the teaching component "checks for understanding," an observer might need to judge how many moments there were in a lesson when such a check should have occurred, and then judge whether the teacher did so at all, most, a few, or none of those moments.

A direct method you can use for measuring interpretation skills is to have observers cite the appropriate rubric language when they submit their sorted evidence. Along with noting that "these were the moments" and "these were the checks," the observer also notes that the rubric says that checking at most key moments indicates a rating of *effective*. This mimics exactly what observers should do in practice—going back to the rubric language before determining what a rating should be.

Scoring observers' interpretations raises some of the same issues as scoring evidence. If the observers' task is to cite the appropriate rubric language, you need a set of criteria for determining the extent to which they do so. Each rubric component includes multiple indicators (e.g., checking for understanding at key moments, and doing so with a range of students). All of your reviewers should know how to correctly score an observer who gets some of the language right, but not all of it.

You might also use proxy measures, so long as they capture sufficient evidence to support the claims you want to make about observers' interpretation skills. You might pose different scenarios and then ask which ratings they reflect. Or you could ask which of several statements must be true to warrant a particular rating (see Figure 18.7).

Whatever method you use, you will find that measuring interpretation skills provides a window on how your observers are thinking. There are multiple reasons why an observer might give the wrong rating, even after collecting and sorting strong evidence. Resolving confusion is easier when you have evidence to suggest the source.

Measuring Accuracy in Rating

Measuring an observer's ability to rate accurately is in many ways straightforward. The number of possible answers is limited to the number of possible ratings. Comparing the ratings that observers produce to the ratings that were determined through the pre-scoring process

FIGURE 18.7   Selected-Response Items to Assess Interpretation Skills

What should be the rating for "checks for understanding," given the following?	Which of the following would be indicators of "effective" use of questioning?
• The teacher checked for understanding with a range of students at most of the moments when doing so would be important; and • The teacher always did so in a way that provided accurate information with which to inform instruction going forward. a) Ineffective b) Minimally Effective c) Effective d) Highly Effective	a) The teacher asked a mix of open-ended and non-open-ended questions. b) The questions asked students to explain their thinking. c) Students posed their own higher-order questions. d) The teacher sometimes used appropriate wait time.

can be done automatically. Consistent scoring doesn't require norming a group of reviewers on how to apply a common set of criteria. By its nature, rating calls for a selected-response approach.

But measuring accuracy does present you with two major challenges: (1) you need to set a standard for sufficient accuracy; (2) you need to make sure your assessment of accuracy is accurate. As we explained earlier in this chapter, the ability to rate lessons accurately on average is not enough. Observers must be able to distinguish effective from ineffective practice for specific aspects of teaching. But how accurate must they be at that level, and how can you know if they really are?

To consider those questions, think of a target with a bull's-eye in the middle, surrounded by three concentric circles (see Figure 18.8). Obviously, someone who hits the bull's-eye every time is accurate. But what about someone who hits the bull's-eye most of the time and isn't far off when she misses it? An observer who gets the correct rating most of the time and otherwise gets a rating that's close to correct still might be able to identify where a lesson was strongest and where it was weakest, based on your rubric.

In assessment lingo there are three "agreement statistics" for describing sufficient accuracy. One is the number or percent of *exact* matches with the correct rating. The second is the number or percent of ratings given that are *adjacent* to—that is, one higher or one lower than—the correct rating. The last is called "discrepant," and generally refers to the number or percent of ratings that were more than one point off from the correct rating (e.g., the observer

FIGURE 18.8   Measures of Agreement

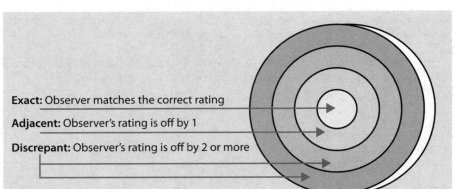

Exact: Observer matches the correct rating

Adjacent: Observer's rating is off by 1

Discrepant: Observer's rating is off by 2 or more

gave a rating of 4 for the teaching component "use of questioning" when it really warranted a rating of 2).

There are good reasons to include all three statistics—exact, adjacent, and discrepant—in your standard for accuracy. It might seem acceptable for observers to get just the adjacent score most of the time, but that means an observer could fail to get any ratings correct and still be considered "accurate enough." If that's not acceptable, you need to specify a standard for exact matches. You may also need a limit on the acceptable number of discrepant scores so that observers can't be way off in their rating of multiple rubric components.

But where you set each threshold depends in large part on the structure of your observation rubric. What it means for someone to get the exact rating, an adjacent rating, or a discrepant one is different when there are four possible ratings from when there are seven. When the target has seven concentric circles, an arrow that hits adjacent to the bull's-eye is closer to it than when there are four. With seven circles (in a target of the same size) the bull's-eye is also smaller, and so harder to hit.

Another factor is the number of teaching components in a rubric. A stipulation that no more than three ratings are discrepant implies something different when applied to a nine-component rubric than when applied to one with twelve components. In the latter case, three ratings represent 25 percent of what an observer needs to evaluate in a lesson; in the former, it's one-third. Being way off on one-third of all aspects of teaching might not be acceptable if your goal is to improve teaching and learning.

> *To set a standard for accuracy the first time, a good approach you might use is to see how others have defined accuracy for similarly structured rubrics, and then consider the implications of those definitions. Ask: what does this ensure, and what would it allow?*

To set a standard for accuracy the first time, a good approach you might use is to see how others have defined accuracy for similarly structured rubrics, and then consider the implications of those definitions. Ask: what does this ensure, and what would it allow? Would it ensure that observers can correctly identify a teacher's strengths and weaknesses? Would it allow observers to provide many ratings that are off the mark, or even way off the mark? How you answer may lead you to define things somewhat differently.

 TIPS FOR ASSESSING WITH PRE-SCORED VIDEO

- Videos for assessment should include enough material so the assessment activity resembles what an observer does in the classroom. Although videos may be edited, they should be long enough (usually around 20 minutes) to include evidence from the lesson for rating most, if not all, rubric components.

- Remember that retakes require more assessment videos. You shouldn't reassess an observer with the same video they rated the first time. The same goes for all assessment (including written material)—but given all that's involved in pre-scoring video, it's especially important to plan ahead to produce enough videos for initial assessments and for retakes.

- Make sure to include videos from the range of contexts in which observers will find themselves. Don't assess someone only with videos of English language arts instruction if they'll also be observing math lessons.

- Some videos may need to be augmented to provide sufficient evidence. For example, observers may need lesson plans, or copies of student work, to make certain judgments.

- Some observers simply aren't comfortable rating video. Always begin assessing with video, but before making a claim that someone can't rate accurately in a live observation, you should have them observe in a classroom alongside an expert observer, to see if they perform much differently.

SNAPSHOT:
STANDARDS FOR ACCURACY IN THE MET PROJECT

For its major study of classroom observations, the MET project trained and certified some 900 raters so they could review and score thousands of lesson videos using
different observation instruments. ETS and Teachscape developed the online system
used to build and assess the raters' understanding of how to apply each rubric to
the video. To be included in the pool that produced ratings for the study, raters had
to meet specific performance standards. These standards varied depending on the
instrument's structure. Figure 18.9 shows the standard that the MET project used for
one instrument.

FIGURE 18.9   A Standard for Accuracy in the MET Project

Observation Instrument: MET version of Framework for Teaching	
Number of rubric components	8
Number of possible ratings/ performance levels	4
MET standard for accuracy for this instrument	At least 50% exact; No more than 25% discrepant
Percent of trained raters who met the standard after two tries*	83%

*This speaks to only MET raters' accuracy—not their abilities to collect evidence or
provide feedback, which were not measured in the study.

Over time, your own data should suggest if your standards need to be changed. Are
observers who meet your standard for accuracy producing ratings from the classroom that
seem credible? Or are they, for example, giving the highest ratings for rubric components
that represent the most challenging aspects of teaching? Are untrained observers just as
likely to meet your standard as those you train? Such inquiry may prompt you to revisit how
you define proficiency.

An approach that's not recommended is to make it easier for observers to meet a standard
simply because you want more of your observers to meet it, or because it's making them
stressed. The right response in those cases is to make the changes needed in your training

and support—and communication—so that you and your observers feel confident that they can demonstrate a level of proficiency that supports better teaching and student learning. You can't elevate practice by lowering expectations.

> *Keep in mind your own obligation for accuracy in measuring the accuracy of your observers. To make a claim about someone's ability to rate correctly you need to know your measure is a reliable indicator.*

Keep in mind your own obligation for accuracy in measuring the accuracy of your observers. To make a claim about someone's ability to rate correctly you need to know your measure is a reliable indicator. Whether or not an observer gets the correct rating for "checks for understanding" in one lesson is not a reliable indicator of the observer's ability to correctly rate that component when observing other lessons. Recall the earlier rule of thumb, on page 244, about assessing each skill with at least two similar items.

Measuring Feedback Skills

In Chapter 15, "Coaching Teachers," we explained why feedback skills must be explicitly taught. Few instructional leaders have had the opportunity to practice applying a consistent set of ideas about what effective feedback looks like. Whether or not observers develop the skills to provide effective feedback should not be left to chance. If it is, teachers' experiences with observation most likely will be highly uneven. Some teachers will get great value from observations, but many will not.

In the same vein, don't leave to chance whether or not your feedback training was successful. Just because observers can justify a set of sufficiently accurate ratings doesn't mean you've built a shared vision of effective feedback. Some may still think teacher feedback is telling the teacher: "Here's why you got these ratings." You need to assess observers on their ability to use evidence and ratings as a starting point for an effective conversation with the teacher about ways to improve instructional practice.

An effective post-observation conference with a teacher meets several criteria. It prioritizes just one or two areas for improvement, and it provides specific techniques for addressing them. Observers should also deliver feedback in a way that encourages teachers to analyze their own instruction. These criteria, and how to help observers develop an understanding of them, are described in detail in Chapter 15. Your assessment should measure the extent to which observers can provide feedback to teachers that meets the criteria.

Your assessment of observers' conferencing skills will most likely involve some direct measures. It's very difficult to assess interpersonal skills without observing someone interacting with someone else. This might entail having observers prepare and deliver feedback to a teacher after a live observation, or having them review a lesson on video and then take part in a role-play. This lets you see, for example, if observers are promoting reflection, or if they're quickly answering their own questions.

Before choosing lessons or developing scenarios for role-plays, you should consider what kinds of situations make the most sense to include in your assessment. What are observers likely to encounter? Will they encounter teachers who are highly skilled, teachers who are defensive, or teachers who aren't reflective (i.e., they struggle with reflective prompts.)? You can't make a claim about an observer's ability to adjust feedback to teachers' dispositions with evidence that is based on teachers' responding to just one situation.

These role-plays can be supplemented with a review of written feedback. Written feedback doesn't capture interpersonal skills, but it can be used to judge an observer's ability to prioritize areas of focus and to suggest specific actions that a teacher might take. It's also logistically easier to evaluate written feedback because the evaluators don't need to be physically present when the observer is preparing it; this also makes it easier for multiple evaluators to review the same feedback.

Scoring feedback is in some ways trickier than scoring evidence. There's no way to say what the feedback should be in any one situation. Two observers may prioritize different areas of focus after reviewing the same lesson, and each may nonetheless support positive change in the teacher's practice. What matters is that an area of focus is narrow, addresses an opportunity for improvement clearly evidenced in the lesson, and takes into account the teacher's skill level and stage of development.

You can help reviewers of written feedback by giving them examples prepared by expert observers. Those who pre-score video may also prepare examples of possible feedback based on videos that you then use to assess newly trained observers on their feedback skills.

> *Although assessing feedback presents special challenges, it's nevertheless essential. An observer assessment that stops short of feedback skills fails to ensure a critical step in the improvement process.*

But these would just represent some examples of what might constitute quality feedback. You'll know your reviewers can apply your criteria for quality feedback consistently when different reviewers produce similar scores for the same feedback.

Although assessing feedback presents special challenges, it's nevertheless essential. An observer assessment that stops short of feedback skills fails to ensure a critical step in the improvement process. It's a waste to invest all the effort needed to develop observers' abilities to identify effective teaching if they can't also help teachers employ more of it in their instruction.

TOOL:
CRITERIA FOR ASSESSING FEEDBACK

Reviewers in DCPS use a rubric to evaluate examples of written feedback provided by trained observers. The rubric includes three criteria: use of evidence; clarity and professionalism; and suggestions for improvement. Figure 18.10 shows the indicators of different performance levels for an observer's suggestions.

The full DCPS rubric for written feedback, along with an annotated feedback example, may be found in the Appendix, page 331. DCPS uses a different rubric to assess peer evaluators on their post-observation conferences. Also in the Appendix are two checklists for reviewing feedback: The Post-Observation Assessment Checklist used in Hillsborough County (Florida) Public Schools (see page 328); and the RIDE Feedback Quality Review Tool created by the Rhode Island Department of Education (see page 327).

FIGURE 18.10   Excerpt from DCPS Rubric for Rating Written Feedback

1	2	3	4
There are no suggestions in the written feedback.	The feedback includes only suggestions that are either not meaningful, unclear, simply copied language from the rubric, or not actionable.	The feedback contains at least 1 suggestion across all rubric components that is meaningful, clear, and "bite-sized."	The feedback contains 2 or 3 suggestions across all rubric components that are meaningful, clear, and bite-sized.

Planning for When Observers Miss the Mark

When planning a lesson, teachers ask themselves three questions: What do I want students to learn, how will I know when they've learned it, and what will I do when they don't? The same should be asked when planning how to build the knowledge and skills of your observers. Some observers—perhaps many—will not demonstrate proficiency when first assessed. Without a plan in place for what to do when that happens, you may very well find yourself without good options.

The first thing you should do when observers do not meet the determined standard is to figure out why. Maybe they are confused about what kinds of evidence are relevant to different but related rubric components. Or they might be unclear about the conditions that call for one rating versus another. The lines of inquiry that may reveal the source of an error are described in the previous chapter, where we explain how to analyze observers' attempts to practice rating and use evidence as part of their training. (See the "Peeling the Onion" section in Chapter 17, "Collecting and Using Data from Training," page 228.)

Remember, the problem could be with the observer, the training, or the assessment. If lots of observers make the same mistakes, then the problem is likely among the latter two. Perhaps your training didn't do a good job clarifying the difference between descriptive evidence and generalizations. Or maybe it didn't help observers understand what constitutes a feedback suggestion that's specific and actionable. Alternatively, the video used in the assessment may have lacked clear evidence of some components, causing observers to make big inferences about performance.

> *The first thing you should do when observers do not meet the determined standard is to figure out why.*

When deficiencies are limited to a few individuals, your response should be targeted support for those individuals (see Figure 18.11). This support might include additional opportunities for practice, going back through the relevant training materials, or one-to-one coaching by an expert observer. Plan ahead to make sure such resources are available for those who need them. Also, make sure there's sufficient time for observers to take advantage of the support, and to retake your

FIGURE 18.11   Options When Observers at First Don't Meet Standards

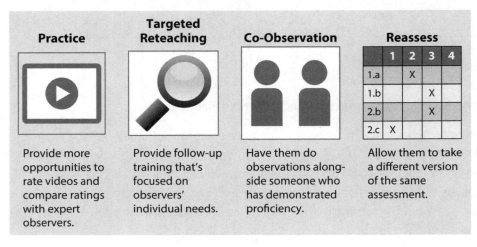

Practice	Targeted Reteaching	Co-Observation	Reassess
Provide more opportunities to rate videos and compare ratings with expert observers.	Provide follow-up training that's focused on observers' individual needs.	Have them do observations alongside someone who has demonstrated proficiency.	Allow them to take a different version of the same assessment.

For the Reassess column:

	1	2	3	4
1.a		X		
1.b			X	
2.b			X	
2.c	X			

assessment, before they need to start carrying out observations in the classroom. You might train and assess in the early summer, allowing mid-summer for reteaching and reassessment before the next school year begins.

Of course, at some point, for some individuals, you'll face a difficult question: Should someone who continues to fall short of your performance standards—even after extensive initial training, additional support, and retakes—be carrying out observations as part of teachers' formal evaluations? Ultimately, that's a policy question, and your school system's response must take into account the rules that govern the job responsibilities of your school administrators and other instructional leaders.

Whatever your decision, it should be made with the right people at the table, and with an understanding of the implications. Your teachers, administrators, and students all have a stake, and all their interests should be considered. What happens when someone provides an inaccurate assessment of a lesson? If the ratings are accurate "on average," the lesson won't unfairly affect the teacher's overall evaluations, especially if other measures are factored in, including observations by other, more accurate observers.

The real consequences are bad feedback, bad information on the state of teaching, and the eventual erosion of trust as teachers get conflicting messages. It doesn't advance the goal of better teaching and student learning when observers produce inaccurate judgments of practice and give poorly delivered feedback. It's arguably not even fair to administrators to be told they needn't meet a meaningful standard for a key part of their jobs; doing so takes the system off the hook for helping them succeed.

 TIP

When training is new, you will likely need to reteach the whole group of observers some skills to get them over the performance bar. Schedule, and allocate resources, accordingly.

Where to Start and How to Build

Start small, and humbly. It is critical to avoid making any claims about observers' proficiency levels before your training and assessments are proven. You need to know that those who complete your training have a reasonable chance of passing, and that passing is a reliable indication of their ability to carry out observations with sufficient quality. Holding people to an untested standard of performance doesn't make sense—and may very likely prompt a backlash.

As part of their development, assessment items and activities should be tested to see how they perform. Do trained or expert observers do better on them than novice or untrained ones? Do observers who do well on one item or activity also do well on items or activities that measure the same skills or closely related ones? Do individual observers perform similarly when they take different versions of the same assessment? If the answer is "no," then this may call for revisions, and further testing.

Once you settle upon a set of items, you should conduct a pilot with just a few observers, followed by similar types of analyses. Only once you have confidence in your observer assessment and in your training should you trust your ability to identify who is ready, and who's not, to carry out observations that meet your expectations for quality. But you should continue to test your claims using other measures, including information on observations in classrooms (which we discuss in Chapter 19, "Monitoring Your Observation System").

> *Your principals and other observers need to appreciate assessment as a means to equip them with the knowledge and skills needed to support improvements in teacher practice. They can't just see a performance bar they must surmount.*

Stakeholder understanding is especially important when it comes to implementing observer assessments. Your principals and other observers need to appreciate assessment as a means to equip them with the knowledge and skills needed to support improvements in teacher practice. They can't just see a performance bar they must surmount. You need to involve them in your assessment planning. Show them, early and often, all that you're committed to do to help them succeed.

Lastly, keep in mind that if you assess observers only after their initial training, then your evidence about what they know and are able to do is based on just one moment in time. In reality, how someone applies a set of criteria will drift over time from how the criteria were meant to be applied. The only way to check for this drift and counter it is to periodically (at least annually) reassess observers. We explain how in the next chapter.

 **TECHNIQUES:
ASSESSING THE KNOWLEDGE AND SKILLS FOR OBSERVATION**

To Lay the Foundation:

- Convene stakeholder representatives to forge a shared understanding of the important role observer assessment plays in improving observer training, in improving observers' knowledge and skills, and in improving teaching and student learning.

■ With such a group, reach agreement on what observers need to know and be able to do to carry out quality observations (e.g., evidence collection and sorting, interpretation and rating, and coaching teachers to change their practice). Use Figure 18.2, "Identifying Assessment Needs," on page 239 to ground the discussion.

■ Identify your system's constraints regarding how you might administer and score an observer assessment. (See the table "Comparing Assessment Approaches" in this chapter, on page 240.) Consider the implications of these constraints for the type of assessment you use (with direct or proxy methods, or both), and what capacities you may need to address to implement your preferred method.

■ Examine how other school systems with similar objectives, constraints, and observation instruments have assessed their observers. What activities are included, how are they scored, and how do they ensure reliability? Include at least two items to measure each skill in your assessment.

■ Plan to pilot any assessment to see how it performs with a small number of observers before administering it at a wider scale. Define proficiency standards that advance the goals of better teaching and student learning, but don't use them as an absolute cutoff before you have confidence in your training's effectiveness and in your assessment's ability to indicate who is ready and who is not.

■ Plan ways to help observers meet your standards when at first they don't. Assume that many will need additional time, training, and practice after their first attempt at an assessment. Let observers know from the outset that you'll make every effort to help them meet the standards.

To Build and Improve:

■ Consider if there are additional skills and aspects of observation knowledge that your assessment needs to include to ensure that observers are equipped to support improvements in teaching and learning. Involve stakeholders in decisions about changes, and make sure to pilot and collect data on any new assessment elements before holding observers to an absolute cutoff.

■ Review assessment results for signs that assessment activities may need revision, or that assessment materials may need replacing. Are observers performing very differently on items that measure the same thing? Are lots of observers unable to determine certain correct ratings when reviewing particular videos?

(TECHNIQUES Continued)

- Also review assessment results for indications of where you need to do a better job in your training. Are there certain skills they struggle to develop without additional support?

- To ensure the integrity of results, establish an ongoing process for refreshing your supply of assessment items and materials. Using the same version of the same assessment over time opens the door to observers sharing what's included, intentionally or not.

- Examine information on observations carried out in the classroom for signs that observers who meet your performance standards are able to carry out quality observations. This may include the distribution of the ratings they produce (do they seem inflated or inconsistent?), information from co-observations with expert observers, and teacher surveys.

- Communicate to all stakeholders any improvements in observers' general performance on the assessment, and point out how assessment results are supporting improvements in observer training and in the quality of observations.

💡 Putting It into Practice

To Lay the Foundation:

What steps can you take to begin the conversation in your system about the need for observer assessment, and how to approach it?

To Build and Improve:

What gaps do you see in your assessment of observers, and what steps could you take to address them?

⬇ This item can be downloaded from www.wiley.com/go/betterfeedback

CHAPTER 19

Monitoring Your Observation System

ESSENTIAL QUESTION

How Will You Ensure That Teachers Are Getting Fair and Helpful Observations?

No matter how authentic you try to make your observation training and assessment, they can never fully replicate the experience of actual observation. Unlike in actual observations, observers generally aren't familiar with the teachers they are observing during their training and their assessment. While they are being trained, observers also needn't contend with numerous other demands for their time as they do in real life. For these reasons, observers may perform differently in the field than they did during their training and assessment.

Moreover, how observers perform at one point in time is not a good indicator of how they will perform over the long run. Gradually, and unconsciously, an observer may start assigning higher or lower ratings to teacher practice than is warranted. This "drift," as it's called, is a natural tendency. Over time, how someone performs any task will deviate from expectations, but without any ongoing comparison with expected norms, the person won't recognize this deviation.

> *The only way for you to know what's actually happening in the field is to check—and check repeatedly.*

The only way for you to know what's actually happening in the field is to check—and check repeatedly. When you monitor the work of your observers over time, you can take steps to counter drift and to provide the guidance and support observers need to ensure that teacher observations are taking place as intended (see Figure 19.1). Without monitoring, you won't know if some observers' ratings are influenced by their past experiences with the teacher—including past observations of the teacher—or if they're rushing through their observations—and cutting corners—to meet deadlines at the last minute. Nor can you do anything to correct the situation.

In the last two chapters, we explained how you can collect and use information from training and assessment to support and improve the quality of your observation system. In this chapter, we describe how you can gather and use information on your observers' work after they've initially demonstrated sufficient mastery. Many of the tools and activities you will use for monitoring your observers are similar to those used for assessment and for checking

FIGURE 19.1   Monitoring Questions

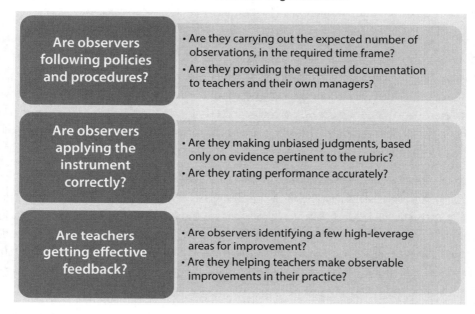

observers' understanding during training. Like assessment and checking for understanding, monitoring is a matter of capturing the right information, looking for patterns, and asking what might be going on when the data seem off.

Monitoring Policy and Procedures

The first question you should ask is whether observations are even happening. The question is so basic it's easily overlooked. But anyone familiar with the work lives of principals and other instructional leaders knows how easy it is for even important issues to get deprioritized and left undone. Your school leaders face constant interruptions and unpredictable problems that need to be solved. Scheduling and protecting the time for observations is a major challenge. Further, if no one's checking whether observations are taking place, then that sends a message that your system leaders don't see teacher observations as especially valuable.

Of course, another big reason why policy and procedures aren't followed is that they're not understood. You need to clarify, with written guidelines, what your observers are supposed to do, how they are to do it, and when they are to do it. Set clear windows for when each observation cycle should take place (e.g., teachers should get their first observation of the school year between October 1 and November 7, the second one between February 1 and March 15, etc.). Provide your observers with a timeline of the steps within the cycle (e.g., they should agree with the teacher on a time for observing at least one week ahead; they should schedule post-observation conferences for two to three days afterward; etc.).

You will need to monitor adherence to those expectations with an online system. This can be done simply with free software, like Google Forms or Microsoft Excel. For every teacher who is expected to be observed, observers should enter the key dates (for observations and conferences, etc.) into your online system and submit the same documentation they provide to teachers. Assign someone the task of reviewing this information weekly and flagging those who fall behind. Sometimes all it takes is a friendly reminder—in the form of an e-mail or phone call—for an observer to give the process a higher priority.

Before you start holding observers accountable for schedules, you need to get their managers on board. Your school chiefs, area superintendents, and others who supervise principals and instructional leaders need to communicate the importance of giving observations sufficient attention and of completing them on time. When observers fall behind schedule and must catch up at the end of the year, the process becomes one of compliance rather than professional growth. Rushed observations damage both teacher trust and the quality of the information produced. Enlist those who manage observers to contact stragglers.

If your observers are missing deadlines, ask why. Do they need help managing their time? Do they not understand the procedures, or do they think following these procedures is not important? Such questions may reveal where more support is needed. Some of your observers may need coaching on how to plan and pace themselves—say, by identifying early in the cycle those teachers for whom they'll need a co-observer (e.g., inviting a translator to co-observe a Mandarin class). Your managers may also suggest ways to streamline the process without sacrificing quality; some observers may be over-documenting (e.g., including far more notes from an observation than needed) and a little coaching could help them home in on what is most relevant.

> *When observers fall behind schedule and must catch up at the end of the year, the process becomes one of compliance rather than professional growth.*

Keep in mind, though, that your observers may be legitimately overwhelmed. A full teacher observation may take three of four hours, including pre-work, observing, conferencing, and drafting documentation. Ideally, your system leaders planned ahead of time to ensure that there is a sufficient pool of trained observers available to carry out the required number of teacher observations. (For more on this subject, see Chapter 2, "Finding Enough Observers.") But if many of your observers are struggling, you may need to revisit your assumptions about how many observers are needed and how many observations one person can do within a certain time period. How can you free up more of people's time for observations?

TIPS FOR MONITORING POLICY AND PROCEDURES

- Look for fixes in time management first. Observers often feel overwhelmed because they haven't paced themselves well, leaving many observations to the last minute, or because they're including too much documentation in their written feedback. Provide observers with examples to show that effective feedback can be given without writing an opus.

- Know that observers get significantly more efficient with time and experience. The more they observe, the quicker they become at preparing and delivering targeted and meaningful feedback.

- More complicated observation procedures require more guidance for observers. For example, some school systems differentiate the number of required observations a teacher gets based on his or her past performance (i.e., a teacher with low initial ratings gets observed more than does one with higher ratings). It may be necessary, at least initially, to provide schools with the appropriate observation timing for each teacher as observers get acclimated to such procedures.

Checking for Drift and Bias

Mitigating drift takes pre-scored video. The only way to know if your observers are deviating from the correct interpretation of your rubric is by comparing ratings that they produce to ratings for the same lessons that you know are accurate. Using video that has been pre-scored by multiple expert observers gives you greater confidence that you're judging accuracy against the correct interpretation of a rubric. With live observations it's much harder to say, with consistency, that you know where observers were accurate and where they weren't.

Monitoring with pre-scored video is similar to how you allow for practice during observer training and how you assess for accuracy after the initial observer training. (This process is discussed in detail in the previous two chapters.) Generally, you need to create a rating activity that mirrors what your observers do during and after a classroom observation: reviewing enough of a lesson to collect, sort, and interpret evidence for all rubric components and to determine a rating for each component.

When you monitor for accuracy, you should include both formative and summative elements (see Figure 19.2). For the former, you give observers multiple opportunities during the school

FIGURE 19.2 Getting and Keeping Observers Accurate

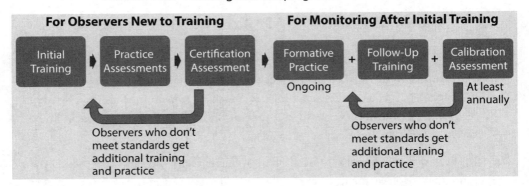

year to rate practice videos and to receive feedback on their ratings. The feedback should include the correct ratings for the video, plus the correct justifications for the ratings. This helps your observers not only to recognize when they're rating a component too high or too low, but also to understand why. Tracking your observers' results on formative activities lets you quickly identify those components for which observers may need additional support to get re-normed.

Summative monitoring for accuracy involves a similar kind of rating activity, but there are stakes attached to the results. This is much the same as when you assess your observers at the end of their initial training to see if they're ready to carry out classroom observations as intended or if they need more preparation. This periodic reassessment is sometimes called "calibration," while the assessment after initial training is for "certification." You use the same performance standard in both to determine who has demonstrated sufficient accuracy. Setting performance standards is explained on pages 244–248 in Chapter 18, "Assessing Observers to Ensure and Improve Quality."

A key difference between formative and summative monitoring is that in the latter you don't tell observers what the correct ratings are. Telling observers the right answers after they've submitted their ratings compromises the integrity of the assessment—at least it does if you will use the video to assess other observers. The purpose of calibration assessment is not to provide feedback to your observers but to gather evidence as to who has maintained an acceptable level of accuracy. You should assess for calibration at least once a year for all your observers, and more often for those observers for whom you see evidence of significant drift.

But don't rely entirely on pre-scored video to do this. Some observers who rate videos correctly may nonetheless veer from the correct interpretation of what they see and hear in their own schools. They may fear conflict with their teachers. Just as likely, without realizing it, they may allow their rating of a lesson to be influenced by their past experiences with the teacher or with the students in the class. Seeing a teacher do something exceptionally well, or poorly, in one observation may color how an observer interprets what happens in subsequent observations. Monitoring with pre-scored video won't catch this.

One way you can monitor for accuracy in live observations is through co-observation. For each observer, you send an expert observer along on a handful of observations at different points during the year. You can draw these experts from among those who pre-scored your videos, those who train observers, or those identified as highly accurate based on your assessments. In a co-observation of a lesson, each observer should independently collect and sort the relevant evidence—and interpret and rate the lesson—before they compare notes.

The other method you can use to monitor live observations is to look for patterns in ratings that your observers produce. Here are some of the patterns that may suggest drift or bias:

■ *An observer consistently gives ratings to teachers that are significantly different from the results from other effectiveness measures used for the same teachers.* Some mismatch is expected; different measures capture different aspects of teaching and learning. But it may be an issue if an observer consistently gives the highest ratings to teachers whose students make the least gains in achievement compared with similar students, or vice versa.

■ *An observer almost always gives one or two adjacent ratings to teachers, on every rubric component* (e.g., 90 percent of all the ratings that an observer gives are 2s or 3s). Sometimes called "non-differentiators," these observers may be playing it safe by giving very similar ratings.

■ *An observer consistently gives different ratings for teachers than other observers give for the same teachers.* This applies to situations in which individual teachers are observed by more than one person.

Some observers who rate videos correctly may nonetheless veer from the correct interpretation of what they see and hear in their own schools.

None of these patterns can tell you for sure that an observer is misapplying your instrument. You need to dig further. This might entail sending an expert observer to someone's school to do co-observations. Reviewing the evidence and other documentation an observer submits also may reveal if he or she is interpreting correctly, or if the observer is assigning a set of ratings that don't match your rubric's descriptions for the performance levels (see Figure 19.3).

FIGURE 19.3   Signs of Possible Inaccuracy in Rating

MISALIGNMENT
The ratings an observer gives differ greatly from other evaluation data for the same teachers.

NONDIFFERENTIATION
An observer almost always gives teachers 1 of 2 adjacent ratings for every rubric component.

INCONSISTENCY
The ratings an observer gives differ from the ratings given to the same teacher by other observers.

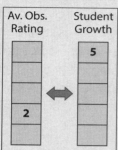

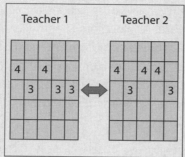

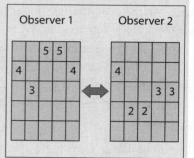

Note: Patterns shown are simplified examples. In actual practice, a teacher's observation results should be based on multiple observations.

🖈 TIPS FOR REASSESSING ACCURACY

- Explain to observers the reason for reassessment. They're more likely to accept the idea if they understand that drift is a natural tendency, and that the purpose is to help them maintain their accuracy.

- Assessment for calibration needn't be as extensive as the assessment after initial training. For example, assessment for initial certification may include items that collect evidence of an observer's knowledge of the instrument's structure. But that knowledge isn't likely to diminish among those who carry out observations on a regular basis. For calibration assessment, you might also require all observers to review and rate just one video, and only require two videos of those who didn't do well on the first attempt; when doing this, make sure observers know well before the assessment that the purpose is to be respectful of their time while still giving more chances to demonstrate proficiency to those who need it.

SNAPSHOT:
TARGETING SUPPORT FOR IMPROVED ACCURACY
IN TENNESSEE

The Tennessee Department of Education compares teachers' achievement gains with their observation scores to identify places where observer accuracy may be a problem. The state looks for schools in which large numbers of teachers have observation ratings that are widely different from their results on the value-added measure that Tennessee uses to estimate teachers' contributions to students' achievement gains. A school is identified if many of its teachers have average observation ratings that are three or more points off from their value-added scores (both are given on a five-point scale).

Identified schools receive an invitation to work with an evaluation coach. Working under contract with the state, these coaches are expert observers with deep knowledge of the observation instrument. Through co-observation and additional training, they make sure the school's observers are able to apply the instrument correctly. Evaluation coaches also work with district-level staff to build their capacity to support quality observation within their system's own schools. In one recent year, roughly 80 schools received such support, and in nearly 90 percent of them the discrepancies were reduced.

IN FOCUS:
IS YOUR INSTRUMENT MEASURING WHAT MATTERS?

Our focus in this book is on making sure observers can apply an observation instrument as intended. But it's also important to make sure your observation instrument is measuring the right things. It doesn't advance your goal of improving student learning when feedback and evaluation are based on criteria that have no relation to student learning. Nor does it build trust among teachers and evaluators.

It's beyond the scope of this book to detail how to develop an observation instrument and test its validity for a particular use. But we can offer a few suggestions. When adopting an existing instrument, ask the developers for results from validation studies that compare teachers' observation ratings with student learning measures. Did the students taught by teachers who rated well tend to make greater gains than did similar students taught by teachers who rated poorly? Whether or not you adopt an existing instrument, you should use the data from your own students and observers to ask the same question.

An example of the relationship to look for is in Figure 19.4, which compares the observation scores of Tennessee teachers to their results on the state's measure of student learning gains, the Tennessee Value-Added Assessment System, or TVAAS. Sharing such visuals with teachers and observers builds credibility for the instrument; they can immediately see its relevance to student learning.

FIGURE 19.4   Average Observation Score by TVAAS Level

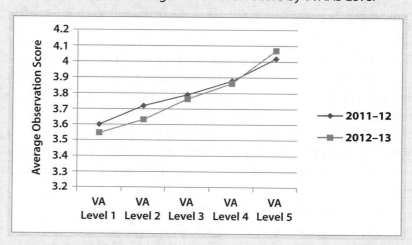

Source: Tennessee Department of Education, Teacher Evaluation in Tennessee: A Report on Year 2 Implementation, 2013.

If you find there's no relationship, a few things could be happening:

■ Your observers might not be applying the instrument correctly, and so your analysis isn't really comparing the student learning gains to the instrument's criteria for effective teaching. You can't evaluate the validity of an observation instrument with observation results that aren't accurate. The assessment and monitoring techniques in this book will suggest if this is so.

■ The observation instrument may in fact emphasize teaching that promotes important aspects of student learning, but those may not be aspects of learning that your student assessment was designed to measure (e.g., your instrument stresses critical thinking, but the student assessment does not). If so, you should look for other measures of student learning with which to make the comparison.

■ The observation instrument may not be a valid measure of the kind of teaching that promotes the student outcomes you care about. If your observers are accurate and your student assessments really do capture what stakeholders consider to be most important, then you may need a different instrument. Choosing or developing a new instrument begins by considering what kinds of teaching will support the student outcomes you seek.

Evaluating an instrument's validity for a particular use is not a one-time activity. The relationship between observation results and student learning gains can weaken over time. This can happen when teachers change their behavior in ways that result in their getting higher observation scores, but without improving the underlying practice in their classrooms. This may call for a different set of indicators, or different observation procedures (e.g., more frequent, or unannounced observations). In addition, you may find that when your student assessment changes, the relationship with teachers' observation results changes as well.

Monitoring Feedback Quality

Of all the steps in the observation process, feedback delivery is the one most likely to get short shrift. Preparing, providing, and following up on feedback takes a good deal more time than the observation itself. Quality feedback is also the part of the observation process that many observers struggle with the most; few school and instructional leaders have experienced effective feedback themselves. If all you track is accuracy and whether observations are taking place, then chances are many teachers will receive feedback that's overly vague and lacking in actionable advice. Moreover, you won't know how to support your observers to provide better feedback.

You should review the written feedback that observers provide to teachers. For each observer, review three or four examples each year, using a common set of criteria to judge quality. To what extent did the observer provide clear and appropriate evidence for strengths and areas for improvement? For the latter, did they give specific suggestions of techniques and resources the teacher could use to make small changes in practice? Consider reviewing feedback after the first observation cycle in the fall so that you have time to provide additional guidance to observers who need it before much of the school year has passed. We discuss the elements of effective feedback in detail in Chapter 15, "Coaching Teachers." Reviewing feedback examples tells you which observers need more help employing these elements.

If all you track is accuracy and whether observations are taking place, then chances are many teachers will receive feedback that's overly vague and lacking in actionable advice.

Teacher surveys are another important tool you can use to monitor feedback. When you ask teachers if they're getting useful information from observations, it signals to them that quality feedback—and not just evaluation—is your primary objective. Base the questions you ask on the same criteria that you use to audit written feedback. Give respondents the chance to explain their answers, and consider using focus groups to probe survey results more deeply. Make sure also to share results with your observers and teachers so they can see which aspects of feedback need the most attention, and which are improving over time.

 ## TIPS FOR MONITORING FEEDBACK

- Create annotated examples of written feedback that meet your criteria for sufficient quality. Use these to clarify expectations with observers before you start auditing their feedback; then use the examples to guide the auditing process.

- You can also use surveys to gauge interest in different observation procedures. You might test whether teachers would be comfortable having their lessons reviewed by video, instead of live. Video makes it easier for multiple observers to review the same lesson—another form of co-observation—and lets observers pause and rewind to confirm they've captured the evidence correctly. Video also enhances the post-observation conference, allowing teachers and observers to see again what happened. (For more, see the "Incorporating Video in the Feedback Conversation" box on page 207 in Chapter 15, "Coaching Teachers.")

 ## TOOL:
RHODE ISLAND'S TEACHER SURVEY

Each year the Rhode Island Department of Education (RIDE) surveys teachers across the state on their experiences with evaluation. Questions related to observation ask about timeliness, frequency, and utility. RIDE uses the anonymous survey to inform changes in evaluator training. Figure 19.5 is a slide from observer training in which the department shared some of the results. See page 338 for the full set of questions on observation. For more on how the agency defines its criteria for effective feedback, see the write-up on Rhode Island's Feedback Quality Review Tool on page 195 in Chapter 15, "Coaching Teachers."

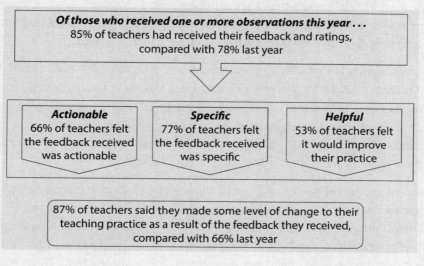

FIGURE 19.5   Sharing Teacher Survey Results in Rhode Island

Of those who received one or more observations this year . . .
85% of teachers had received their feedback and ratings, compared with 78% last year

Actionable	*Specific*	*Helpful*
66% of teachers felt the feedback received was actionable	77% of teachers felt the feedback received was specific	53% of teachers felt it would improve their practice

87% of teachers said they made some level of change to their teaching practice as a result of the feedback they received, compared with 66% last year

IN FOCUS:
EVALUATING SUPPORTS FOR BETTER TEACHING

Quality feedback is the most direct and perhaps the most visible way in which observations support better teaching. But it's hardly the only way. To get the full benefit of a trustworthy observation system requires using the data produced from the classroom to evaluate and improve the full range of instructional supports in a school system. Good information on the state of teaching practice in your schools empowers you to make better decisions about where to invest, which investments to keep making, and which to stop. Consider these three potentially high-impact examples:

- *Professional development offerings.* If teaching in your system is stronger in some areas of practice than in others, then that should inform where to invest your professional development dollars. In addition, whether or not you continue with a particular investment should be informed by whether or not you see changes in related ratings of teacher practice.

- *Teacher recruitment pipelines.* Which teacher preparation programs, and other sources of new hires, are producing the teachers with the highest observation ratings? This tells you where to focus recruitment. Showing teacher preparation programs how their graduates are performing in specific areas of instruction also creates an incentive for them to make their own improvements.

- *Teacher retention policies.* Are you retaining the most highly skilled educators? Are those with the highest observation ratings staying in your system, or are they moving on after a few years? If the latter, find out why. Maybe they see a lack of growth opportunities where they are, or feel the need for a better work environment. Whatever the reasons, take steps to address them, and track whether or not those with the highest ratings wind up staying longer.

It would take another book to explain all the ways in which observation data should drive more strategic decision-making at the system level. But such uses should be part of your planning, at each stage of implementation. A first step is to communicate to all your stakeholders—teachers, observers, and system leaders—the intent of using observation data to assess and improve supports for better teaching. Later, you can share with them how you've put the data to such uses. Teachers and observers alone can't shoulder all the responsibility for improving teaching and learning.

 SNAPSHOTS:
PLANNING PROFESSIONAL DEVELOPMENT INVESTMENTS IN HILLSBOROUGH COUNTY, FLORIDA

The Hillsborough County Public Schools in Florida has shifted investments in teacher professional development based on system-wide observation data. District leaders saw that most teachers were proficient in classroom management but performed lower in areas of practice related to teaching of higher-order thinking skills. As a result, they decreased the amount of professional development offerings for the former and increased it for the latter. They realized it made little sense to invest heavily in developing skills that most teachers had mastered.

EVALUATING PROFESSIONAL DEVELOPMENT INVESTMENTS IN TENNESSEE

The Tennessee Department of Education has used observation results and other measures of effective teaching to evaluate the impact of teacher professional development. In 2012, the agency provided nearly 200 teachers with eight days of training on instructional coaching and on teaching techniques aligned to Common Core State Standards in math. Those teachers then served as coaches to colleagues, for whom they provided three days of training on the same instructional methods. To assess the training's impact, the state examined the subsequent changes in the observation ratings of the coaches, of the teachers they coached, and of teachers without any direct involvement in the program. Compared with nonparticipants, the teachers who coached their peers improved by about one-fourth of a point more, on the state's five-point scale for observations, on aspects of teaching that were most relevant to the training (see Figure 19.6). The teachers they coached showed less improvement, but still more than nonparticipants.

FIGURE 19.6   Improvements in Observation Ratings for TNCore Math Training Participants, Relative to Nonparticipants*

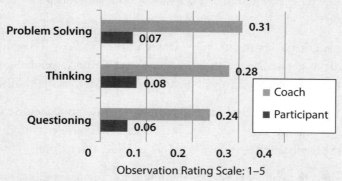

*Controls for teachers' past ratings

Source: Tennessee Department of Education, The Impact of the 2012 TNCore Math Training on Teaching Practices and Effectiveness, 2013.

✓ TECHNIQUES: MONITORING OBSERVATIONS

To Lay the Foundation:

- Distribute to observers clear guidelines for when observations should take place, the steps included within each observation cycle, and the documentation they need to submit.

- Create an online system for observers to enter all the key information from each teacher they are to observe, including: dates for scheduled observations and post-conferences, ratings, and written feedback. Assign someone the task of reviewing this information weekly, and follow up with observers who are falling behind.

- Provide observers with opportunities to practice reviewing and rating pre-scored video throughout the school year. Observers should get feedback on their practice that includes the correct ratings for video, as well as the evidence and justification provided by the expert observers who pre-scored it.

- During observers' initial training, make sure they are aware of the need to participate in calibration assessments at least once every year. Explain how drift in rating is a natural tendency, and that reassessment is meant to help them maintain their proficiency.

- When planning assessments, allow enough time for those who don't meet your standards to get additional training and support, and to retake the assessment, before they need to begin carrying out more observations in the classroom.

- Set up a process to audit observers' written feedback to make sure it meets your criteria for quality. Plan to survey teachers across your system on the extent to which the feedback they receive is timely, specific, and helpful.

- Communicate to all stakeholders the intent to use observation results to evaluate and improve supports for better teaching. Identify some early opportunities for doing so (e.g., to inform and evaluate investments in targeted professional development for teachers, or to identify the most promising teacher preparation programs).

To Build and Improve:

- Continue to expand opportunities for observers to practice observing and giving feedback with pre-scored video throughout the school year.

- Begin assessing observers at least once a year to identify those who need additional training and support to become proficient.

- Share with observers in training the results of monitoring activities to communicate common strengths, areas for improvement, and progress made in following procedures, accuracy, and delivering quality feedback.

- Also share with stakeholders how you've used observation results to improve systemic supports for better teaching (e.g., if they've prompted improvements in teacher preparation programs, or been used to demonstrate the effectiveness of a professional development program).

- Identify a cadre of expert observers to carry out a small number of co-observations at each school annually.

- Look for patterns in the ratings observers produce that may suggest deviation from accurate interpretation (e.g., when an observer at one school tends to give much higher or lower ratings than observers at most other schools). Where patterns suggest a possible problem, send experts to do co-observations.

- Review all results from monitoring annually to inform changes in your initial and follow-up observer training.

- Supplement teacher surveys with focus groups to probe more deeply on their experiences with observation. Look for any unintended consequences that may need to be addressed in observer training or clarifying guidance.

Putting It into Practice

To Lay the Foundation:

What steps can you take in your school system to implement the techniques under "To Lay the Foundation" in "Techniques: Monitoring Observations"?

To Build and Improve:

What gaps do you see in your monitoring of observations, and what steps can you take to fill them?

This item can be downloaded from www.wiley.com/go/betterfeedback

Concluding Thoughts
Getting It Right

Think back to the two teachers we introduced at the beginning of this book—Mr. Smith and Ms. Lopez—whose experiences with teacher observation were so different. Recall that Mr. Smith saw observation as unhelpful and subjective, while Ms. Lopez saw it as trustworthy and having great value.

Now, picture a point in the future when the teachers in both their districts see observation as clarifying, supportive, and central to their work. In countless conversations each year, teachers and observers are analyzing instruction and exchanging ways to improve it. Principals see such value in teacher observation and feedback training that they demand more of it. District leaders trust observation data enough that they use it to plan and assess their investments in professional development.

Most important, Ms. Lopez, Mr. Smith, and all their colleagues are getting the support they need to achieve as much success as possible with their students.

Translating What Works

Every part of this picture is already happening in districts across the country. It's just not all happening at scale. Preparing all students for the world of tomorrow is often less about identifying as-yet-undiscovered methods than about finding ways to spread what works. The trick is maintaining quality as practice transfers from one place to others. Too often, critical understandings are lost in translation. What worked in one place doesn't appear to work in another, when in reality what worked in the first place was never really replicated.

The fact that the implementation of observation systems has been uneven is understandable. Observations in their current form are still relatively new. Getting to the future we want, however, will require getting it right everywhere.

We see this happening with teacher observations. District leaders who have implemented observation and feedback systems recognize the need for training, monitoring, and ongoing support for their observers. But what that looks like in practice varies greatly. In one district, observers may engage in close study of each part of a rubric to understand what evidence they need to collect, but in another they may get only a cursory explanation of the rubric's structure. In some places, trainees get to practice analyzing instruction with carefully pre-scored video, while in others they may review video without being able to compare their work to that of expert observers. Some districts require their observers to demonstrate proficiency—and provide additional training to those who don't—while other districts don't assess their observers at all.

The fact that the implementation of observation systems has been uneven is understandable. Observations in their current form are still relatively new. There's a lot to learn in order to do them well. Not long ago, the standard practice for classroom visits was to pop into a teacher's room for a few minutes with a simple checklist in hand. The widespread adoption of observation instruments that clarify important teaching aspects is a big step forward. Getting to the future we want, however, will require getting it right everywhere.

Learning from Experience

Our goal for this book is to build a common understanding of how to ensure that observers have the full set of knowledge and skills required to identify and develop effective teaching. We've tried to be clear and complete about what needs to happen, why, and in what order. But to fully understand something, you need to experience it. Only after you try to apply some of these lessons to your own system will this guidance be fully clear. Indeed, we expect that after you've learned from a few iterations you'll be better able to help others understand good practice than we were. We expect you'll learn many lessons we didn't teach, and we hope you'll share them with practitioners in other states and districts.

Some advice as you go forward: Collect data, and don't go it alone. Every section in this book includes ideas for analyzing information for the sake of improvement. With good information on effectiveness, you can find ways to become more effective. But you still need a coach. Like the teachers we all aim to serve, those charged with implementing observations need those with experience to look at what they're doing and offer practical ways to improve. There are many school systems and organizations with expertise in quality observation, including ones we've mentioned in this guide. Find experts who understand the challenges you face, and seek out their help.

It's About Growth

Finally, remember that the point of a quality observation system is not just to produce trustworthy observation results. It's also to build the instructional leadership skills of those who support teachers so that all teachers—at all levels of performance—can change practice in ways that improve student learning. If observations don't lead to professional growth, then the pace of change in teaching won't catch up to the rapidly changing needs of students. Now more than ever, teachers need reliable feedback to adjust their practice to these needs. With a shared understanding of effective teaching, the future we need becomes possible.

APPENDIX
Observer Training Checklist

Use the checklist on the next two pages to identify any gaps and weaknesses in your observer training. Consider whether your training addresses the knowledge and skills described. Questions and examples are provided to clarify each item; for more detail, refer to the pages listed in the right-hand column. Specifically:

■   If you already train observers, consider whether or not your training addresses each item under the six key elements of knowledge and skills needed for quality observation.
  - Knowing the rubric
  - Evidence collection
  - Understanding bias
  - Recognizing relevant evidence
  - Using the criteria for rating
  - Coaching teachers to change practice

■   If you are building a new training program, review these items, and in the margins or white space write down your biggest questions about how training should address them.

 This checklist is available for download from www.wiley.com/go/betterfeedback.

✐ **TIP**

Before adding any checks or questions, circle what you see as the key words in each item. This will help you to better consider what's being described.

	Knowing the rubric. Training develops an understanding of the key rubric elements that define each teaching component and performance level.	**pp. 115–126**
❏	**It helps observers see that what they value in teaching is reflected in the rubric.** Does training connect what they see as good practice with aspects of teaching emphasized in the instrument?	p. 116
❏	**It clarifies how use of a rubric supports fair evaluation and meaningful feedback.** Does training explain how the objective criteria allow different observers to make the same judgments?	p. 116
❏	**It explains how a rubric's structure organizes indicators of performance.** Does an overview point out the key rubric elements that define practice at each level for each component of teaching?	p. 118
❏	**It points out text features and annotations that clarify how to make judgments.** For Example, key words that define the critical attributes of practice; notes that list related teaching practices or behaviors.	p. 121
❏	**It explains how evidence of different indicators is interpreted and weighed in rating.** For example, the general rules and types of exceptions for considering all evidence for a component of teaching.	p. 121
	Evidence collection. Training develops the skills to record objective description—efficiently and without judgment—of what occurs in a lesson.	**pp. 127–137**
❏	**It develops an understanding of what is evidence.** That is, evidence is descriptive, as opposed to opinion, summary, or judgment.	p. 128
❏	**It explains why evidence is essential for accurate evaluation and meaningful feedback.** Evidence is the basis of judgment based on a common set of criteria, and it gives meaning to feedback.	p. 128
❏	**It provides opportunities for collecting different types of evidence.** For Example, teacher and student statements, descriptions of behaviors, and how often they occur.	p. 130
❏	**It suggests techniques for efficient and accurate note-taking.** For Example, scripting key statements, capturing anecdotes, tally marks.	p. 131
	Understanding bias. Training builds awareness of how observer preferences may influence observation and of ways to reduce the impact of bias.	**pp. 139–148**
❏	**It describes how different types of personal preferences (or bias) can influence rating.** For Example, unconsciously inflating judgments of a lesson that includes a preferred teaching method.	p. 142
❏	**It provides techniques to help observers identify their personal preferences.** For Example, by reflecting on and taking note of their tendencies.	p. 144
❏	**It suggests strategies for minimizing the effects of preferences on rating.** For Example, by keeping one's own list of things that might trigger bias, positive or negative.	p. 145

	Recognizing relevant evidence. Training builds the ability to identify in a lesson all the evidence related to each teaching component in a rubric.	**pp. 149–166**
❑	**It unpacks the rubric components to clarify what to look and listen for.** Does training help evaluators understand what kinds of evidence are important for each aspect of teaching?	p. 153
❑	**It provides for modeling and practice collecting relevant evidence using pre-scored video.** Are there opportunities to see and attempt the correct collection of—relevant evidence?	p. 156
❑	**It provides for modeling and practice aligning evidence to the right rubric components.** Are there opportunities to see and attempt correct sorting or categorizing of relevant evidence?	p. 159
	Using the criteria for rating. Training develops the ability to apply a rubric's rules for rating teaching components correctly and without influence of bias.	**pp. 167–185**
❑	**It includes close study of key rubric language distinguishing among performance levels.** For each teaching component, does training call out what the evidence must show for a particular rating?	p. 170
❑	**It uses pre-scored video for modeling and practice interpreting and matching evidence to the right performance levels.** Do trainees get opportunities to see and attempt correct application of the rating criteria for each component of teaching?	p. 174
❑	**It provides feedback on trainees' ratings, evidence, and rationales.** Do trainees get to see the extent to which they rated accurately, and why their ratings were accurate or not?	p. 175
❑	**It provides for practice reviewing and rating whole lessons on all components of teaching.** Do trainees get opportunities to practice doing full observations?	p. 177
	Coaching teachers to change practice. Training builds the feedback skills required to help teachers implement specific techniques in areas for growth.	**pp. 187–219**
❑	**It includes protocols that support practical, specific, and improvement-focused post-observation conferences.** That is, they begin with strengths and end with co-planning how to implement specific suggestions.	p. 192
❑	**It provides opportunities to practice employing the elements of effective feedback.** For Example, through role-plays and by preparing written feedback.	p. 194
❑	**It provides guidance on how to help teachers implement specific techniques in the classroom.** For Example, on how to model with teachers to help them quickly address focused areas for improvement.	p. 200
❑	**It explains ways to maintain a supportive tone and to adjust feedback for different teachers.** For Example, by showing interest and confidence in teachers and tailoring delivery based on their dispositions.	p. 202

Write notes and questions about the training checklist here:

Planning Worksheet

Use this worksheet to summarize plans for addressing the Essential Questions throughout this book.

⬇ This worksheet is available for download from www.wiley.com/go/betterfeedback.

Part I: Making the Big Decisions

p. 18   How will you make the case for robust training?

p. 26   Who will you train to ensure sufficient feedback?

p. 36   How will you deliver training?

p. 46   What will be your goal for training this year?

Part II: Pre-Scoring Video

p. 60   How will you create support for pre-scoring video?

p. 65   What is your goal for pre-scoring video this year?

p. 69   What pre-scored video do you need?

p. 76   How will you get the right kind of video to pre-score?

p. 81   How will you pre-screen video for quality and content?

p. 83   How will you share video and collect rating justifications?

p. 86   How will you recruit master coders?

p. 90   How many master coders will you need?

p. 92   How will you train master coders?

p. 102   How will you check the work of master coders for quality?

p. 105   How will you keep track of the process and products?

p. 108   How will you use data for continual improvement?

Part III: Building the Knowledge and Skills for Observation

p. 116   How will you explain your instrument?

p. 128   How will you teach evidence collection?

p. 140   How will you build an understanding of bias?

p. 150   How will you develop the skills to identify and sort relevant evidence?

p. 168   How will you build an understanding of accurate rating?

p. 188   How will you build a shared vision of effective feedback?

p. 212   How will you organize training?

p. 224   How will you use information to improve training?

Part IV: Using Data to Improve Training and Support for Observers

p. 234   How will you know when observers are ready, and what will you do if they're not?

Tools Referenced in This Book

The following pages provide printed copies of the tools mentioned in the chapters. Downloadable versions of these tools are available from the book's website at www.wiley.com/go/betterfeedback.

Chapter	Tool
Chapter 7: Getting the Right Video to Pre-Score	7-1 DCPS Video Quality Checklist
Chapter 8: Recruiting and Training Master Coders	8-1 RIFT Master Coding Worksheet 8-2 DCPS Advice for Facilitating Reconciliation 8-3 DCPS Guidelines for Score Rationales
Chapter 13: Recognizing Evidence	13-1 DCPS Evidence Collection Template
Chapter 14: Using Criteria for Rating	14-1 PUC Evidence Record Rubric 14-2 LDC/TCRP Top Ten Principles of True Scoring 14-3 RIDE Calibration Session Protocol
Chapter 15: Coaching Teachers	15-1 RIDE Feedback Quality Review Tool 15-2 HCPS Post-Observation Assessment Checklist
Chapter 17: Collecting and Using Data from Training	17-1 DCPS Feedback Rubric with Annotated Example
Chapter 18: Assessing Observers to Ensure and Improve Quality	18-1 MPS Rubric for Rating Use of Evidence
Chapter 19: Monitoring Your Observation System	19-1 RIDE Teacher Survey Items on Observation

Tool 7-1: DCPS Video Quality Checklist

This tool, developed by District of Columbia Public Schools Filming Specialist Tamika Guishard, is explained in Chapter 7, on page 82.

Video File Name:

Video Content:

Time stamps for the calibration clip you've identified (Start to Finish):

Tier 2 Criteria	
	☐ An observer can identify the lesson objective (stated or implied).
	☐ An observer would have enough information about student understanding to score this lesson. Evidence:
	☐ Teacher Actions ☐ Student Body Language
	☐ Student Verbal Responses ☐ Student Work
	☐ There was no more than one moment where an inability to hear the teacher would affect the scoring of multiple standards.
	☐ During whole-group lessons, student responses are heard clearly enough to capture useful evidence as necessary.
	☐ During teacher/student exchanges, both parties are heard clearly enough to capture useful evidence as necessary.
	☐ When a visual was necessary for rating purposes, a clear shot of the visual is seen at the appropriate time.
	☐ The two cameras provided a good sense of what was happening in the room.

(*Tool continues on next page*)

(Continued)

Tier 1 Criteria	☐ Most student faces are visible.
	☐ Extraneous audio (hallway noise, necklace against lapel mic, etc.) does not inhibit one's ability to hear the lesson and collect evidence.
	☐ An observer would have enough information about student understanding (teacher actions, student body language, verbal responses and work products) to score this lesson **with confidence**. Evidence:
	
	    ☐ Teacher Actions ☐ Student Body Language
	    ☐ Student Verbal Responses ☐ Student Work
	
	☐ An observer can see whether or not differentiation is happening.

Time stamps for subtitles	*If you transcribe all or part of this video, please include script when e-mailing this checklist.*
Additional Notes	

Final Evaluation:

☐ This is a Tier 1 clip.

☐ This is a Tier 2 clip. The following standards might be difficult to rate:

☐ This clip is not ratable and should not be re-edited.

☐ This clip needs revisions. Note time stamps and revisions necessary:

☐ This footage should be used for training videos. The time stamps and Teach standards for those sections are:

Tool 8-1: RIFT Master Coding Worksheet

The Rhode Island Federation of Teachers and Health Professionals created this worksheet to guide the work of master coders as they review video, record evidence, and come to agreement on ratings. The Rhode Island coders work in pairs to add their evidence and rationales to the worksheet for each component of teaching (or "focus area") evident in a video. As an additional check, each pair presents (or "defends") its rationales to other coders who have reviewed the same video before submitting their completed worksheets. For more on this tool, see page 97 in Chapter 8.

Master Coders' Names:		
Video Name:	Focus Teaching Component for This Clip:	
Clip Start Time:	Clip End Time:	
Evidence:		
Master Coder Rating:	It is not *lower*, because …	It is not *higher*, because …
Defended in Whole Group ☐	Consensus Reached ☐	Consensus Not Reached ☐

⬇ This item can be downloaded from www.wiley.com/go/betterfeedback

Tool 8-2: DCPS Advice for Facilitating Reconciliation

Lindsay Wallace Michael, a member of the District of Columbia Public Schools (DCPS) evaluator support team, drafted this advice for guiding discussion among master coders, called "anchor raters" in DCPS. The goal is to reach agreement on the ratings for videos of teaching on each component (called "Teach standards") in the DCPS rubric, the Teaching and Learning Framework (TLF), by considering the evidence of the performance indicators (called "rows") for each standard. As noted in the advice, facilitation may include reminding raters of a "scoring policy" in the rubric (e.g. when one indicator should be given more weight than others). For more on this tool, see page 97 in Chapter 8.

Open the session by reminding raters of the meeting's purpose

"Thanks so much for the time you took to submit scores for this video, and for setting aside time this afternoon for our call. It's exciting for me to have the opportunity to discuss this video with two really smart evaluators. Before we dive into our discussion, I'd like to quickly touch on a couple of norms for the call that will help our conversation go smoothly. First and foremost, remember that we have a common goal today—to come to agreement about what the best scores for this video are—and it's Okay if those scores are different from the ones you initially assigned it. In addition to creating a powerful tool for the district, we hope that the experience of participating in score reconciliation will be a rich professional development experience for all of our anchor raters—so, in that spirit, please be willing to challenge your colleague respectfully to consider the evidence from a different perspective, and also be willing to be challenged yourself so that together the two of you can come to the best final score. Let's also agree to hold each other accountable to maintaining a rigorous focus on evidence and the TLF standards as we work through scores for this video, and to apply the scoring policies when relevant."

Roadmap: Provide an overview of the work to be done

"We'll go through the evidence for each Teach standard one at a time. We have several scores with agreement, and we have disagreement for Teach standards 2, 3, 5, 6, and 7. We need to ensure that we have enough evidence to fully support all of the scores, but we'll spend the majority of our time reconciling the standards for which we're starting with disparate scores."

It might be helpful to set time limits. Share the time limits with the raters at the beginning of the meeting, and monitor the time/provide time cues throughout the call.

⬇ This item can be downloaded from www.wiley.com/go/betterfeedback

Summarize Teach standards with agreement

"You both scored Teach 1 as a 2, and your evidence was similar … "

When raters agreed on the score—and perhaps much of the evidence, as well—start by summarizing what they agreed on, then focus on ensuring that the evidence fully supports the selected score. Evidence should be collected and discussed for every row of every Teach standard, including standards on which the raters agreed from the start.

Guide the conversation on Teach standards with discrepancies

Provide an overview: "For Teach 2, we have a disagreement in scores—a 1 and a 3. Heidi, could you please start by sharing the evidence you saw for this Teach? Matt, after Heidi shares her rationale, you can share your evidence." Try to let the first rater finish his/her thoughts before the other rater jumps in.

OR, if the evidence raters submitted allows: "For Teach 2, we have a disagreement in scores—a 1 and a 3. It looks like you both noted that the teacher did (fill in the blank), and so it appears that the difference in scores might be due to different perspectives on the evidence for (insert relevant rows). Heidi, could you please share about the evidence you saw for (insert relevant rows)?"

Raters do not need to agree on every row score, as long as they agree on the overall score for the standard. However, evidence should be discussed and recorded for every row of every Teach standard.

Remind raters of the scoring policies when necessary

If raters are leaning toward a score that diverges from a scoring policy, gently remind them: "This is one of the scenarios for which we have a scoring policy. Since, the teacher had a 1 in (insert relevant row), s/he cannot receive an overall 4 for the Teach standard, unless the weight of the evidence provides a compelling reason to deviate from this policy. Do we have compelling evidence in this video?" Require the raters to articulate the evidence—if evidence cannot be clearly and convincingly articulated, the evidence is not compelling enough to deviate from the policy.

When raters don't come to agreement

When raters are having a difficult time coming to agreement, remind them that it is not necessary to agree on every row score—overall agreement for the standard is the goal. Provide a quick summary and then highlight the area of disagreement: "You've both noted that the teacher did (fill in the blank), and so it appears that the difference in scores is due to different perspectives on the evidence for (insert relevant rows). Let's focus in on these points. Heidi, could you please share about the evidence you saw for (insert relevant rows)?"

If difficulty reconciling persists, guide the raters to move on to a different Teach standard and then come back to the difficult one later. If raters still are unable to come to agreement, consider the reason. Is it because of evidence collection challenges that are unique to video (e.g., audio/visual quality issues)? If so, this video may not be useful for training or calibration for the Teach standard in question and no more time should be spent attempting to reconcile the score.

When raters agree on a questionable score

If you have serious reservations about a score that the raters agree on, please note this in the comment box when submitting final scores. Please be as specific as possible when explaining your concerns so that the next pair of anchor raters can pay particular attention to this area.

When scores don't feel quite right

Sometimes the final scores might not feel quite right. For example, it might seem that if the rater had been in the classroom, s/he would have been able to see important evidence that could have led to a different score. However, because the video is the common experience/data set for every viewer, it is important to base scores only on the evidence that we have access to.

Remember that our goal is to create replicable, gold standard scores. To accomplish this, our video scores and evidence must align as precisely as possible to the language of the TLF rubric and the observable evidence in the video. If a score doesn't feel quite right, but the evidence matches the description of that score in the rubric, support raters in resisting the urge to change the score.

Tool 8-3: DCPS Guidelines for Score Rationales

Leah Levine, a member of the District of Columbia Public Schools' (DCPS) evaluator support team, created these guidelines for drafting score rationales as part of the district's process for master coding videos (called "anchor rating" in DCPS). Included are criteria for language, organization, specificity, and reference to the components (call "Teach standards") and indicators (called "rows") in the DCPS observation rubric. For more on this tool, see page 97 in Chapter 8.

Rationale: The goal of anchor rating is to set the gold standard for teacher observation. Videos scored through this project support consistent scoring expectations across the district. Strong evidence is the most effective way to provide insight into a rater rationale and to ensure practices are replicated across DCPS.

Audience-ready evidence criteria includes:

Professional Writing	Ensure there are no mechanical errors. ■ A Word template has been provided for your convenience.
Consistent Language	Submit evidence in the third person, past tense. ■ *Teach 9, Row 4, Level 2:* **The teacher** sometimes reinforced positive behavior and good academic work. For example, during the summary portion of the lesson **the teacher paused** to say, "You guys are doing awesome." However, she **did** not always provide meaningful, specific praise.
Rubric Language	Begin your evidence with the language of the rubric level that best describes the evidence. ■ *Teach 6, Row 3, Level 3:* The teacher **almost always probed students' correct responses to ensure student understanding**. For example …

Row-by-Row Scores and Organization	You can organize evidence by short paragraphs:
	■ *Teach 5, Row 1:* The teacher checked for understanding at some key moments. For example, she called on students to share their responses to the "Do Now." She also checked for understanding during the group activity. However, she missed a key moment when she did not check for understanding of the group work directions releasing students. Although she said, "Any questions?" this was not an effective check. *(2)*
	
	You can also organize evidence through a bulleted list:
	
	■ *Teach 5, Row 1, Level 2:* The teacher checked at some key moments by:
	  • Calling on students during the "Do Now,"
	  • Questioning during the activity
	■ She missed the following key moment:
	  • After giving directions: "Any questions?" was an ineffective check.

⬇ This item can be downloaded from www.wiley.com/go/betterfeedback

(Continued from previous page)

Context-Specific Evidence	Include student/teacher quotes and names when appropriate:
	■ The teacher asked many questions such as, "Who can use some of our vocabulary to tell me if the experiment was fair or unfair?"
	■ At various points in the lesson, students asked questions that demonstrated movement toward higher-level understanding. For example, Olivia asked, "Are 'parallel' and 'perpendicular' opposites?"
	Note locations and time stamps when appropriate:
	■ Students at the left table passed notes and threw paper while the teacher was addressing the group at the front of the class.
	■ The transition to small groups took almost 7 minutes. The teacher released students to small groups at 13:20. Students did not begin work until 20:13.

Examples of evidence that meet the criteria:

Example 1: Teach 4, Level 1

Row 1 (Level 1): The teacher provided multiple ways to engage with the content, but most ways did not move students toward mastery. The teacher engaged students in the following ways:

■ Interpersonal—Students worked in partners with a dictionary to investigate the multiple meanings of a word. However, this way was not effective because students were not supported on how to effectively use context clues.

■ Kinesthetic—Students were given special words and asked to line up by which word they were given. However, most students were not given the opportunity to engage in the content in this way.

■ Visual ways—The teacher projected the assignment on her Smart board. However the visuals did not support student understanding about how to use context clues in order to select the correct multiple meaning word.

■ Auditory—The teacher offered explanations of the content to students. However, her explanations were not high quality (see Teach 2) and therefore did not move students toward mastery.

Row 2 (Level 2): The teacher included learning styles appropriate to the students, and most students responded positively. Not all were actively engaged, however. For example, two students were observed whispering to each other throughout the lesson and one student had his head in his hands for the majority of the lesson. While some students were able to participate in the kinesthetic line-up activity, most remained at their desks and were not observed participating in the lesson.

Example 2: Teach 2, Level 2

- *(Row 1-2)* Explanations were generally clear with a few exceptions. For example, although her demonstrations were effective, the teacher did not clearly explain the difference between sipping and gulping and how that related to walking and sprinting.

- *(Row 2-2)* The teacher used broad vocabulary like analogy, but her statement that "skill-fully" and "gracefully" were "pretty much the same" was not entirely precise.

- *(Row 3-2)* She sometimes emphasized key points by demonstrating the act of sprinting to show the relationship to gulping. However, she did not explain how the word pairs related to one another.

- *(Row 4-3)* Students showed that they understood the explanations by nodding their heads and repeating her explanations.

- *(Row 5-3)* The teacher made connections to students' prior knowledge by using track as an example and stating, "You all remember, I'm going to be in the Olympics."

Examples of evidence that do not meet the criteria:

Example 1: Teach 8, Level 3

The teacher was effective at maximizing instruction. Routines and procedures ran smoothly with minimal prompting from the teacher. Students were engaged and on task. Inappropriate or off-task behavior did not delay instruction.

Explanation: While this evidence includes rubric language that is organized by row and is written in the third person, past tense, it does not provide specific examples from the lesson that would allow the audience to understand why this teacher was effective at maximizing instruction.

Example 2: Teach 9, Level 2

- Students are generally engaged in their work but not highly invested in it

- Safe environment for students to take on academic risks

- Students are generally respectful of the teacher but need reminders to respect peers

- Sometimes reinforces positive behavior

- Positive rapport; no evidence of negative rapport

Explanation: This evidence includes rubric language and is organized by row. It does not include row scores, provide specific examples, and it is not written in third person, past tense.

Tool 13-1: DCPS Evidence Collection Template

This tool is explained on page 158 in Chapter 13.

Observer	
Teacher	
School	
Grade and Subject	
Observation Date and Start Time/End Time	

TEACH 1: Lead well-organized, objective-driven lessons

Well-organized
Clear to students
Students understand importance

TEACH 4: Provide students multiple ways to move towards mastery

Time	Way students are engaged	Students' response	Student mastery

TEACH 8: Maximize Instructional time

Well-executed routines, procedures, and transitions	Effective classroom management

TEACH 3: Engage students at all levels in accessible and challenging work		
Lesson is challenging	Lesson is accessible	Appropriately balanced/student-centered

TEACH 7: Develop Higher-level understanding through effective questioning		
Higher-Level Questions or Tasks	Student Responses	Teacher Strategies

TEACH 9: Build a supportive, learning-focused classroom community

Students are invested
Safe environment
Students are respectful
Reinforces positive behavior/academic work
Has positive rapport

TEACH 2: Explain Content Clearly

Explanations are clear and coherent
Clear definitions/academic language
Emphasizes key points
Students show they understand
Teacher makes connections

Teach 5 and 6		
Teacher Question	Student Response	Follow-Up

Tool 14-1: Partnerships to Uplift Communities (PUC) Evidence Record Rubric

This tool is explained on page 179, in Chapter 14.

Criteria	Not Yet Certified (1)	Conditionally Certified (2)	Certified (3)	Certified with Distinction (4)
Evidence	Evidence is lacking for many indicators. Evidence includes frequent inference or summary.	Two to three facts are recorded for most indicators. Evidence is mixed with some inference or summary.	Three to four facts are recorded for most indicators. Evidence is free of inference and summary.	*All of Level 3 and …* An abundance of relevant facts are recorded for each indicator. Evidence includes specific numbers and/or time references.
Alignment	Evidence is commonly misaligned to the framework.	Evidence is sometimes misaligned to the framework.	Evidence is aligned to the framework.	Evidence is aligned to the framework and accurately reflects the context of the lesson.
Also, for each criterion …	Frequent issues, multiple types of issues; makes interpretation difficult.	Some problems, often four or five of two or three types, or six or seven of one type; presents issues for interpretation.	Very few problems, often just two or three of one type, and they don't interfere with meaning.	Problems are very rare, and the observer has gone beyond the basics of evidence collection.

EVIDENCE COLLECTION PROBLEMS

Inference or Bias—The observer layers a meaning to something (e.g., labels a strategy) or uses words of judgment or opinion.

Summary—The observer summarizes rather than records evidence.

*Rubric adapted from Teaching Learning Solutions © 2011, www.teachinglearningsolutions. Used with permission.

This item can be downloaded from www.wiley.com/go/betterfeedback

Unclear Citation—The observer collects fine evidence, but you can't tell the source (e.g., teacher versus student).

Lack of Evidence—Too little evidence is collected, or the observer records that evidence was not observed or did not happen.

ALIGNMENT PROBLEMS

Misalignment—The observer assigns evidence to the wrong standard or indicator.

Over-Inclusion—Too much evidence that is not sufficiently edited for specific alignment, or the same piece of evidence aligned to too many indicators.

Under-Inclusion—Too little evidence when appropriate evidence is available elsewhere in the evidence record.

Overly Discrete—The observer collects evidence in such small pieces you can't tell why it belongs in one indicator or another.

Tool 14-2: Literacy Design Collaborative (LDC)/(TCRP) Top Ten Principles of True Scoring

The College Ready Promise (TCRP) based this set of reminders for observers on a similar tool from the Literacy Design Collaborative. For more, see page 180 in Chapter 14.* †

---

1. **Know the rubric.**

   It is your Constitution. Granted, that means it is sometimes hard to interpret, but every score must be an attempt to apply the rubric's language and meaning.

2. **Trust evidence, not intuition.**

   Intuition is a powerful force, but it is also highly subjective (or specific to the individual). Calibration with other scorers requires us to base our judgments on the evidence that everyone can see, not on what a particular person feels.

3. **Match evidence to language in the rubric.**

   A safe rule of thumb: If you dinged the teacher for something specific, be sure you can circle its justification(s) in the lesson plan or script.

4. **Weigh evidence carefully; base judgments on the preponderance of evidence.**

   Within each scoring dimension, the score must be based on the overall performance as evidenced throughout the lesson or lesson plan. Therefore the score is not based on the lesson's best or worst moment; rather, it reflects what is generally true about the lesson's overall quality within each of the analytic scoring dimensions.

5. **Know your biases; minimize their impact.**

   The trick is not to rid yourself of bias; that's impossible. But you do need to recognize what your biases are, and to be mindful of how they can trigger first impressions that color all judgments that follow.

6. **Focus on what the lesson includes, not on what the lesson does not include.**

   Scorers who attend to what is in the lesson, rather than what is not, or what is missing, tend to score more accurately. That shouldn't surprise us: it is easier to agree on what is than on what could be. A score is always based on what is.

---

* Adapted by The College Ready Promise from Top Ten Principles of LDC Module Jurying and Teacher Moderated Scoring Systems "Top Ten Scoring Principles" (Measured Progress and the Stanford Center for Assessment, Learning, & Equity for the Literacy Design Collaborative, 2013).

7. **Isolate your judgment: One bad element does not equal a bad lesson.**

    Problems in the learning objective sometimes affect the overall quality of the lesson. But our rubric is not designed to assess one's overall impression of a lesson. Rather, it is isolating variables, distinguishing between relative strengths and weaknesses. Certain lessons will require that you invest more cognitive work in their scoring. Be sure not to be overly punitive in scoring those lessons, and be mindful that a lesson's low score in one scoring dimension does not cloud your judgment on the scoring of other, unrelated dimensions.

8. **Resist seduction: One good element does not equal a good lesson.**

    It also works the other way. You read a particularly well-designed learning objective, and after that the lesson designer can do no wrong. (This is known as the "halo effect.") One exceptional strength does not cancel out the weaknesses.

9. **Recognize pre-loaded template elements.**

    The lesson plan templates provide standardized language, elements, and often a set of questions that are meant to be selected and adapted for a particular lesson. Focus on how well aligned those elements are to the demands of the learning objective and whether the teacher has sufficiently customized those elements for the specific purposes of the lesson.

10. **Stick to the rubric.**

    Don't measure what is not being measured. Be wary of applying criteria (e.g., personal preferences) that are not evaluated in the rubric.

Tool 14-3: RIDE Calibration Session Protocol

The three versions of the protocol on the next few pages are from the Rhode Island Department of Education, and they are explained on page 181 in Chapter 14.

Reviewing Professional Practice Calibration Framework

Utilizing an Observation Protocol Can Have Many Purposes

- Ensure consistent and uniform scoring of teacher practice during observations within and across schools and districts

- Developing common language and shared expectations

- Supporting educators through high-quality feedback

- Peer observations as a form of professional development, and building a culture of professional learning community within our schools

Why It's Important to Continually Calibrate

Personnel evaluating teachers in all models participated in training and calibration of observations leading up to and throughout the first year of full implementation. Continual calibration is critical as evaluators conduct more and more observations, as personnel evaluating teachers change within schools and districts, and as drift naturally occurs over time. To calibrate observations of Professional Practice a variety of sessions could be utilized. We suggest calibrating multiple times a year at the school level and at least once a year at an LEA level.

Two Levels of Calibration

School Level:	LEA Level:
1. All personnel evaluating teachers' practice watch a video of classroom instruction and utilize Protocol 1.	1. All personnel evaluating teachers' practice watch a video of classroom instruction and utilize Protocol 1.
2. All personnel evaluating teachers' practice (or a team of 2–3) observe a teacher's practice live at their school and utilize Protocol 2.	2. All personnel evaluating teachers' practice observe a teacher's practice live and utilize Protocol 2.
3. All personnel evaluating teachers' practice (or a team of 2–3) observe a teacher's practice live at a different school and utilize Protocol 2.	*Note: These could be completed in grade-span groups (elementary, secondary or elementary, middle, high school), but it is also beneficial to see multiple grade spans

Additional Opportunities for Using Calibration for Professional Development of Teachers

Calibrating with Teachers:

Teachers can also be included in calibration of observations to support their understanding of high-quality instruction and use of the rubric in their evaluation. This can be powerful professional development and can be structured in a variety of ways including, but not limited to, the following:

1. *Teachers in a school within a grade-level team or content area:* Grade-level teams or departments within a school can utilize either of the two protocols. All RI Model districts have a Framework for Teaching Proficiency System (FFTPS) account they can utilize for PD with teachers, and many other websites have video libraries of teaching.

2. *Teachers in a content area across a district:* Teachers could see what teaching looks like at other schools and grade levels. Additionally, if a school has only one or two art teachers, the arts teachers in the district could come together for a calibration session.

3. *Teachers observing different grade-levels and/or content areas:* We encourage teachers to calibrate their observation of subjects and grades outside their own, as this can oftentimes be highly beneficial.

4. *Teachers only focusing on one component in observation:* Each month teachers could focus on a different component of the rubric and observe one another in a focused way to identify a variety of successful strategies in diverse contexts. If utilizing this approach, Protocol 3 would be most helpful.

Protocol 1: Video Observation Calibration Protocol

1. **Identify a video** that you'd like to use.

2. **Observe the video of the teaching episode** as a group and individually record evidence (free of bias and interpretation). Each member of the group is responsible for taking notes in their preferred format (Educator Performance and Support System [EPSS], hand-written notes, iPad, etc). The group can watch the video together or separately.

3. After the observation, individual evaluators should **independently sort evidence and score** for each component based on the evidence they collected. In addition to the rating, evaluators should be prepared to provide rationale to support their score.

4. Once each evaluator has had a chance to score independently and identify evidence, the group should **share and discuss component level ratings and rationale** together.

   Scoring Debrief Norms
   - One member serves as facilitator
   - Establish conversation time limits (e.g., plan to complete Domain 2 by x time)
   - Hold one another accountable to bias and interpretation
   - Every member shares their component scores. One approach is to ask participants to indicate their scores by placing dot stickers on wall charts for each component. This provides a visual of whether ratings are calibrated, adjacent, or discrepant before debriefing.
   - If the scores are the same, name why the score is that level
   - If the scores are different, have a conversation regarding rationale in order to reach consensus by grounding the conversation in two questions:
     - *What does the rubric level descriptor say exactly?*
     - *Where does the preponderance of evidence fall?*
   - Repeat this process for each component

5. After completing the scoring, consider the **reflection questions.**

   Connect, Reflect, and Plan
   - What components were most challenging in reaching consensus? What caused this challenge?
   - Were there instructional practices that were interpreted differently?
   - How was this protocol helpful in aligning our instruction language and expectations?
   - How can others experience this learning?
   - Are there any significant next steps that have come from this conversation that need action steps?

Protocol 2: In-Person Observation Calibration Protocol

1. **Identify a teacher** willing to volunteer for an unofficial classroom visit that will include an observation scored by multiple evaluators (but will not count as an official observation for their evaluation).

2. **Observe a teaching episode** as a group and individually record evidence (free of bias and interpretation). Each member of the group is responsible for taking notes in their preferred format (EPSS, hand-written notes, iPad, etc.).

3. After the observation, individual evaluators should **independently sort evidence and score** for each component based on the evidence they collected. In addition to the rating, evaluators should be prepared to provide rationale to support their score.

4. Once each evaluator has had a chance to score independently and identify evidence, the group should **reconvene to share and discuss component level ratings and rationale**.

    #### Scoring Debrief Norms

    - One member serves as facilitator
    - Establish conversation time limits (e.g., plan to complete Domain 2 by x time)
    - Hold one another accountable to bias and interpretation
    - Every member shares their component score
    - If the scores are the same, name why the score is that level
    - If the scores are different, have a conversation regarding rationale in order to reach consensus by grounding the conversation in two questions:
      - *What does the rubric level descriptor say exactly?*
      - *Where does the preponderance of evidence fall?*
    - Repeat this process for each component

5. After completing the scoring, consider the **reflection questions.**

    #### Connect, Reflect, and Plan

    - What components were most challenging in reaching consensus? What caused this challenge?
    - Were there instructional practices that were interpreted differently?
    - How was this protocol helpful in aligning our instruction language and expectations?
    - How can others experience this learning?
    - Are there any significant next steps that have come from this conversation that need action steps?

Protocol 3: Single Component Observation Calibration Protocol

1. **Select the single component** to be the focus of the observation.

2. **Identify a video of teaching or a teacher** willing to volunteer for an unofficial classroom visit by other teachers (that will not count as an official observation for their evaluation).

3. **Observe a teaching episode** as a group and individually record evidence (free of bias and interpretation) that reflects the selected component. Each member of the group is responsible for taking notes in their preferred format (EPSS, hand-written notes, iPad, etc.).

4. After the observation, individual observers should **independently review evidence and score** the component based on the evidence they collected. In addition to the rating, observers should be prepared to provide rationale to support their score.

5. Once each observer has had a chance to score independently and identify evidence, the group should **reconvene to share and discuss component level rating and rationale.**

   *NOTE: If desired observers can provide structured feedback to the teacher, rather than providing a component score.

   Scoring Debrief Norms
   - One member serves as facilitator
   - Establish conversation time limits (e.g., plan to complete Domain 2 by x time)
   - Hold one another accountable to bias and interpretation
   - Every member shares their component score (if applicable)
   - If the scores are the same, name why the score is that level
   - If the scores are different, have a conversation regarding rationale in order to reach consensus by grounding the conversation in two questions:
     - *What does the rubric level descriptor say exactly?*
     - *Where does the preponderance of evidence fall?*
   - Identify practices that worked well in the lesson and provide suggestions or questions for those that were less successful.

6. After completing the observation, consider the **reflection questions.**

   Connect, Reflect, and Plan
   - What was most challenging in reaching consensus about this component? What caused this challenge?
   - Were there instructional practices that were interpreted differently?
   - How was this protocol helpful in aligning our instruction language and expectations?
   - How can we share our experience and learning with others?

Tool 15-1: RIDE Feedback Quality Review Tool

This tool, from the Rhode Island Department of Education, is explained on page 195 in Chapter 15.

RIDE Rhode Island Department of Education

Feedback Quality Review Tool

Prioritized:

1. Does the feedback reinforce the teacher's strongest practice areas?   ☐ No   ☐ Yes

2. Does the feedback focus on 1 or 2 areas for improvement?   ☐ No   ☐ Yes

3. Will the focus of the feedback have the greatest impact on teacher and student performance?   ☐ No   ☐ Yes

4. Is the feedback appropriate to the context of the classroom?   ☐ No   ☐ Yes

Specific:

5. Are specific examples from the observation cited throughout the feedback?   ☐ No   ☐ Yes

6. Is the feedback aligned to the practice rubric?   ☐ No   ☐ Yes

Actionable:

7. Does the feedback include action steps that offer the teacher a clear picture of what this would look like in his/her classroom?   ☐ No   ☐ Yes

8. Is the feedback feasible to implement successfully in the near future?   ☐ No   ☐ Yes

9. Does the feedback include resources or strategies the teacher can utilize?   ☐ No   ☐ Yes

Feedback Delivery:

10. Is the tone of the feedback supportive?   ☐ No   ☐ Yes

11. Was the feedback provided soon after the observation?*   ☐ No   ☐ Yes

*LEAs may have local policy regarding time frames for feedback

---

⬇ This item can be downloaded from www.wiley.com/go/betterfeedback

Tool 15-2: Hillsborough County Public Schools (HCPS) Post-Observation Assessment Checklist

This tool, from the Hillsborough County Public Schools in Florida, is explained on page 204 in Chapter 15.

Post-Observation Conference

Component	Element (Check All Met by Trainee)	Score (Total Elements Met)	
		Teacher 1	Teacher 2
Sets the Tone	☐ Puts teacher at ease *Seating arrangement, body language, tone* ☐ Explains purpose of meeting *Training purpose, no data into LTM, conference purpose* ☐ Concludes Conference Effectively *Clear conclusion to discussion, connects to previously attained information, pleasant and not abrupt*		
	Component Met?	Choose Yes/No	
	Comments: Click here to enter text.		
Elicits Teacher Reflection	☐ Seeks teacher reflection through questions *Questions asked promote reflection, questions are purposeful* ☐ Collects evidence to rate component 4a *Scripts evidence, clarifies/probes as appropriate, does not lead teacher or sway reflection* ☐ Utilizes appropriate communication skills *Allows teacher to share, restates information to clarify*		
	Component Met?	Choose Yes/No	
	Comments: Click here to enter text.		

Component	Element *(Check All Met by Trainee)*	Score *(Total Elements Met)*	
		Teacher 1	**Teacher 2**
Provides Feedback	❏ Communicates areas of strength clearly *Supports with evidence, ensures teacher understanding, balances with other pieces of feedback, connects to areas of focus when appropriate* ❏ Communicates areas of focus clearly *Supports with evidence, ensures teacher understanding, balances with other pieces of feedback, connects to areas of strength when appropriate* ❏ Makes connections to framework *References language from the framework, clarifies connections between components when appropriate* ❏ Emphasizes impact on student learning *References how evidence collected impacts student learning, shares how changes would enhance student learning*		
	Component Met?	Choose Yes/No	
	Comments: Click here to enter text.		
Next Steps	❏ Attains next steps collaboratively *Seeks teacher input of next steps to enhance practice, has suggestions prepared prior to conference, teacher is aware of next steps at conclusion of conference* ❏ Correlates next steps with identified components/foci *Next steps are aligned with areas identified for focus* ❏ Develops appropriate next steps *Next steps are prescriptive, appropriate to the content area, and specific to the observation; can be used by teacher to enhance practice*		

(*Continued*)

Component	Element *(Check All Met by Trainee)*	Score *(Total Elements Met)*	
		Teacher 1	**Teacher 2**
	Component Met?	Choose Yes/No	
Written Observation Summary	**Comments:** Click here to enter text.		
	❏ Communicates areas of strength clearly *Includes supporting evidence and impact on student learning*		
	❏ Communicates areas of focus clearly *Includes supporting evidence and impact on student learning*		
	❏ Communicates next steps clearly *Includes information to support teacher use*		
	❏ Utilizes appropriate format and written communication *All areas of strength/focus and next steps include rubric language and component name/number, uses correct writing conventions (spelling, grammar), writing is clear and easily understood by teacher*		
	Component Met?	Choose Yes/No	
	Comments: Click here to enter text.		

Tool 17-1: DCPS Feedback Rubric with Annotated Example

This rubric, and the example of written feedback that follows, is explained on page 230 in Chapter 17.

DISTRICT OF COLUMBIA
PUBLIC SCHOOLS

2014–2015 School Leader TLF Report Rubric

Overview

We know that the TLF reports teachers receive are a critical part of IMPACT. This feedback not only provides the essential evidence needed to justify ratings, but it also communicates teachers' strengths and areas for improvement. Along with the post-observation conference, these reports can improve teacher practice in meaningful ways.

Because TLF reports are so important to teachers, school leaders requested additional guidance on this aspect of the evaluation process. In response, the IMPACT team, with the input of principals from across the district, created a rubric which clarifies best practices for ensuring feedback is aligned, specific, and ultimately drives instructional improvement. Reports are reviewed for evidence and suggestions and are considered to meet standards for mechanics unless otherwise noted.

Evidence: *the extent to which evidence is aligned to the Teach standard and justifies the score*

Rating	Criteria
4 - Model Evidence	**ALL Teach standards** are addressed with one piece of aligned and specific evidence, AND the standards which are a focus for suggestions have **multiple pieces of specific, aligned evidence.**
3 - Meets Standard	**ALL Teach standards** are addressed with one piece of aligned and specific evidence.
2 - Sometimes Justifies	**At least 6 Teach standards** are addressed with aligned and specific evidence.
1 - Rarely Justifies	**Fewer than 6 Teach standards** are addressed with aligned and specific evidence, OR all comments are purely copy and pasted with rubric language, OR comments do not contain any specific evidence of lesson taught.

⬇ This item can be downloaded from www.wiley.com/go/betterfeedback

Suggestions: *the extent to which meaningful, clear, bite-sized suggestions are present.* According to *Leverage Leadership*, teacher feedback is about "bite-sized action steps that allow a teacher to grow systematically from novice to proficient to master teacher."

Rating	Criteria
4 - Model Suggestions	**The written report contains 2–3** suggestions across all Teach standards that are meaningful, clear, and bite-sized.
3 - Meets Standard	**The written report contains at least 1** suggestion across all Teach standards that is meaningful, clear, and bite-sized.
2 - Limited Suggestions	**The written report contains only** suggestions that are any of the following: not meaningful, unclear, copied examples from the rubric, or not actionable.
1 - No Suggestions	**The written report contains no suggestions.**

Mechanics: *the extent to which the writing is clear and professional*

Rating	Criteria
Meets Standard	The writing in the report is clear and professional.
Below Standard	There are **several significant errors** across all Teach standards and/or the writing **distracts** the reader.

Sample Feedback, Annotated

DCPS provides observers with a two-page example of written feedback, with annotations, as guidance. Reformatted here to fit on smaller pages, this feedback example scored a Level 3 in Evidence and in Suggestions on the Written Feedback Rubric. Annotations in italics explain why, and offer some ways the feedback could be strengthened.

STANDARD	RATING	COMMENTS
TEACH 1 Lead Well-Organized, Objective-Driven Lesson	3	Your lesson was well-organized to achieve the objective you posted: "Readers pay attention to where characters experience strong emotion or make critical choices to learn from their experiences." As demonstrated by the answers to your questions and the level of participation, your students clearly responded positively and were actively involved in this lesson! *Because this justification cites one specific, aligned piece of evidence for Teach 1 and another for Teach 4, this justification meets expectations (Level 3) on the Evidence measure of the Written Feedback Rubric.* Leverage Leadership *urges school leaders to limit suggestions to a few key areas. Because this standard is the sole focus for suggestions, to receive a Level 4 (Exceeds Expectations) on the Evidence measure, it would be useful to cite additional evidence for why Teach 4 specifically is an area of focus. This could be achieved by supplementing the evidence about students' active involvement (Row 2) with evidence that also addresses the effectiveness of the ways in moving students towards mastery (Row 1). For example, the following sentence could be inserted between the first and second sentence: "By modeling, using an anchor chart, and providing students with multiple practice opportunities (group and independent work), you moved students towards initial mastery of the general lesson content." This additional evidence previews the rationale for Teach 4 feedback since the ways used by the teacher moved students towards mastery (Level 3: Effective) but did not result in students developing deep understanding (Level 4: Highly Effective).*
TEACH 4 Provide Students Multiple Ways to Move Toward Mastery	3	**Suggestion:** Your students' many successful responses suggest that they are ready to develop a deeper understanding of the content. One way you could extend their learning is to ask students to defend which lesson learned was most important to the character's development and to support their argument with additional evidence from the text.

STANDARD	RATING	COMMENTS
		This feedback meets expectations for effective suggestions. It is meaningful, clear, and bite-sized. *It is **meaningful** because focusing on this area will potentially impact the teacher's effectiveness in multiple areas: (presenting students with challenging content [Teach 3], probing student understanding [Teach 6], developing higher-order thinking [Teach 7]) and subsequently have a positive impact on student achievement.* *It is **clear** and **bite-sized** because it is specific and concrete. The teacher likely can act to implement this feedback in an upcoming lesson.*
TEACH 2 Explain Content Clearly	3	Your explanations were clear, concise, and effective. You strategically selected mini-lesson examples to demonstrate how the skill could be applied to realistic fiction, fantasy, and historical fiction. You used the chart and verbal explanations to effectively emphasize key points, such as the importance of meta-cognition in identifying emotions and lessons that characters learned. You also carefully made the distinction between an emotion and a character trait (academic vocabulary), and used a broad vocabulary (e.g., words such as "vulnerable") to explain concepts and to ask questions. Your students demonstrated a high level of understanding throughout the lesson!
TEACH 3 Engage Students at All Learning Levels in Accessible and Challenging Work	3	You made your lesson accessible by modeling with an anchor chart that your students could reference, and almost all of your students were engaged while on the carpet. You then gradually released students to practice such that they had opportunities to show you how they were progressing toward the objective. Your use of leveled texts during independent practice was particularly useful in ensuring that your students could access the content.
TEACH 7 Develop Higher-Level Understanding through Effective Questioning	3	Furthermore, your lesson was inherently challenging, as it required students to make inferences about what a character was learning. You engaged all students with higher-order questions ("What lesson did Rob learn based on Sistine's reaction?" and "What do you notice about Sophie? Is she showing a strong emotion or action?"). Most of your students provided meaningful responses about what characters learned such as when one student shared that what Rob learns is "When you let your feelings out you feel better and the other person will feel better, too."

STANDARD	RATING	COMMENTS
TEACH 5 Check for Student Understanding	3	You checked for understanding at all key moments, using turn-and-talks, whole-class questions, and by observing students at work. You circulated during the first turn-and-talk and were able to gather information from many students about the extent to which they understood the content. During the second turn-and-talk you focused on one student pair. *Since the evaluator noted a missed opportunity to check the understanding of additional students, it may be useful to offer a corresponding suggestion.* *For example:* *"Create increased opportunities for more students to participate and share their thinking with the larger group. You predominately called on volunteers throughout the lesson. To ensure that you check all students' understanding, it will be useful to intentionally call on non-volunteers. Equity sticks, which are a way to ensure you are calling on a range of students by drawing one name from a pile, may be a useful procedure to try!"* *This feedback would be* **meaningful** *because involving more students in the lesson will increase the quantity of information the teacher has about students' current level of mastery (Teach 5) which will influence how the teacher responds (Teach 6), and whether the teacher adjusts lesson pacing (Teach 8) or increases rigor (Teach 7).* *This feedback would be* **clear** *and* **bite-sized** *because it presents the teacher with a single, concrete strategy to try in a future lesson.*
TEACH 6 Respond to Student Understanding	3	When you observed many students conflating emotions and character traits you reminded students of the emotions and traits charts they had made earlier in the year in order to scaffold their understanding. Additionally, when your students provided correct answers, you almost always probed for more thorough responses, such as when you asked, "How do we know that she (Sophie) is angry?"

STANDARD	RATING	COMMENTS
TEACH 8 Maximize Instructional Time	4	Your routines and procedures are a clear strength as students successfully engaged in turn-and-talks, transitioned, and managed their individual materials in Ziploc bags. Students also appeared familiar with the individualized pacing of their independent work and were able to self-monitor accordingly. Furthermore, your students shared responsibility for maintaining an effective classroom environment. For example, during partner work, one student reminded the others, "Get to reading guys, stop talking," which resulted in a positive response.
TEACH 9 Build a Supportive, Learning-Focused Classroom Community	3	Your classroom is a safe and respectful place, and you have a positive rapport with your students. Your students are invested in their work and each other, as they were able to collaborate with partners and respond to higher-level questions in front of the whole group. Throughout the lesson you affirmed your students' thinking and celebrated their effort. It is clear that your students feel supported by you and by the learning environment you have successfully cultivated!

Tool 18-1: Minneapolis Public Schools (MPS) Rubric for Rating Use of Evidence*

This tool is explained on page 251, in Chapter 18.

Score	(1)	(2)	(3)	(4)
Alignment of Evidence	Evidence is misaligned to the criteria or evidence is repeated in multiple indicators without attention to context of the evidence.	Evidence is only partially aligned to the criteria and/or is repeated in some indicators without attention to context of the evidence.	The majority of the evidence is aligned to the appropriate criteria and any repeated evidence reflects the accurate context of the evidence.	All evidence is both aligned to the criteria and accurately reflects the context of the evidence.
Objectivity of Evidence	Evidence includes frequent bias, opinions, summary statements, and/or judgments.	Evidence includes occasional opinions, summary statements, or judgments.	Evidence is largely free of bias, opinions, summary statements, and judgments.	Evidence is quantifiable when appropriate, includes specific numbers and/or time references. The evidence is completely free of bias, opinions, summary statements, and judgments.
Representation of Evidence	Evidence/facts are scant or missing for some criteria and/or do not accurately represent the lesson and associated artifacts.	Minimal evidence/facts are recorded for each criterion and/or partially represents the lesson and associated artifacts.	Sufficient evidence/facts are recorded for each criterion and accurately represents the lesson and associated artifacts.	A preponderance of evidence/facts are recorded for all criteria and accurately represent what occurred in the class and in the associated artifacts.

---

* Rubric adapted from Teaching Learning Solutions © 2011, www.teachinglearningsolutions. Used with permission.

⬇ This item can be downloaded from www.wiley.com/go/betterfeedback

Tool 19-1: RIDE Teacher Survey Items on Observation

This tool is explained on page 278, in Chapter 19.

Rhode Island Educator Evaluation Systems Teacher End-of-Year Survey

2. In which district do you currently teach (2012–2013) school year)?

[▼]

3. What grade level(s) do you primarily work with? (Check all that apply)

☐ Preschool

☐ Grades K–2

☐ Grades 3–6

☐ Junior High/Middle School

☐ High School

4. What area(s) do you primarily teach? (check all that apply)

☐ Preschool or Elementary teacher responsible for multiple content-areas (you do not have to check any further options)

☐ Arts

☐ Career and Technical

☐ English Language Arts

☐ English as Second Language/Dual Language/Bilingual

☐ Health

☐ Library/Media

☐ Math

☐ Physical Education

☐ Science

☐ Social Studies/History

☐ Special Education

☐ World Languages

Other (please specify)

[   ]

5. Not including this year, how many years have you been teaching?

[▼]

Rhode Island Educator Evaluation Systems Teacher End-of-Year Survey

PROFESSIONAL PRACTICE

6. During the 2012–13 school year, how many times were you observed for evaluation purposes?

	Number of Observations
Announced observations	[▾]
Unannounced observations	[▾]

7. How do you feel about how often you received each type of observation during the 2012–13 school year?

	Too frequently	Just right	Not frequently enough
Announced observations	○	○	○
Unannounced obser	○	○	○

8. Which type of observation did you prefer?

○ Announced observation(s)

○ Unannounced observation(s)

9. Please explain your response above.

[▲]
[▼]

10. When you were observed by your evaluator, how consistently were observations accompanied by the following?

	Always	Frequently	Sometimes	Rarely	Never
Post-observation conversation	○	○	○	○	○
Formal written feedback	○	○	○	○	○
Informal oral feedback	○	○	○	○	○
Informal written feedback	○	○	○	○	○
Other	○	○	○	○	○

Rhode Island Educator Evaluation Systems Teacher End-of-Year Survey

11. Please indicate your level of agreement with the following statements related to feedback you received from your evaluator(s):

	Strongly Agree	Agree	Somewhat Agree	Somewhat Disagree	Disagree	Strongly Disagree
I received more specific feedback about my performance this year compared to my past evaluations.	○	○	○	○	○	○
The feedback I received this year helped me identify strengths in my teaching.	○	○	○	○	○	○
The feedback I received this year helped improve my instruction.	○	○	○	○	○	○
My evaluator(s) helped me identify concrete steps to take following an observation.	○	○	○	○	○	○
The feedback I received this year helped me identify strengths in my teaching.	○	○	○	○	○	○
The component scores and rationales I received were accurate.	○	○	○	○	○	○
I received enough feedback on my instructional practice.	○	○	○	○	○	○

12. Typically, how promptly have you received written feedback following an observation?

○ Within one day following the observation

○ Within three days following the observation

○ Within one week following the observation

○ Within two weeks after the observation

○ More than two weeks after the observation

○ I don't typically receive feedback after an observation

13. Did any particular aspect of your teaching improve this year as a result of working with your evaluator(s)?

○ Yes

○ No

14. If yes, what aspect of your practice did you improve on?

Notes

1. For more discussion of these activities, see the MET project brief, "Building Trust in Observations: A Blueprint for Improving Systems to Support Great Teaching." Seattle, WA: Bill & Melinda Gates Foundation, 2014.

2. For descriptions of the rubrics in the MET project's study of classroom observations, see pp. 18–27 in the research paper, "Gathering Feedback for Teaching: Combining High-Quality Observations with Student Surveys and Achievement Gains." Seattle: WA: Bill & Melinda Gates Foundation, 2012.

3. See "The Irreplaceables: Understanding the Real Retention Crisis in America's Urban Schools." TNTP, 2012.

4. See "How Much Are Districts Spending to Implement Teacher Evaluation Systems?" J. Chambers, et al. RAND Education & American Institutes for Research, 2013.

5. See "Does Better Observation Make Better Teachers? New Evidence from a Teacher Evaluation Pilot in Chicago," M. P. Steinberg & L. Sartain. *Education Next*. Winter 2015.

6. See "An Interaction-Based Approach to Enhancing Secondary-School Instruction and Student Achievement." J. Allen et al. *Science* 333, 1034. 2011.

7. See "Ensuring Fair and Reliable Measures of Effective Teaching: Culminating Findings from the MET Project's Three-Year Study." Bill & Melinda Gates Foundation, 2013.

8. For key steps to address all components of an observation system—including observation rubrics, observer assessment, and monitoriting—see the MET project brief, "Building Trust in Observations: A Blueprint for Improving Systems to Support Great Teaching." Cited above.

9. For key steps to address all components of an observation system see the MET project brief, "Building Trust in Observations: A Blueprint for Improving Systems to Support Great Teaching." Cited above.

10. See "Evaluating Teachers with Classroom Observations: Lessons Learned in Four Districts." G. J. Whitehurst and K. Lindquist. Brookings Institution, May 2014. In a blog post with the report's release, Whitehurst clarified that for the lowest-performing teachers, observer bias had very little effect on their performance rankings; see "Teacher Dismissals under New Evaluation Systems," in The Brown Center Chalkboard, No. 67, May 22, 2014.

11. See "Strategies for Enhancing the Impact of Post-Observation Feedback for Teachers." Carnegie Foundation for the Advancement of Teaching. J. Myung and K. Martine, 2013.

12. See "Rethinking Teacher Evaluation in Chicago." Consortium for Chicago School Research Report. L. Sartain et al., 2011.

13. For an excellent discussion on identifying and measuring the key drivers of specific educational outcomes, see the chapter "We Cannot Improve at Scale What We Cannot Measure," in the book *Learning to Improve: How America's Schools Can Get Better at Getting Better*, A. Bryk et al. Harvard Education Press Cambridge, MA, 2015.

References

Allen, J., et al. (2011). An Interaction-Based Approach to Enhancing Secondary-School Instruction and Student Achievement. *Science*, 333, 1034.

Bryk, A., et al. (2015). *Learning to Improve: How America's Schools Can Get Better at Getting Better.* Cambridge, MA: Harvard Education Press.

Bambrick-Santoyo. (2012). *Leverage Leadership: A Practical Guide to Building Exceptional Schools.* San Francisco: Jossey-Bass.

Brookings Institution. (2014). "Evaluating Teachers with Classroom Observations: Lessons Learned in Four Districts." Washington, DC: G. Whitehurst and K. Lindquist.

Carnegie Foundation for the Advancement of Teaching. (2013). "Strategies for Enhancing the Impact of Post-Observation Feedback for Teachers." Stanford, CA: J. Myung and K. Martine.

Consortium on Chicago School Research. (2011). "Rethinking Teacher Evaluation in Chicago: Lessons Learned from Classroom Observations, Principal-Teacher Conferences, and District Implementation." University of Chicago. L. Sartain et al.

McClellan, Catherine (2013). "What It Looks Like: Master Coding Videos for Observer Training and Assessment." Seattle, WA: Bill & Melinda Gates Foundation.

MET Project. (2014). "Building Trust in Observations: A Blueprint for Improving Systems to Support Great Teaching." Seattle, WA: Bill & Melinda Gates Foundation.

MET Project. (2013). "Ensuring Fair and Reliable Measures of Effective Teaching: Culminating Findings from the MET Project's Three-Year Study." Seattle, WA: Bill & Melinda Gates Foundation.

RAND Education & American Institutes for Research. (2013). "How Much Are Districts Spending to Implement Teacher Evaluation Systems?" Pittsburgh & Washington, DC: J. Chambers, et al.

Sartain, L., and Steinberg, M. (Winter 2015). Does Better Observation Make Better Teachers? *Education Next*, Vol. 5, #1. http://educationnext.org/better-observation-make-better-teachers

TNTP. (2012). "The Irreplaceables: Understanding the Real Retention Crisis in America's Urban Schools." Brooklyn.

Whitehurst, G. (May 22, 2014). Teacher Dismissals under New Evaluation Systems. (Blog entry). The Brown Center Chalkboard, No. 67. Brown Center on Education. Brookings Institution. http://educationnext.org/teacher-dismissals-new-evaluation-systems

Index

Page references followed by *fig* indicate an illustrated figure.

DATE DUE